MADONNA

...RAW

All text and photos by George DuBose

Art direction and design by George DuBose

An imprint of Wonderland Publishing
©2015 George-DuBose.com

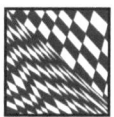

Madonna - Raw
First Edition
ISBN 978-0-9863-0451-4

Printed in the United States of America
Library of Congress cataloging-in-publication data

All of the images in this book are available
as signed, numbered limited edition fine art prints
for more information contact: boss@george-dubose.com

Other books from Wonderland Publishing

"I Speak Music	-	Ramones" (English Edition)	ISBN 978-0-9889-2340-9
"Hablo Musica	-	Ramones" (Españoles Edición)	ISBN 978-0-9889-2341-6
"Eu falo Música	-	Ramones" (Português Edição)	ISBN 978-0-9889-2345-4
"Parlo Musica	-	Ramones" (Edizione Italiana)	ISBN 978-0-9889-2347-8
"I Speak Music	-	Hip Hop - Old School Volume One"	ISBN 978-0-9889-2342-3
"I Speak Music	-	Hip Hop - Old School Volume Two"	ISBN 978-0-9889-2343-0
"I Speak Music	-	Hip Hop - Old School Volume Three"	ISBN 978-0-9889-2344-7
"The Big Book of Hip-Hop Photography" First Edition			ISBN 978-0-9889-2346-1
"Renovate a Sailboat and Cross the Atlantic" First Edition			ISBN 978-0-9889-2348-5

It seemed like a strange request from a manager I had never met or heard of before.

Take a train to Roslyn, NY, go to a club called Uncle Sam's Blues and photograph the singer of the band performing there. Just photograph the singer, not the band members.

Huh?

Since I had moved to New York in 1975, it had taken me a couple of years to get my act as a photographer together. By 1978, I had photographed the B-52's for Andy Warhol's "Interview" magazine and I used another uncommissioned photo for a street poster that I printed a thousand copies to advertise B-52's upcoming gigs. In 1979, the street poster photo of these photos became the B-52's first album cover and mine...

Other album cover assignments soon followed and by going out to the music clubs, CBGBs, Max's Kansas City, Hurrah's, I was meeting other musicians, photographing their live shows and generally becoming "known" as a NYC nightlife and music photographer.

John Phillips, a six foot plus brother who guarded the door at Hurrah's and I became friends, often chatting before the evening's entertainment started. Apparently, John had been asked

if he knew a competent music concert photographer and he recommended me.

I received a phone call from a woman named Camille and she outlined her need for photographs of this yet, unnamed singer.

"$250 bucks, plus film and processing costs, plus train fare." I told Camille. She didn't question the costs and told me the date that the concert would be taking place. Again, she just told me to shoot "only the singer". I had been hired many times to photograph bands in concert for their publicity use, but never "just the singer".

Unfortunately, the actual date of this concert is lost in the "fog of war". I have spoken to several experts who are quite knowledgable about the biographical data of this "singer", but I have yet to learn when I actually was at Uncle Sam's Blues and made these photographs.

Roslyn, NY is quite a distance from Manhattan. I had never heard of Uncle Sam's Blues, there is another more famous nightclub in Roslyn, called My Father's Place and years later MFP actually thought that their venue had hosted this early performance.

I don't recall anything about the club or the guests that were there that evening. Luckily, my photos help me recall the performance of this singer.

I saw many debut acts in my early photography career in New York City. American New Wave music was exploding in the late '70s. Punk wasn't so interesting to me at the time, Disco had become a little one dimensional for me, but New Wave was not really a single style. Anything goes seemed to be the directive of the times...

Klaus Nomi and his contra-tenor voice, the B-52's, Talking Heads, Kraftwerk, Trio, Plastic Bertrand, all had radically different sounds. I even thought that early Hip-Hop was just another style within the New Wave sounds.

As I watched, listened and photographed the performance of this band that night at Uncle Sam's Blues, I quickly became aware that this singer was indeed unique.

First, she was quite cute in a punky way, but she wasn't dressed as a punk. Female punks tend to dress in a uni-sex style and one can be hard pressed to describe that look as sexy. The woman on stage this evening was...sexy. She was dressed in fishnet hose (punky), but she was wearing a little leather miniskirt and matching leather top. These leather garments were not tailored, but rather looked like rough cut hides. Something that Jane (Maureen O'Hara) wore in the famous Tarzan films with Johnny Weissmuller. Tribal chic...

I was quite enthralled. She had a unique and appealing vocal style, she dressed and acted in a sexy, but not slutty manner. She was quite acrobatic, dancing and rolling around on the stage.

I was happy that I didn't to pay ANY attention to the rest of the band.

How long was the first set, I don't recall. I remember going backstage after the set and asked one of the musicians if there was going to be a second show. There was...

I walked further into the backstage area and when I looked into an open door, I saw the singer sitting alone in her dressing room.

Knocking on the door frame, I introduced myself.

"Hi, my name is George. I am your photographer for the evening.

What's your name?"

"Madonna", she replied.

"What's your real name?" I asked.

"Madonna".

I told her that I had enjoyed her show quite a bit. I had seen many new groups performing in Manhattan. I saw which bands were getting publicity and subsequent recording contracts. I told Madonna that I thought her act was great, her material and delivery were unique and she didn't sound like one thousand other bar band singers doing cover songs for suburban teenagers.

I went on to say that I thought her outfit and performance was quite sexy, but I had the impression that she wasn't sure herself how it was "coming across". I told her that I just wanted to assure her that the whole thing was working...

Camille, the manager, obviously heard me saying that or part of that and started yelling at me.

"How dare you speak to my artist! Get out of here this minute!" She screamed.

Grabbing my gear, I quickly exited the dressing room and backstage and went back to the club.

The second show, Madonna wore a series of costume elements. A white University of Michigan athletic sweater with a big "M" on it for Michigan? or Madonna? She wore a jacket from a marching band and then a simple white

man's dress shirt, complete with somebody's laundry marks. Clearly, she was looking for a look, but that would come later...

After the second set, I returned by Long Island Rail Road to Manhattan. The following day, I processed the four rolls of Ilford XP-1 B&W film that I had exposed at her show.

What may be "interesting" to photographers and lovers of photographic art, is that this XP-1 film was new to me, I had never used it before. The film, itself, was a new technology and the emulsion of the film was made of two layers. Both layers together produced a single image, but one layer was more sensitive to light than the other and the sensitive layer produced quite a grainy structure, the second emulsion layer was not so sensitive to light and produced an image with a finer grain structure. As you look over the images in this book, you will notice that the black background is sometimes filled with tiny white spots. This is the grain structure of the emulsion layer that is not as light sensitive.

I phoned Camille the day that I had the film contact sheets ready to be delivered or picked up, but she never returned my call.

...and I was never paid.

I wrote the date of the film development on each roll and in this instance, the rolls are numbered 102081-1 to 102081-4. This leads me to believe that I shot Madonna at Uncle Sam's Blues on October 19th, 1981.

Madonna had made a new fan at her concert in Roslyn. Even if the manager never returned my call to pickup the contact sheets, I thought Madonna was an act worth watching. Her star potential was quite clear to me that night in Roslyn. I began to keep my ears open for upcoming Madonna shows. There was a show at the Underground, a disco in the cellar of the building where Andy Warhol's Factory was. I "think" I was there (Oh! The Fog of War!), but I don't have any photos from that night.

I did take a couple of snapshots at a subsequent gig Madonna had on the roof of the building where Danceteria was.

Danceteria was a very popular nightclub in the early '80s. There would often be an art films viewing early in the evening, to be followed by a night of dancing to Manhattan's hottest DJs. In the summer, there was a BBQ on the roof where one could have a burger while watching Flock of Seagulls or in this case, an up-and-coming Madonna.

I had brought Michael O'Brien and Yuki Watanabe to see this woman that I had been raving about.

Michael was promoting a monthly event in Boston called "New York Nights". Michael and Yuki would scout Manhattan for the newest of the newest New Wave artists, they would then book these hippest acts from Manhattan and expose them to the folk in Boston that were open-minded and curious about new things...

Soul Sonic Force (I told you I thought that Hip-Hop was New Wave), Man Parrish, New York City Breakers, live graffiti painting by Bil Blast, were booked in consecutive months. One event a month. We even tried to book Klaus Nomi after his successful European debut, but Klaus had become terminally ill.

Madonna had impressed Michael and Yuki so much that they arranged a three camera video shoot at a club called "Metro". I flew up to party and photograph this event. This time I was on to another "new" film, color diapositive or slide film that was being produced by Polaroid. This was a new film in a standard 35mm cassette, but the film could be processed immediately with the help of a little processing machine. The film could then be cut, mounted into film holders and immediately put into a slide projector. I thought this was the "cat's ass". To be able to shoot musicians and the general public in a nightclub and then within 15 minutes be projecting the same with a slide projector. This was the state of the art prior to digital photography and beamers.

The downside of the Polaroid film was the emulsion had lines in it, why or for what reason, I have no idea. The second problem is that the emulsion of this color diapositive film is very delicate and susceptible to scratches. I have been only able to salvage a couple of frames from that night in Boston.

Madonna's first Boston show was a memorable concert for two reasons. It was the second concert I saw where Madonna was now dancing to tracks of her tunes. No more band. She had two dancers, another woman and her brother. I guess the "dancer" in Madonna was coming more to the front of the entertainment.

Madonna's stage look was now solidified and focussed. Her work with the influential Maripol gave Madonna a unique look that started her own fashion trend.

After the concert at the Metro, I went to the dressing room where Michael O'Brien and Yuki Watanabe were holding court with Madonna.

When Madonna noticed that I was in the room, she asked me, "What are you doing here?"

I guess she remembered me from Roslyn?

"I got you the gig," I told her.

Eventually, I turned my negatives over to my resale agent, London Features International, who started licensing my Madonna images to various publications and books. I never knew exactly which Madonna photos LFI was releasing or to whom.

I recall an incident several years later. I received a telephone call from someone who said that they were calling from Maverick Records, Madonna's record label. They asked me how much I would charge for a 16 x 20 inch print from the Roslyn show.

I told them, "One thousand dollars". I was still a little sore about being stiffed by Camille. That was a lot of money then and is a lot of money today, but my prices today have gone even higher

Maverick Records never bought that photo that they had enquired about. A year or two later, Maverick called me again and asked me what was my price for a 16 x 20 inch print from the Roslyn show.

I told them, "Two thousand dollars".

Time goes by...so slowly...

On February 16th, 2015, I received an email from one Matthew Rettenmund. He told me that he was the editor of the "Encyclopedia Madonnica, Madonna A-Z"

Matthew told me that he wanted to see all my "unpublished" photos of Madonna.

Right!

I wrote back that I had scanned several of the images that I liked from the 1981 show in Roslyn and I would be happy to send him .jpegs of those images for him to peruse. I wasn't actually sure which of the scanned photos had been published.

That didn't satisfy Mr. Rettenmund.

He wrote back that he wanted to see all of the images from that evening.

I wrote him that that wasn't going to be possible, I didn't have all the images scanned.

He wrote he would pay me to scan all the films again.

I agreed to a price and thought, "What the hell. I can scan two

rolls of 135-36 film, that's only 72 scans."

Ha! Ha! Ha! I had forgotten that here were four rolls, I had double the work to do.

In the end, Matthew licensed quite a few images for the second edition of his Encyclopedia Madonnica, which is actually quite a fascinating book.

I, on the other hand, knew that now I had all of those images from Roslyn scanned and while retouching away any dust and scratches, I became aware that there were many images that I had either never seen before or had forgotten about entirely. I saw a couple of images that were better than I recalled. New favorites.

Often, in interviews or just meetings with fans of the Ramones, B-52's or other groups that I had worked with, I get a lot of "what was it like" questions. Makes me think I should write a book, which I have done in the case of the Ramones and my 12 year relationship producing still images for their covers and publicity use and an even bigger book of the work I did in the Hip-Hop genre.

So here is my book on Madonna, I am including each and every photo I took of her that evening in Roslyn, Long Island, New York in

October of 1981. I don't know if it was Madonna's first concert as a front woman, but I know it was one of her earliest shows. She was still looking for a "look" for her stage image, she was still looking for the right song material in the right context.

I have even included a shot of Madonna from the roof of Danceteria and a couple from her gig at the Metro.

This is my Madonna, warts and all.

My warts, not hers.

Occasionally a shot of mine is out of focus, more often Madonna's movements in the dim stage lighting caused my slow shutter speeds of my camera to allow her to blur in motion, some images were just too dark.

But I have decided to show all of the images just to end any further discussion.

In the interest of Freedom of Information.

Earlier in 2015, I was contacted by Jon Gordon, the guitarist who played with the band supporting Madonna at the Uncle Sam's Blues club in Roslyn. He asked me if I had any photos from that gig that showed the guitar player.

I told him that I was contracted to only shoot the singer that evening and I didn't think that I had any shots of the guitarist. I had seen several images where the bassist was visible, but didn't recall any of the guitar player.

After I had scanned all of the images again for Matthew Rettenmund and was diligently removing all the dust and scratches from the scans, I did see one frame that showed a guitar player.

I sent this image to Jon and indeed, it was him.

I asked Jon if he would kindly answer some questions, specifically whether or not the shots that I had were from Madonna's first concert as a frontwoman.

Here is our conversation:

GDuB: 1. When Madonna's manager contacted me and asked me to go to a club in Roslyn, NY called Uncle Sam's Blues, she explicitly told me to only take pictures of the singer. When did you start playing with Madonna and was it clear to you and the other band members that she was the front person?

JG: I started to play with Madonna sometime in the spring of 1980. I auditioned for the job. It was clear that Madonna was the front person. The rest of the band were "hired guns", paid for their services by Camille and her partner, Adam Alter.

GDuB: 2. Do you remember the names of the other musicians?

JG: Drums: Bob Riley (later replaced by Steve Bray) Bass: John "K" Kumnick Keyboards: David Frank

GDuB: 3. Were you musicians well compensated for your efforts?

JG: We were paid for rehearsals and performances at rates commensurate with the standards of that time. It should be clear that we were in no way shorted in our compensation, to my knowledge.

GDuB: 4. Were any of these musicians in the band called the Breakfast Club?

JG: Steve Bray, who played drums after Bob Riley left, was in a band called "Breakfast Club" that had a subsequent record deal and some degree of success and exposure. I believe that the band had been around off and on in various lineups. I have heard that Madonna herself was with them at one time, prior to their record deal.

GDuB: 5. How many concerts did you and this lineup of musicians play with Ms. M before and after the show at Uncle Sam's Blues?

JG: I would guess that we did a total of 8 to 12 NYC area shows in mid to late 1981. Some of the later shows would have been with Steve Bray on drums.

To the best of my recollection the venues were:

U.S. Blues - 2 appearances
The Underground (Union Square) - 1 appearance
Max's Kansas City - 1 appearance
Cartune Alley - 1 appearance
Venue (?) in a bank building in Soho - 1 appearance
Queens College Student's Union - 2 appearances
Other Local College student's unions - 1 to 3 appearances

GDuB: 6. Were there any other concerts with a band after the show I photographed at US Blues?

JG: Yes, US Blues was one of the first shows we did. There were several afterwards.

GDuB: 7. The second time I saw Madonna was her performance on the roof of Danceteria. There was no band, she was now performing to a dance track with her brother and another woman. How were you and the other musicians informed that your services were no longer needed?

JG: I was no longer affiliated with her by that time, so I can only speculate. I had been replaced by another fine guitarist, Paul Pesco. My own position with her was terminated somewhat earlier by mutual agreement between myself and Camille. At the time I was a very busy freelancer and nobody, except possibly Madonna herself, had a crystal ball to see where her career was going.

Madonna's backup band was bankrolled by Camille's management company. There was eventually a split and Camille ceased to represent Madonna.

It is unlikely at that time that

Madonna would have had the resources to continue to retain the band. That would have been self-evident to the band members. I believe that her dance-club appearances would have been subsequent to that.

Some of her sidemen from that period - notably Steve Bray and Paul Pesco, did work with her later on.

GDuB: 8. Were any of the songs that were performed at US Blues co-written by any of the band members?

JG: I do not believe so. Subsequently we performed some songs that Madonna had co-written with Steve Bray, but not at US Blues.

GDuB: 9. I know Madonna was performing as a drummer early in her career, did she play any other instruments?

JG: She played guitar and keyboards and anything she could get her hands on. Camille owned the rehearsal studio we used and Madonna would have the run of it in off-hours. She used to record really cool rough demos of her songs, using whatever instruments struck her fancy.

GDuB: 10. So who wrote bass lines and melodies to the lyrics of the songs that were performed at this show?

JG: To the best of my knowledge Madonna had written the lyrics and melodies herself, excepting the one or two songs she had written with Steve Bray. I acted as her musical director and prepared the written music that the band used in rehearsal. It was all based on her demo tapes.

At one time we worked on a cover of Buffalo Springfield's "ForWhat It's Worth", but I don't honestly recall if we performed it at US Blues.

As for bass lines - that is an element of the musical arrangement - not the song itself. There might have been bass lines on the demos that we used, I may have suggested lines, or John K might have come up with them himself. Most likely a combination of all three.

GDuB: You may or may not know, but after the first set, I went backstage and found Madonna sitting alone in a dressing room. I was chatting her up, giving her some encouraging words and Camille heard me.

"How dare you talk to my artist!", she cried.

I went back to the venue and shot the second set.

I called Camille and left a message a day or two later, telling her that the four rolls of film had been made into contact sheets and that they were ready for a pickup. I never heard from Camille again.

JG: I did not know that. I think it is a matter of record that Camille's business relationship with Madonna was ultimately a troubled one and that Camille took Madonna to court at one point.

As for my relationship with Camille, she saw to it that I was fairly compensated for my work and she was instrumental in giving me the opportunity to co-produce a demo of Madonna's songs - some of which have been leaked online and are now known as the "Gotham Tapes". I worked for Camille some years later for another artist, Tatiana Cameron. While we have had some disagreements, we have had an essentially cordial relationship for quite few years.

Ultimately, I have no complaints about Camille.

GDuB: I am trying to put Madonna in a good light with this book, it ain't no biography, just shots from one of her early gigs.

JG: The Madonna I knew was talented, very driven, very self-possessed. I did not overestimate my value to her, but I liked her quite a bit.
Sorry if I misunderstood some of your questions.

1) The entire time I was working with Madonna she was clearly the front person of the band. We were hired specifically to be her backup band.

2) Regarding the time frame: I was hoping to find an appointment calendar from those years, but I appear to have disposed of them. I just looked over that period in what appears to be a well-researched bio of Madonna ("Madonna" by Andrew Morton). It does appear that the bulk of my employment with her occurred during 1981. It says that we commenced work at Mediasound studios on her demo in August of 1981. At that point Steve Bray was established as the drummer in the band. If the US Blues appearance was in October, then Steve Bray would have been the drummer. If you have a shot of the drummer and he is black, that would settle it, as Bob Riley was white.

3) I was originally under the impression that the bulk of my employment with Madonna was in 1980, not the "Mid '80s". Please re-read my answer to your first question - I said "spring of 1980".

However, I appear to have been off by a year, because all the events I remember are attributed to 1981 by independent sources. It is entirely possible that I worked with Madonna primarily in 1981 and I accept that as accurate.

Hope that answers your questions.

Best,

Jon

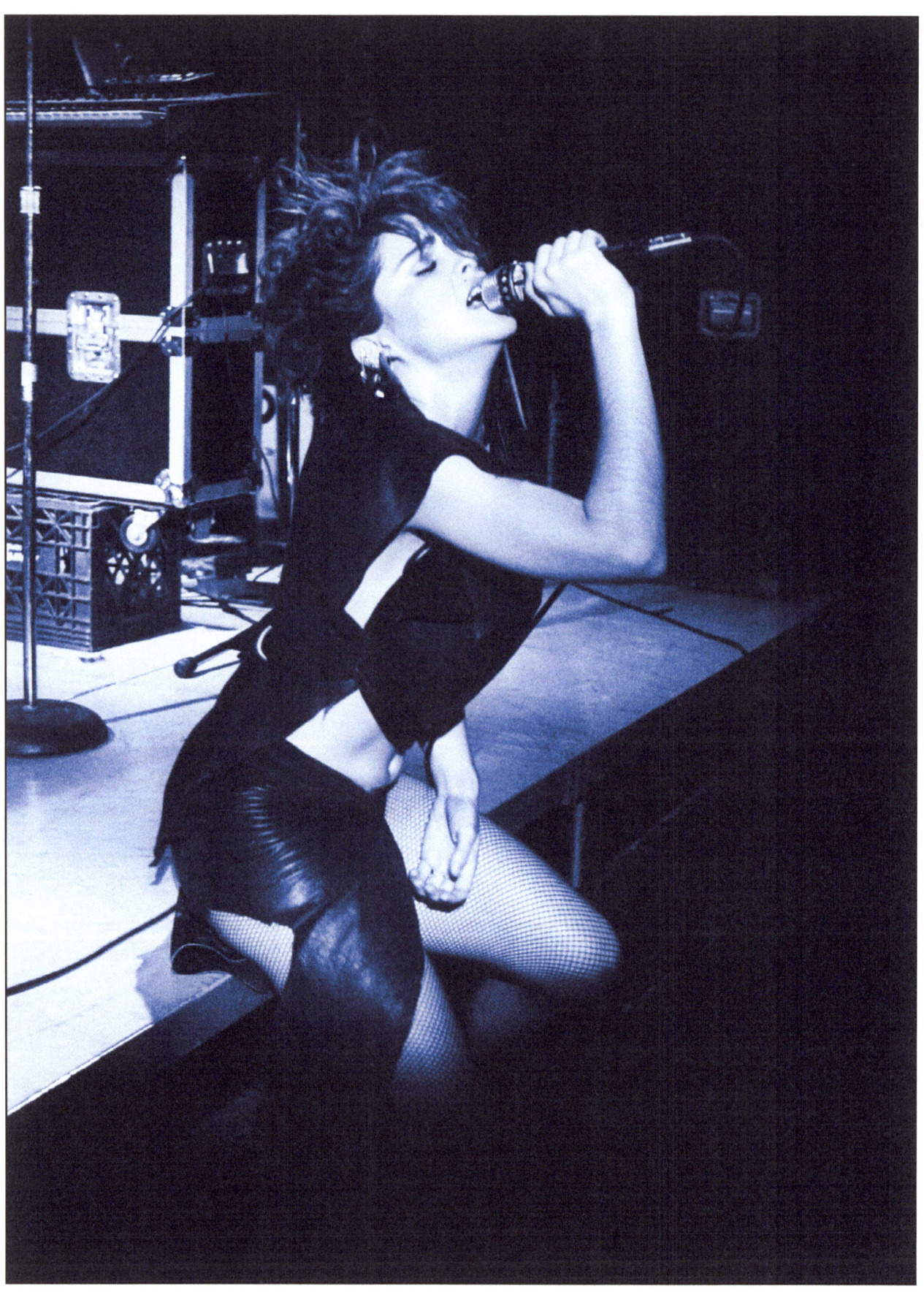

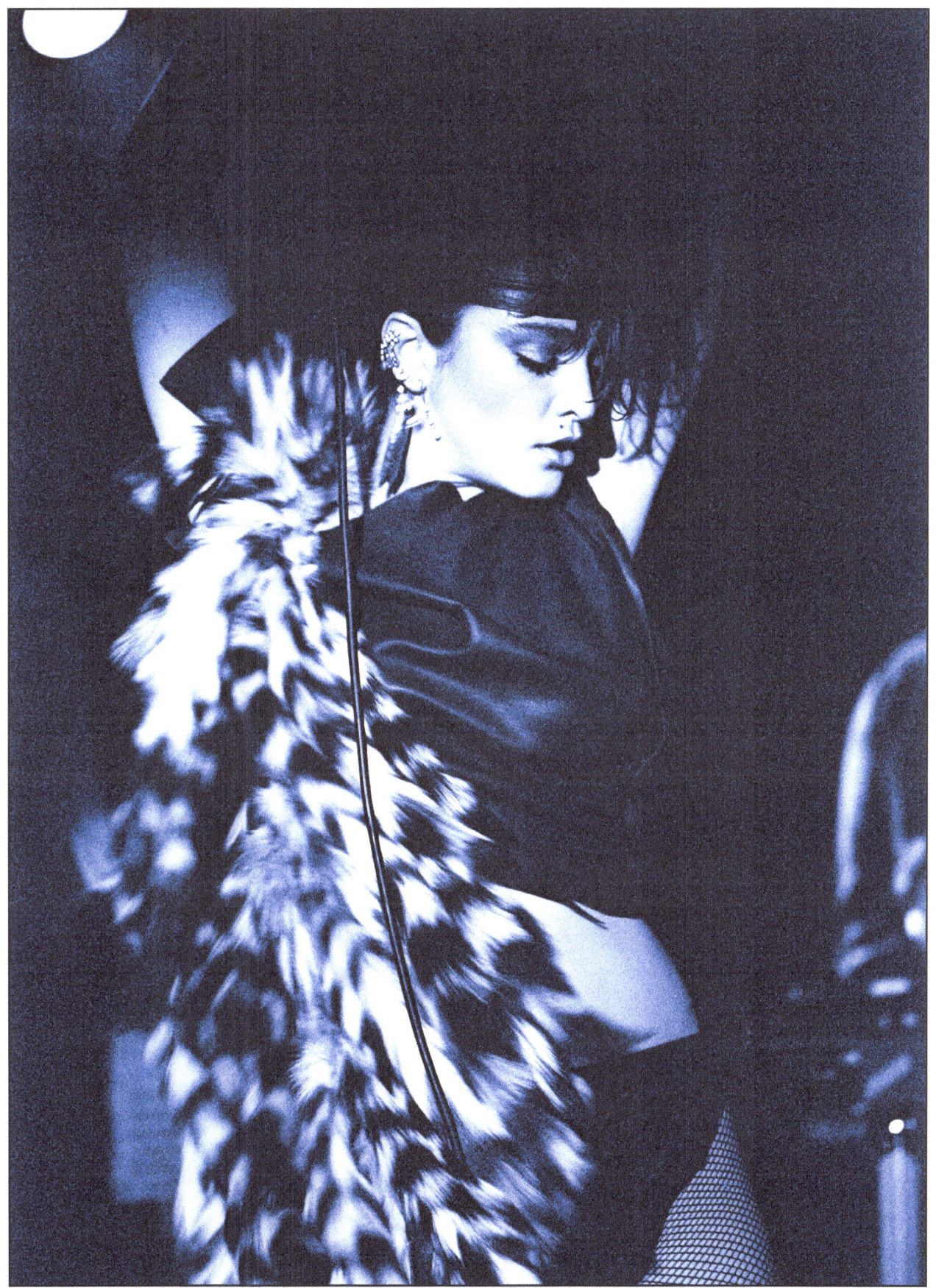

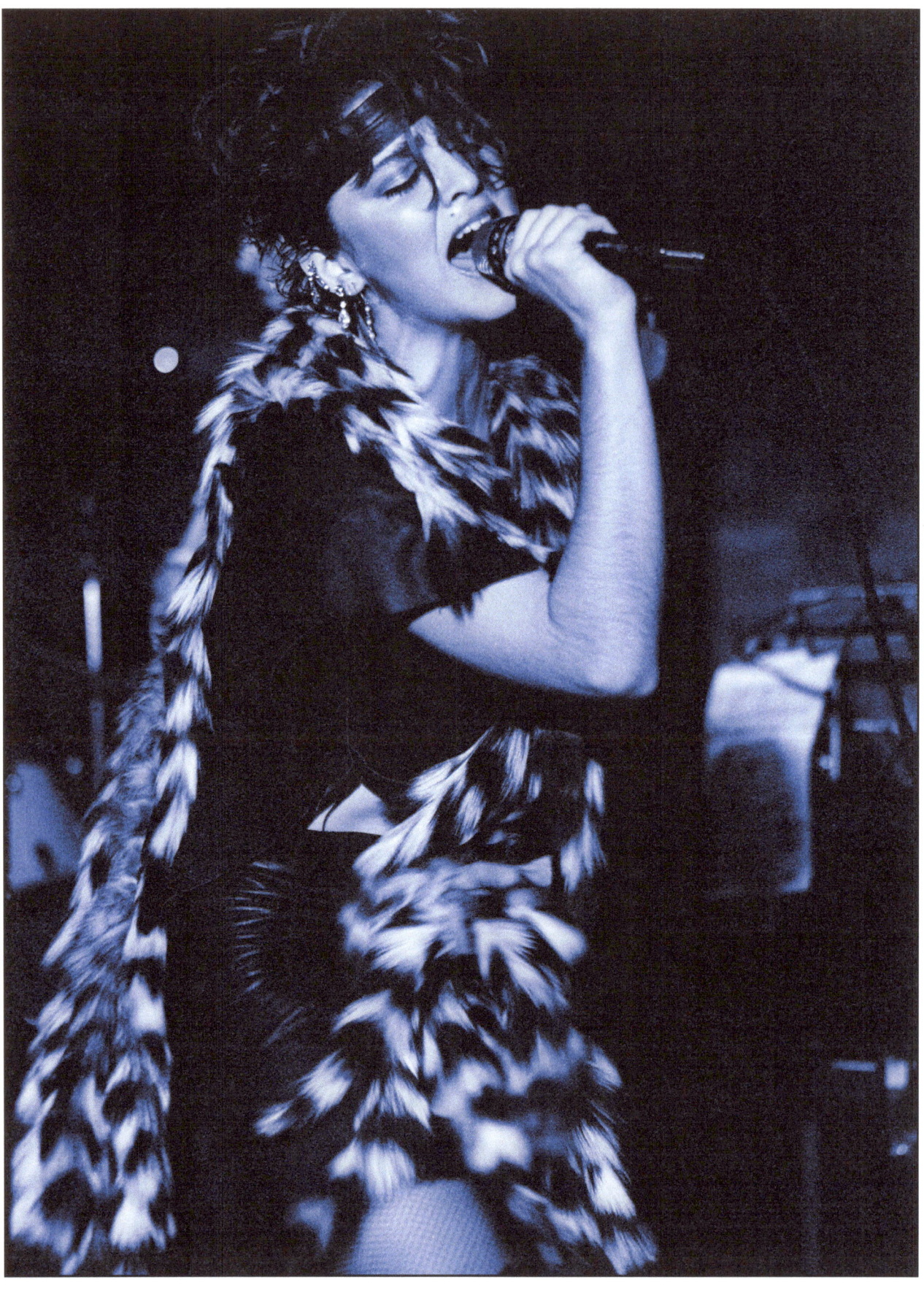

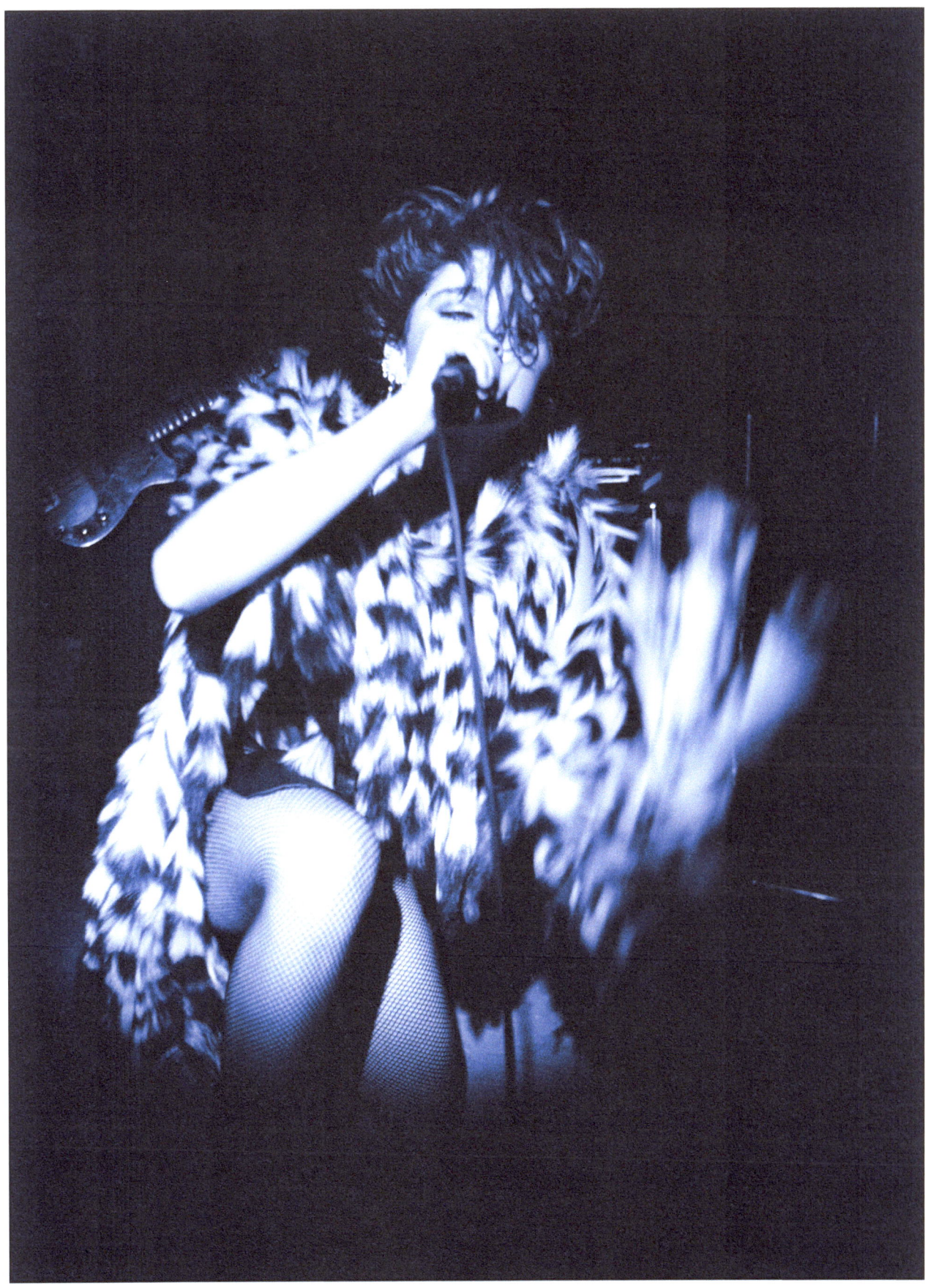

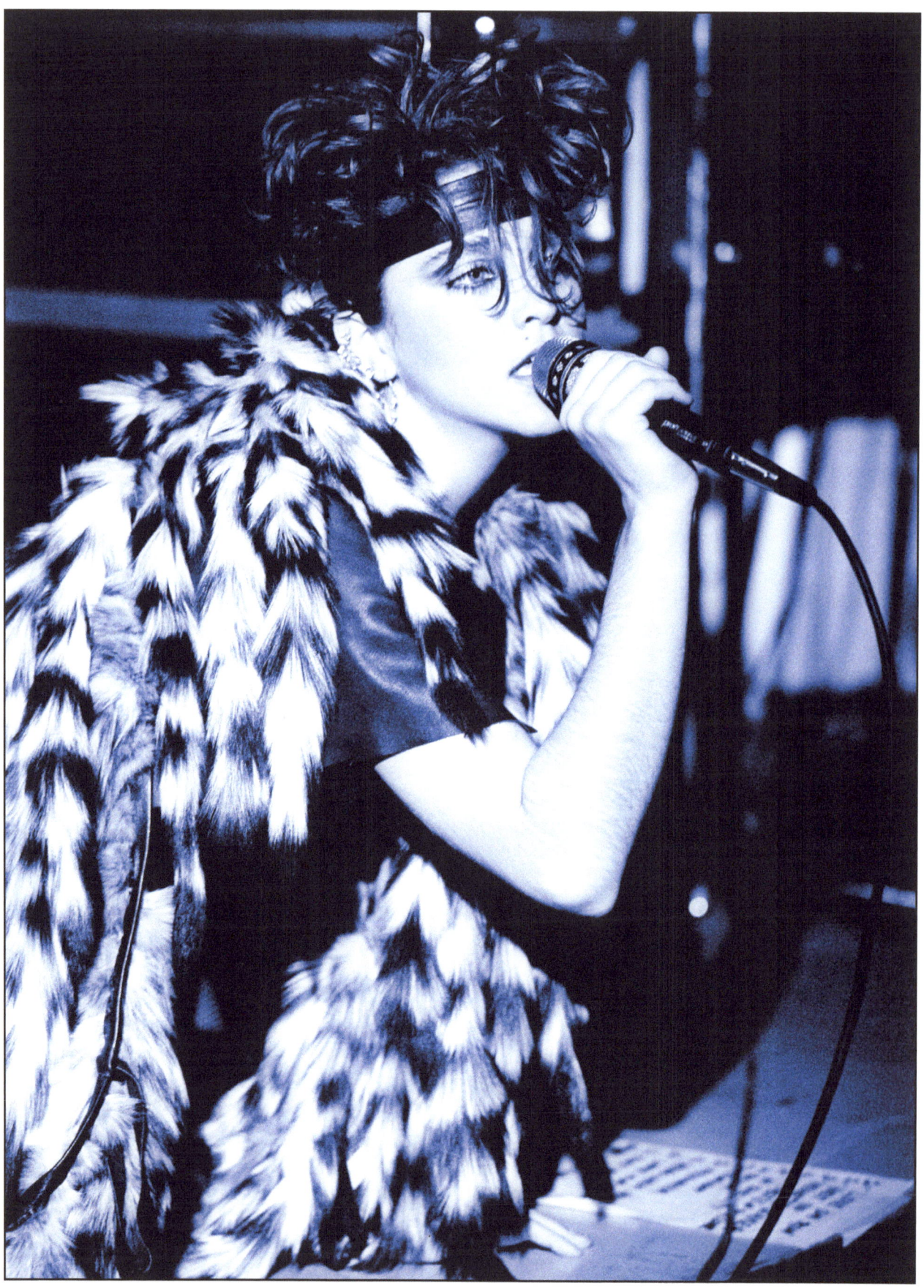

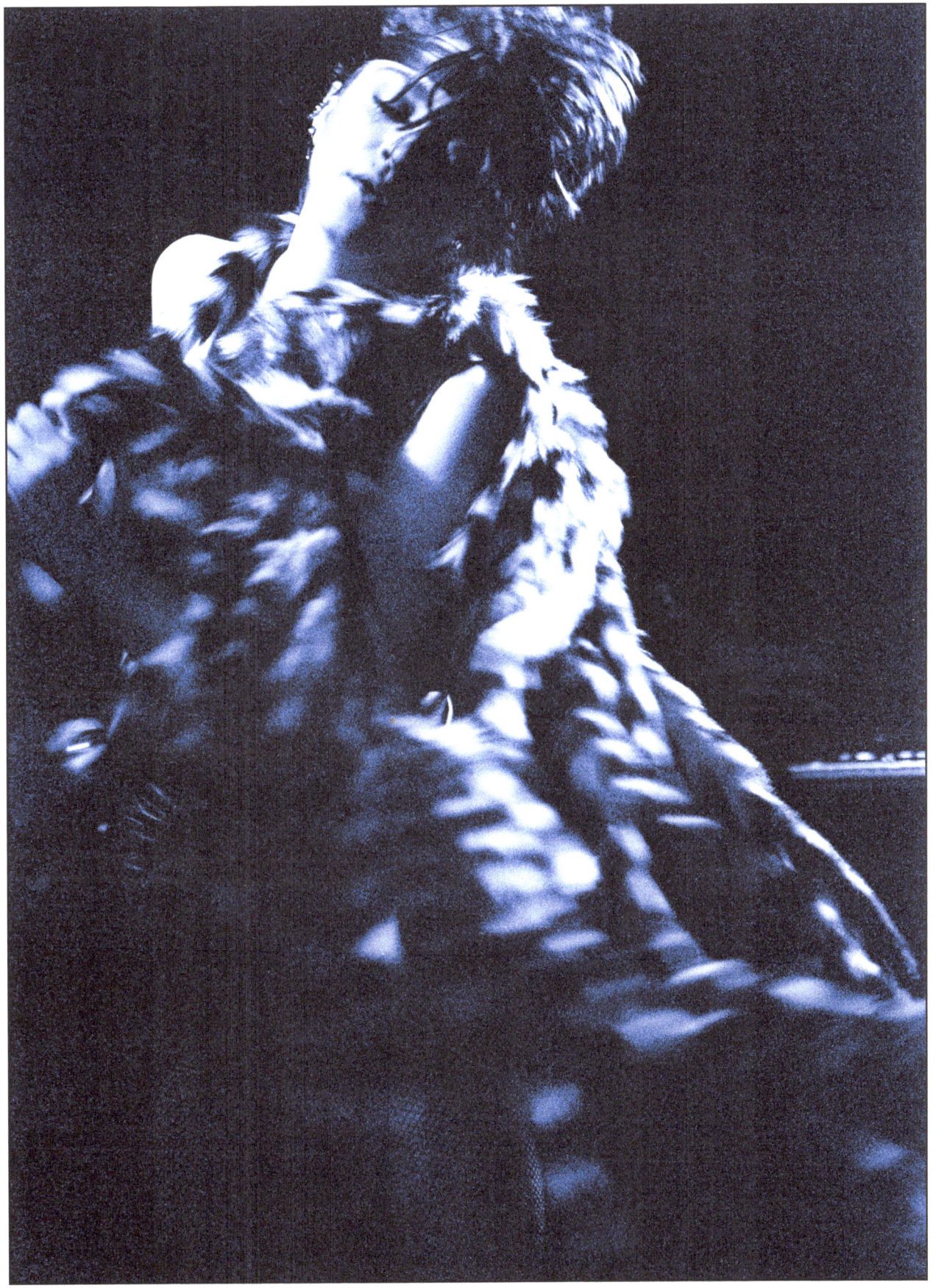

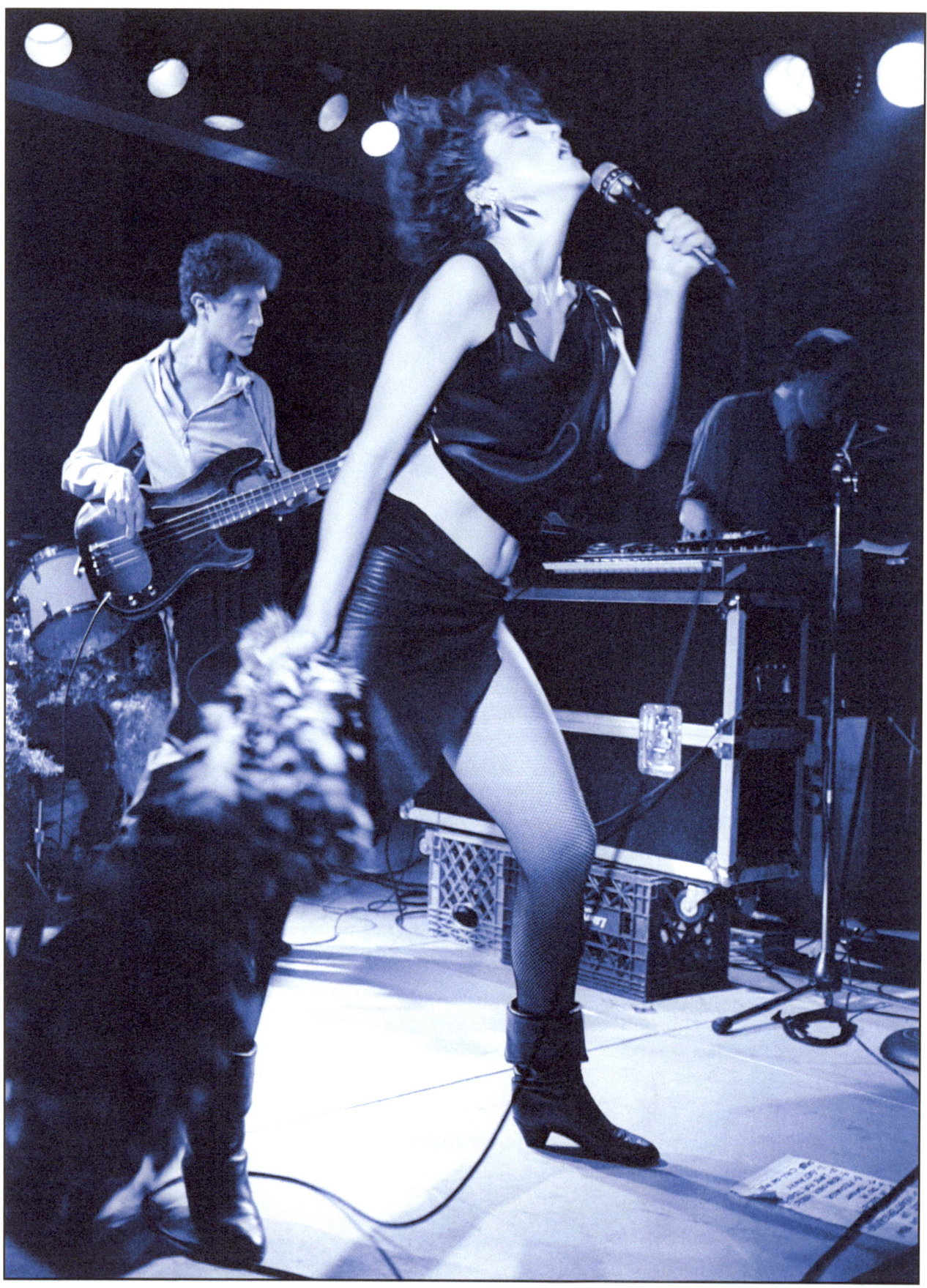

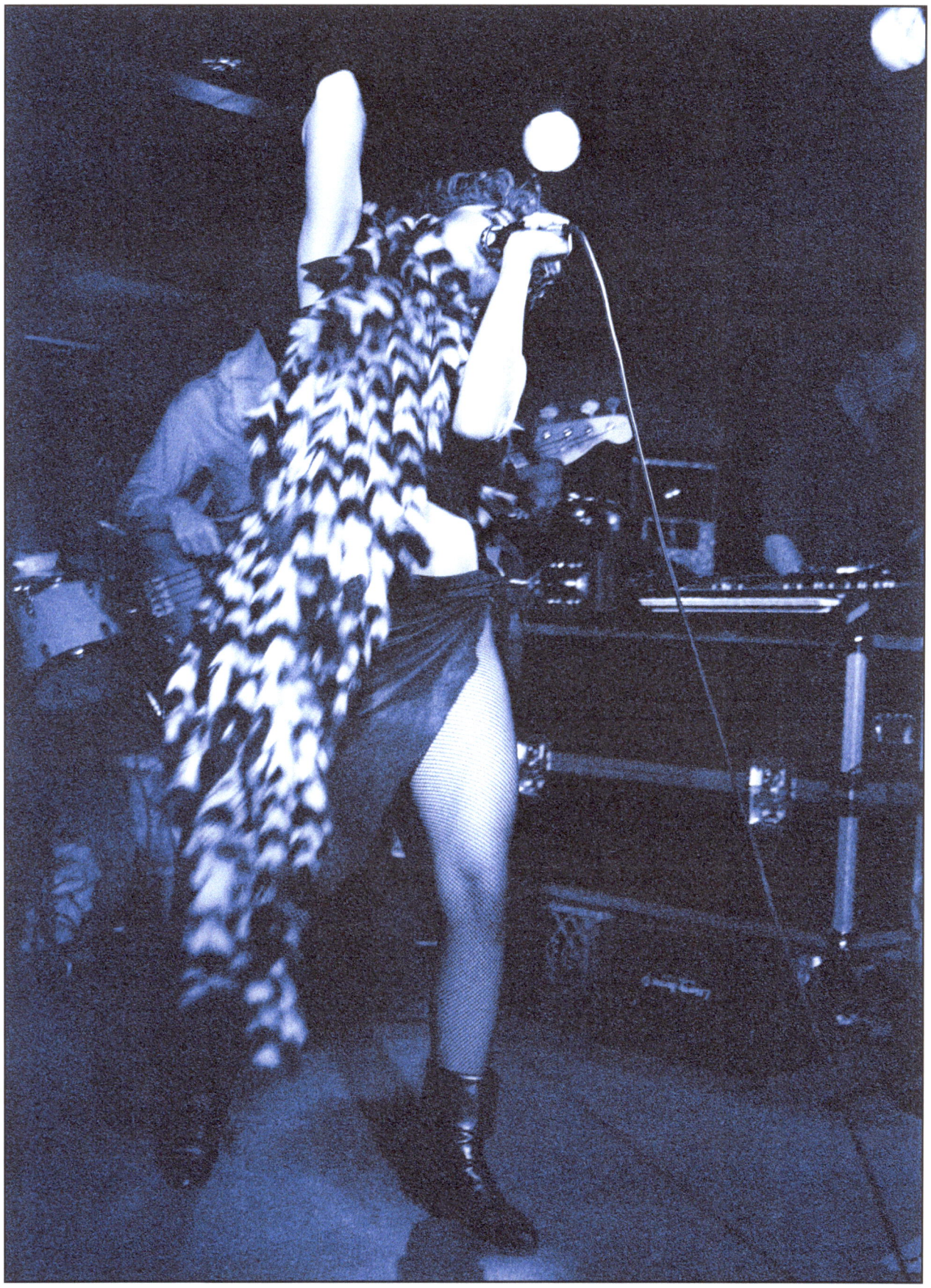

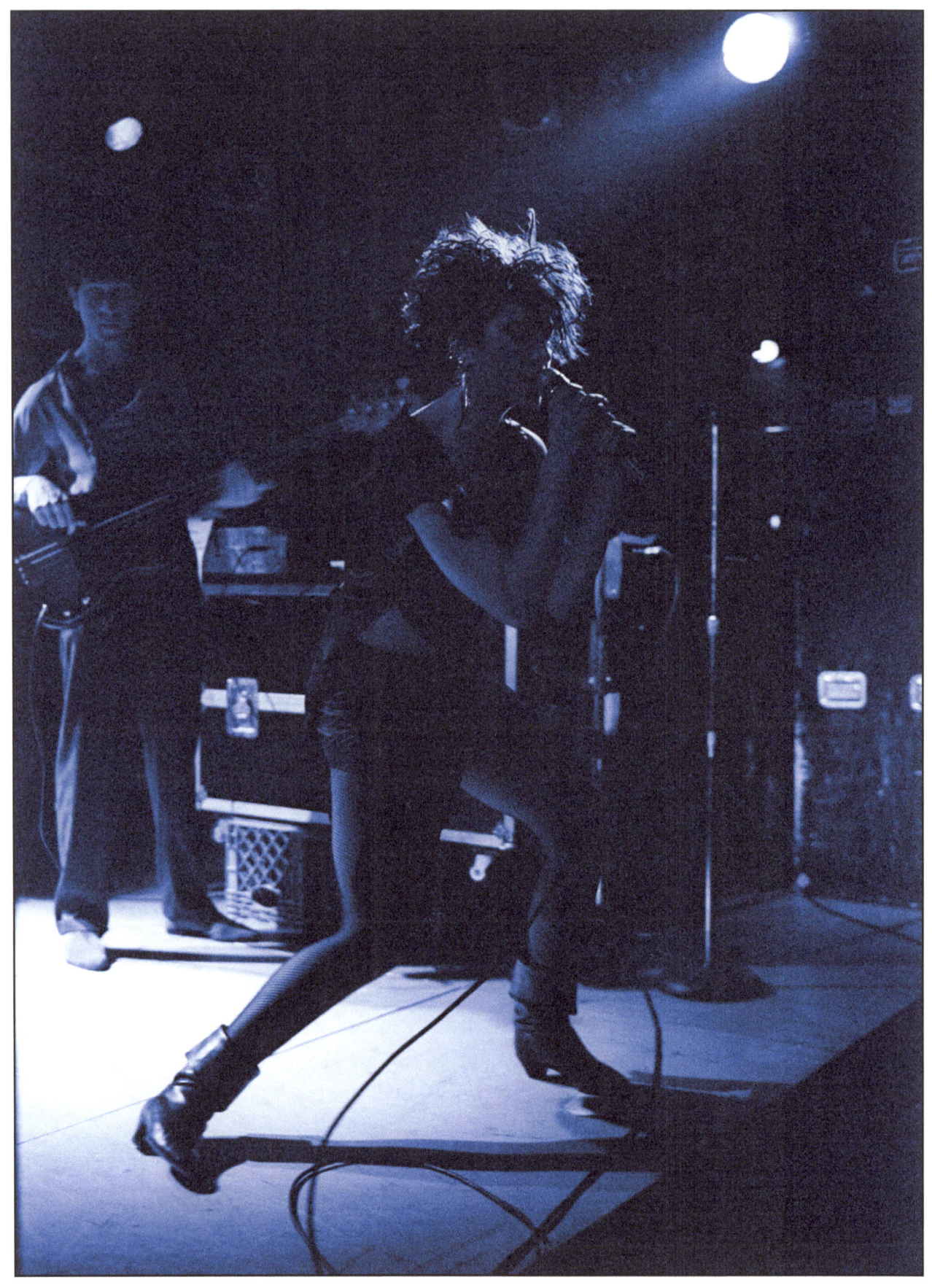

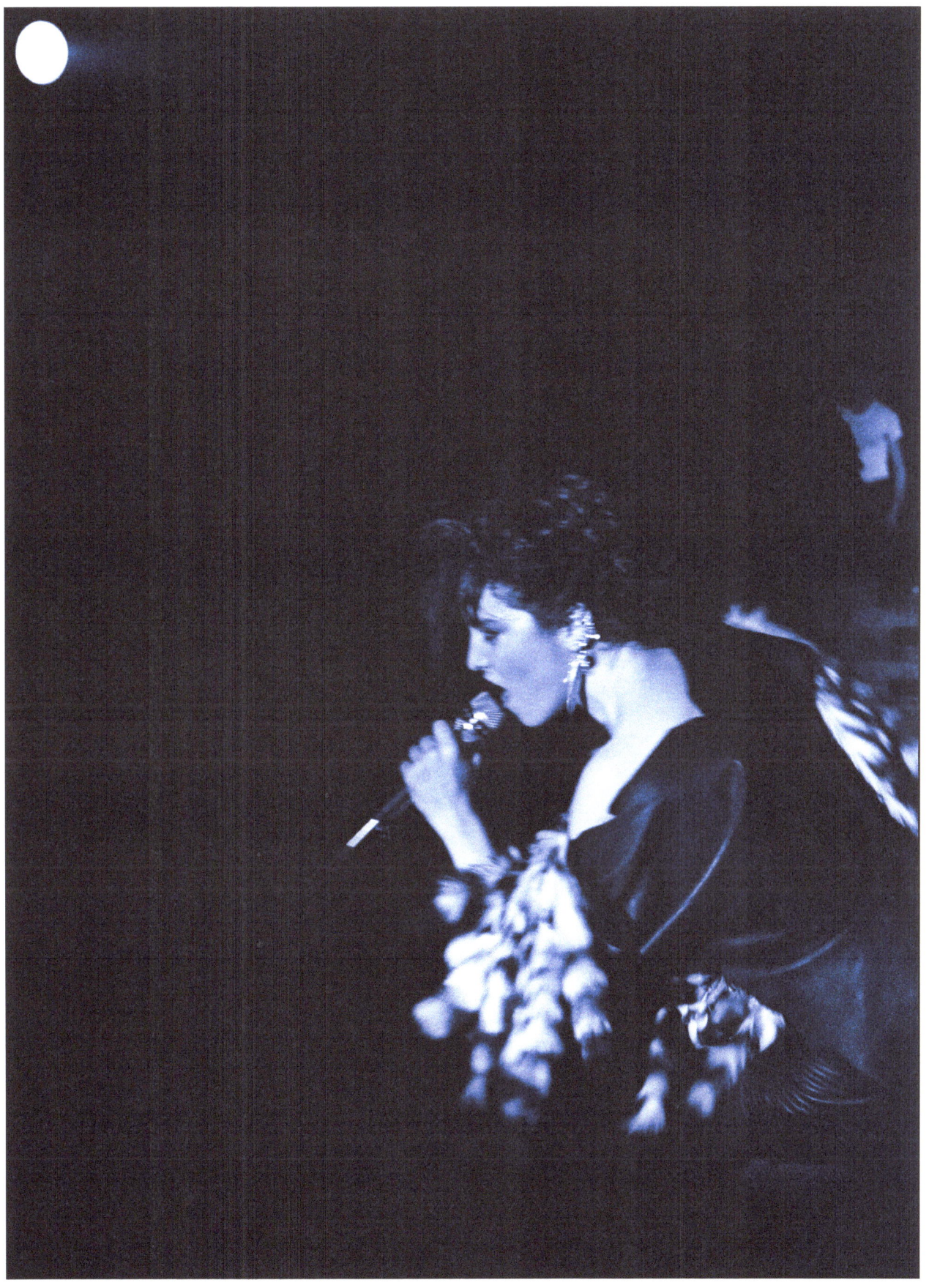

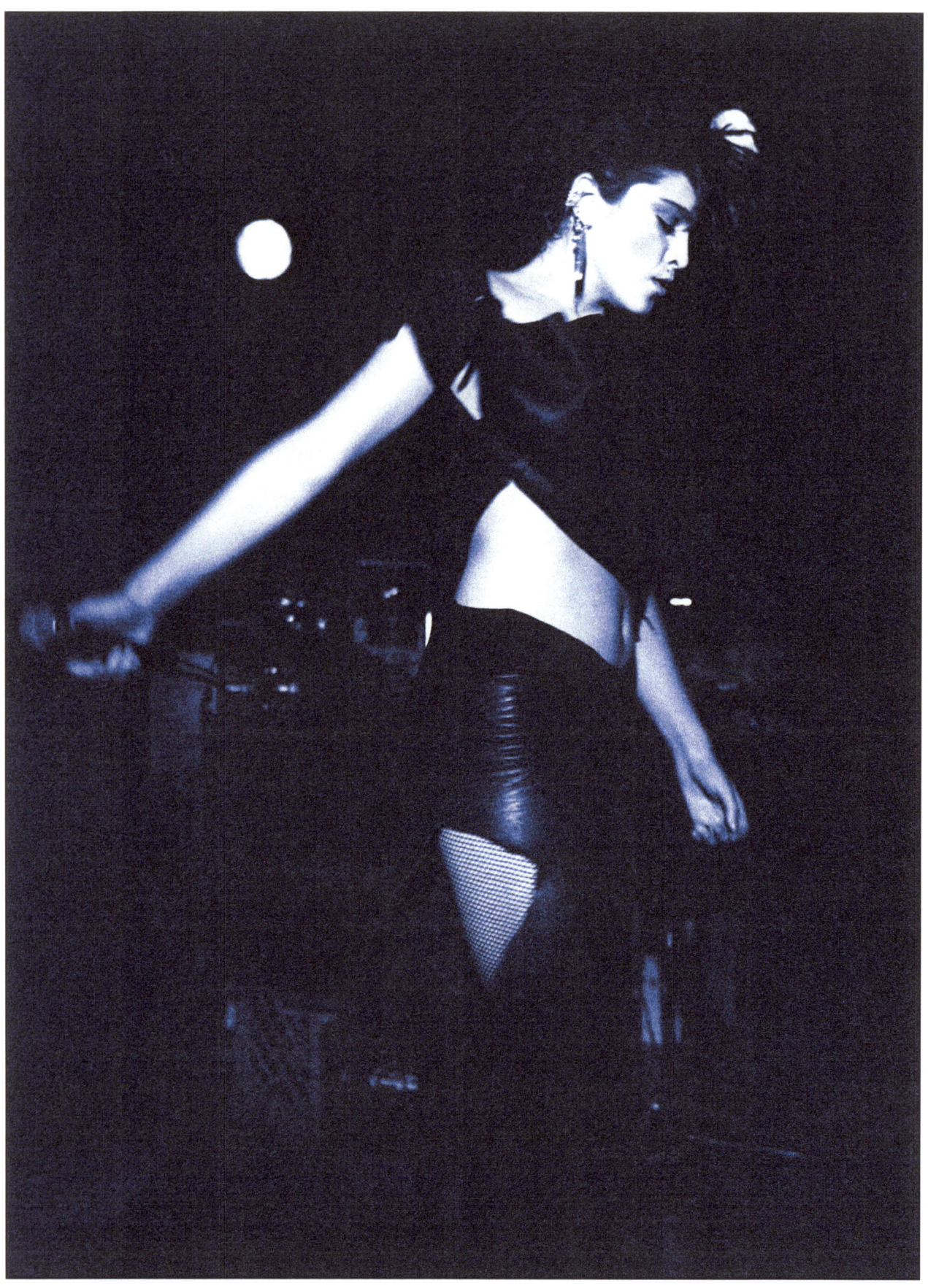

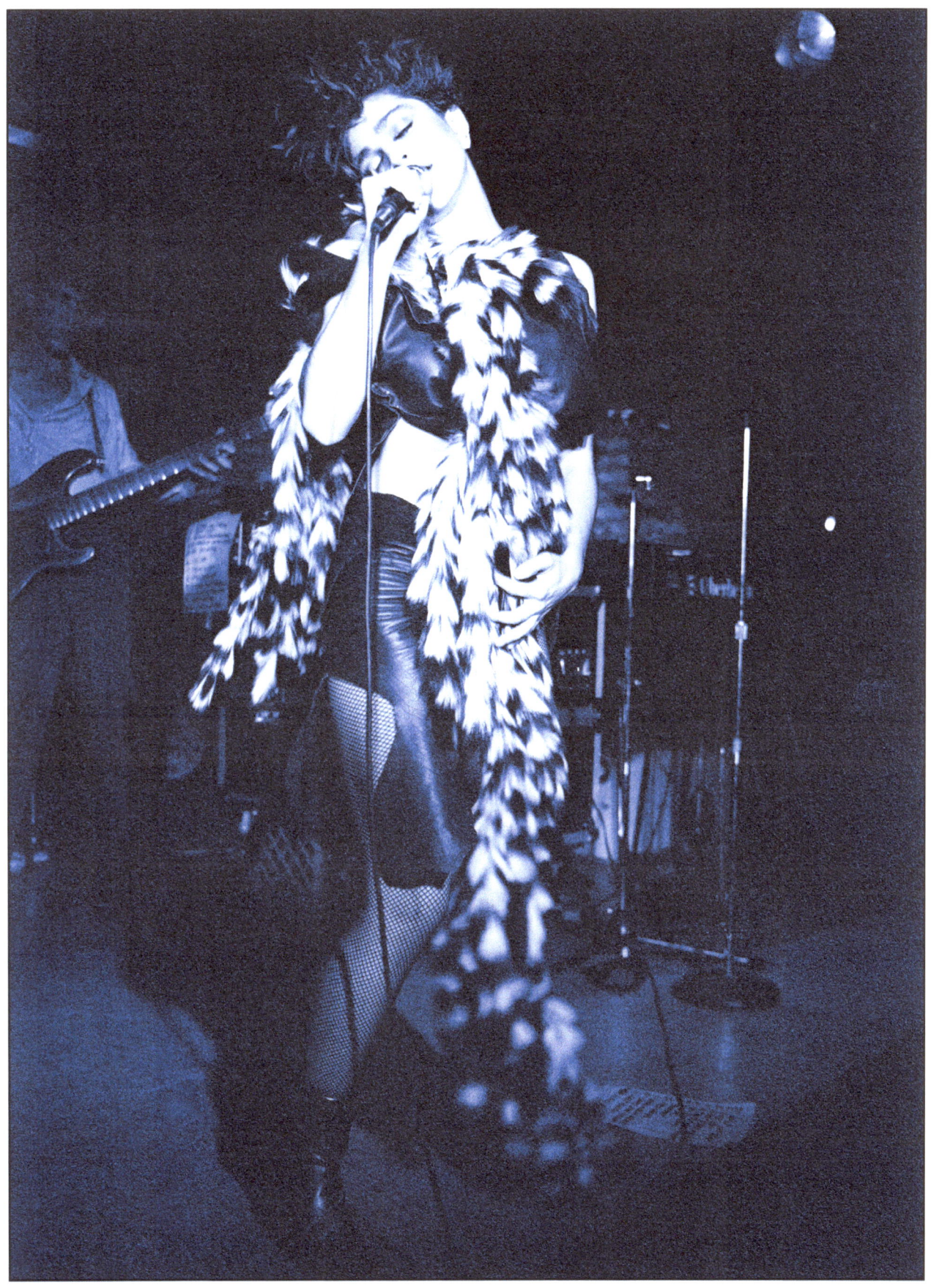

29

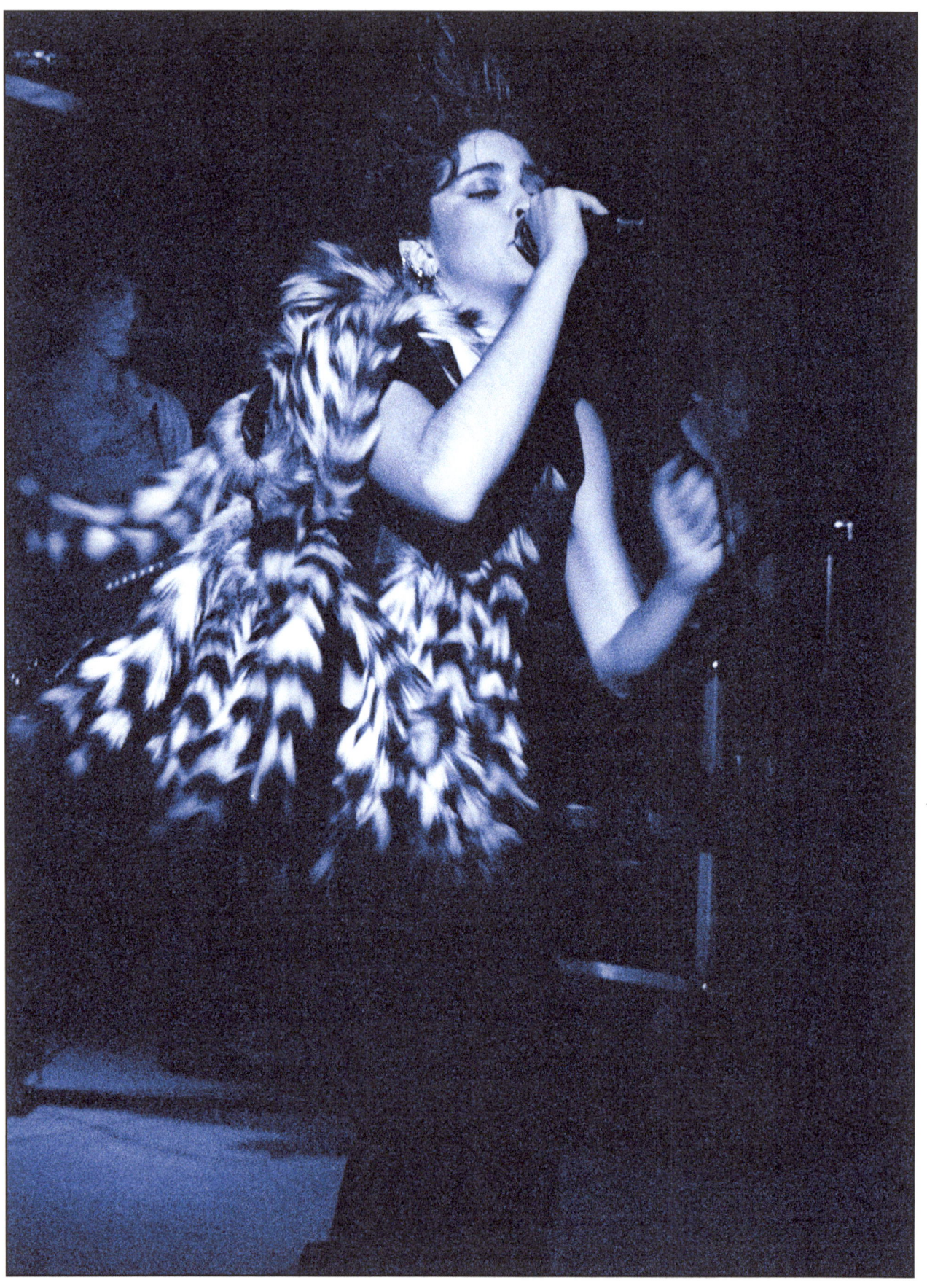

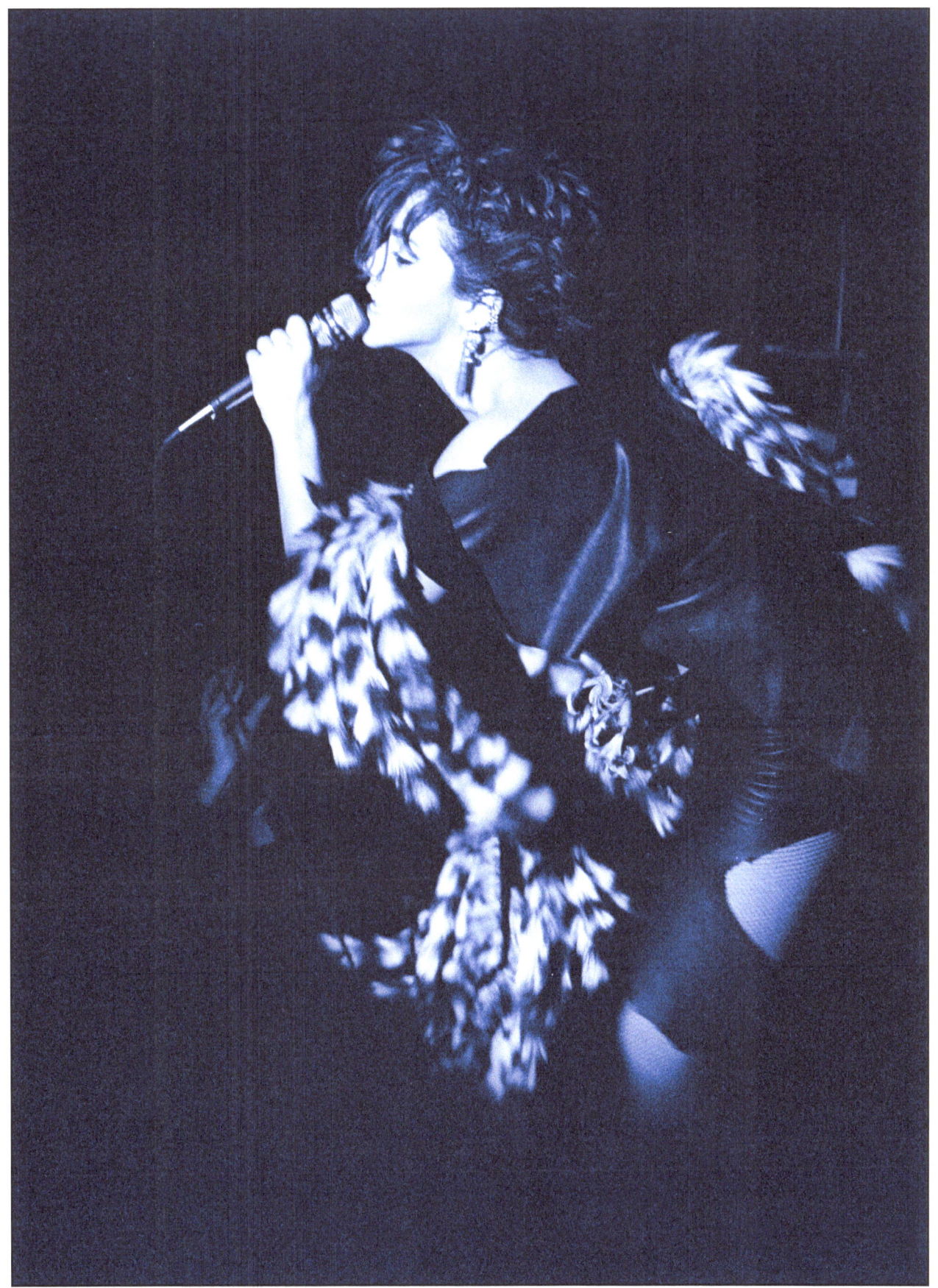

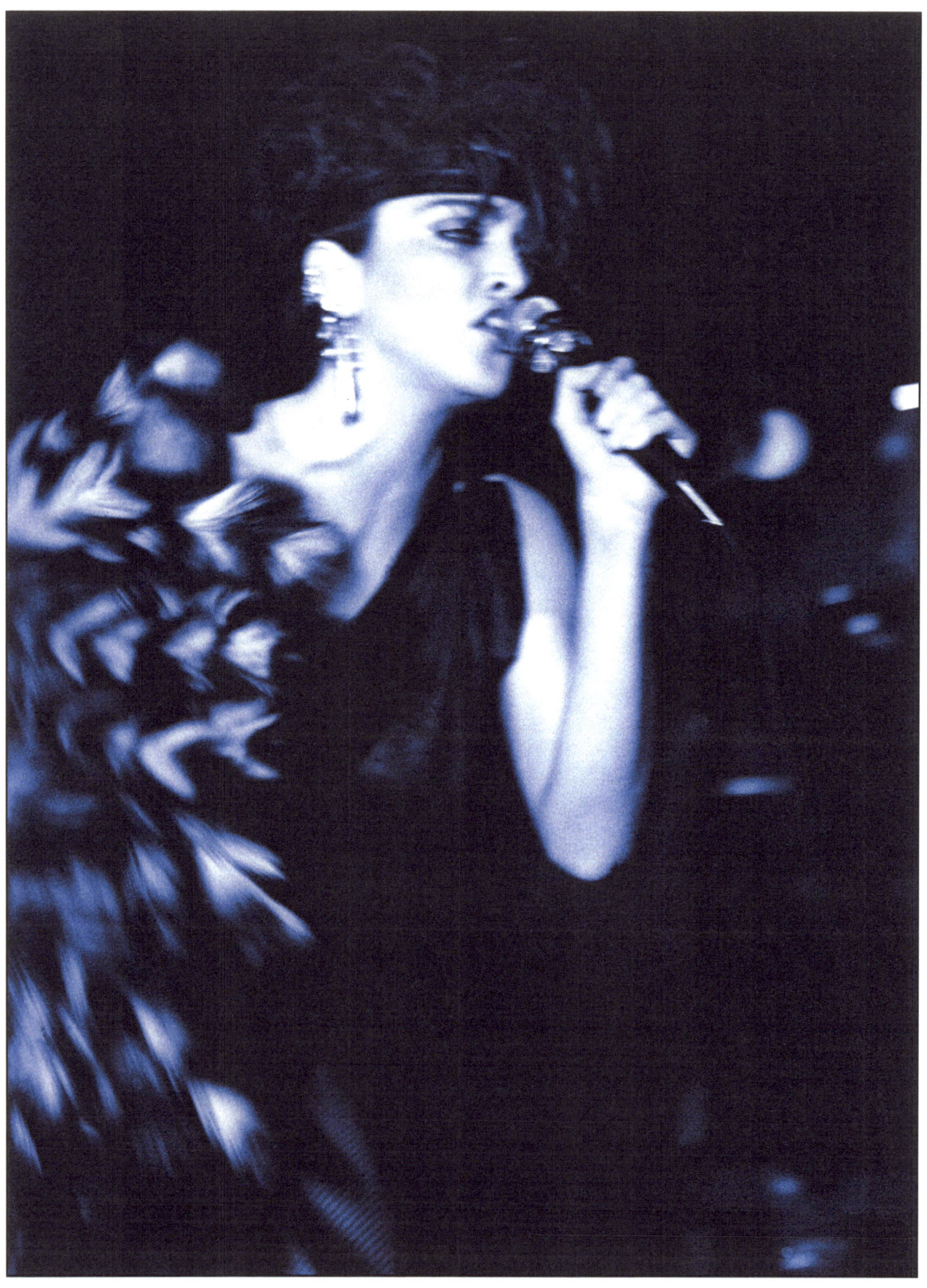

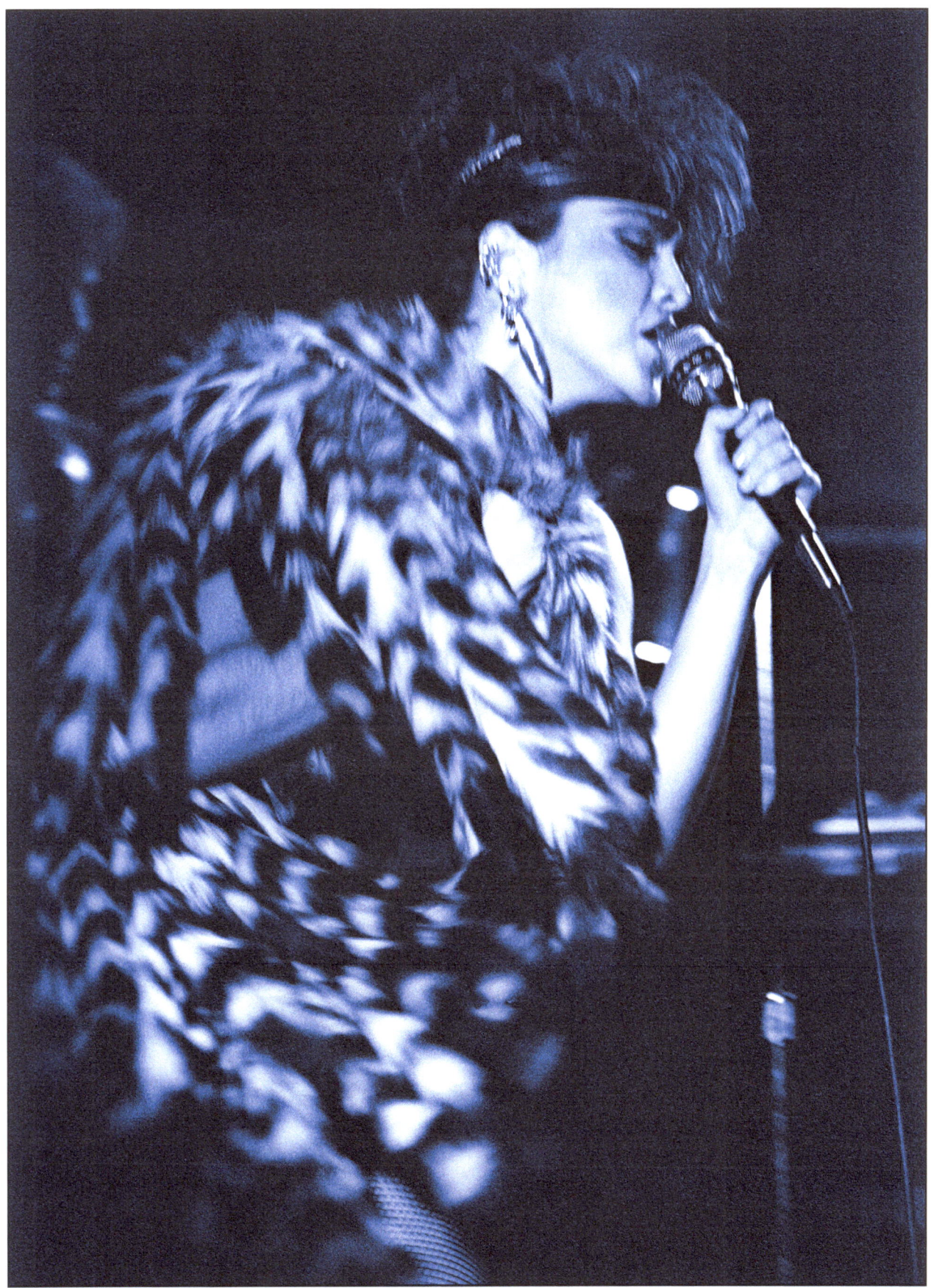

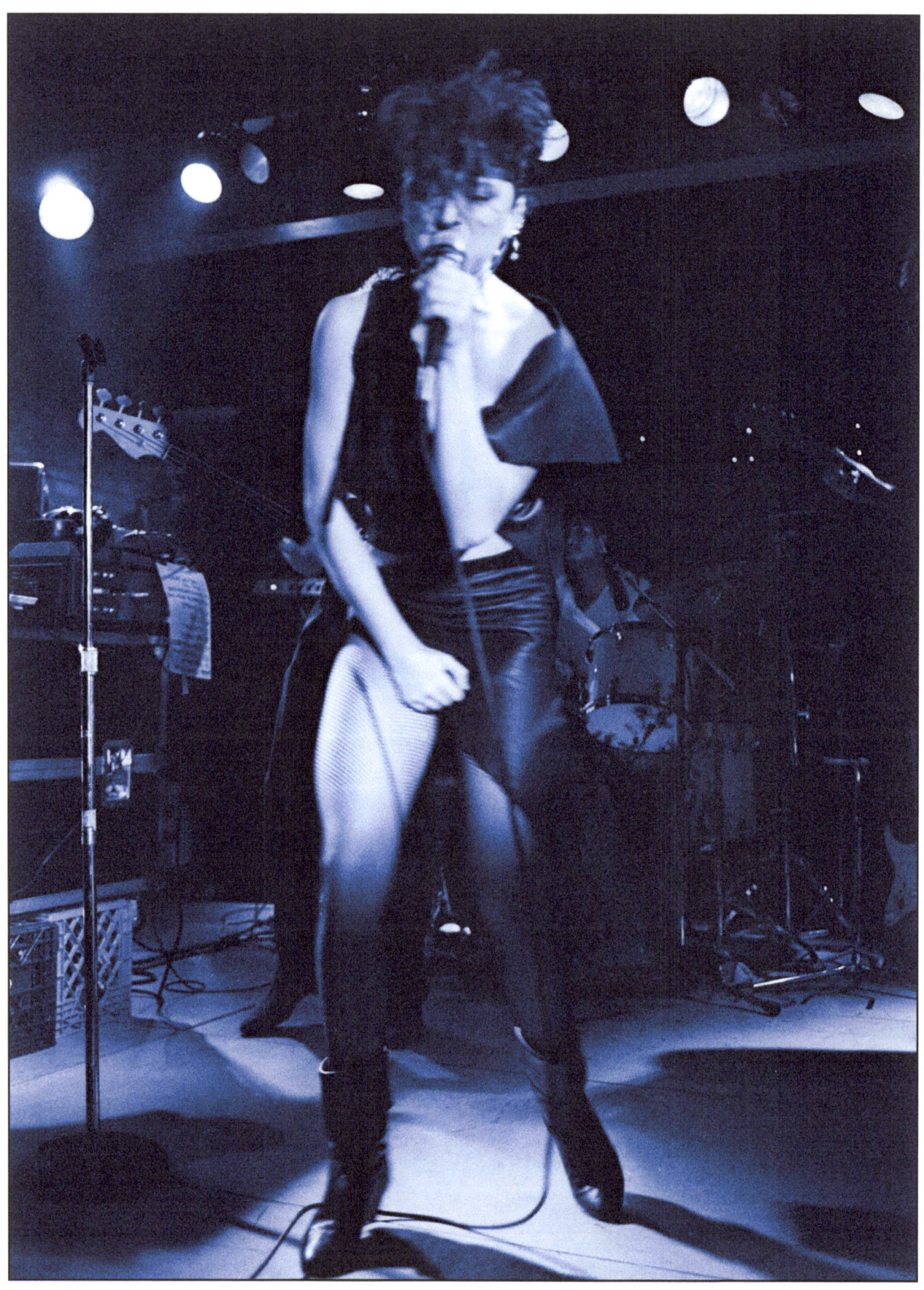

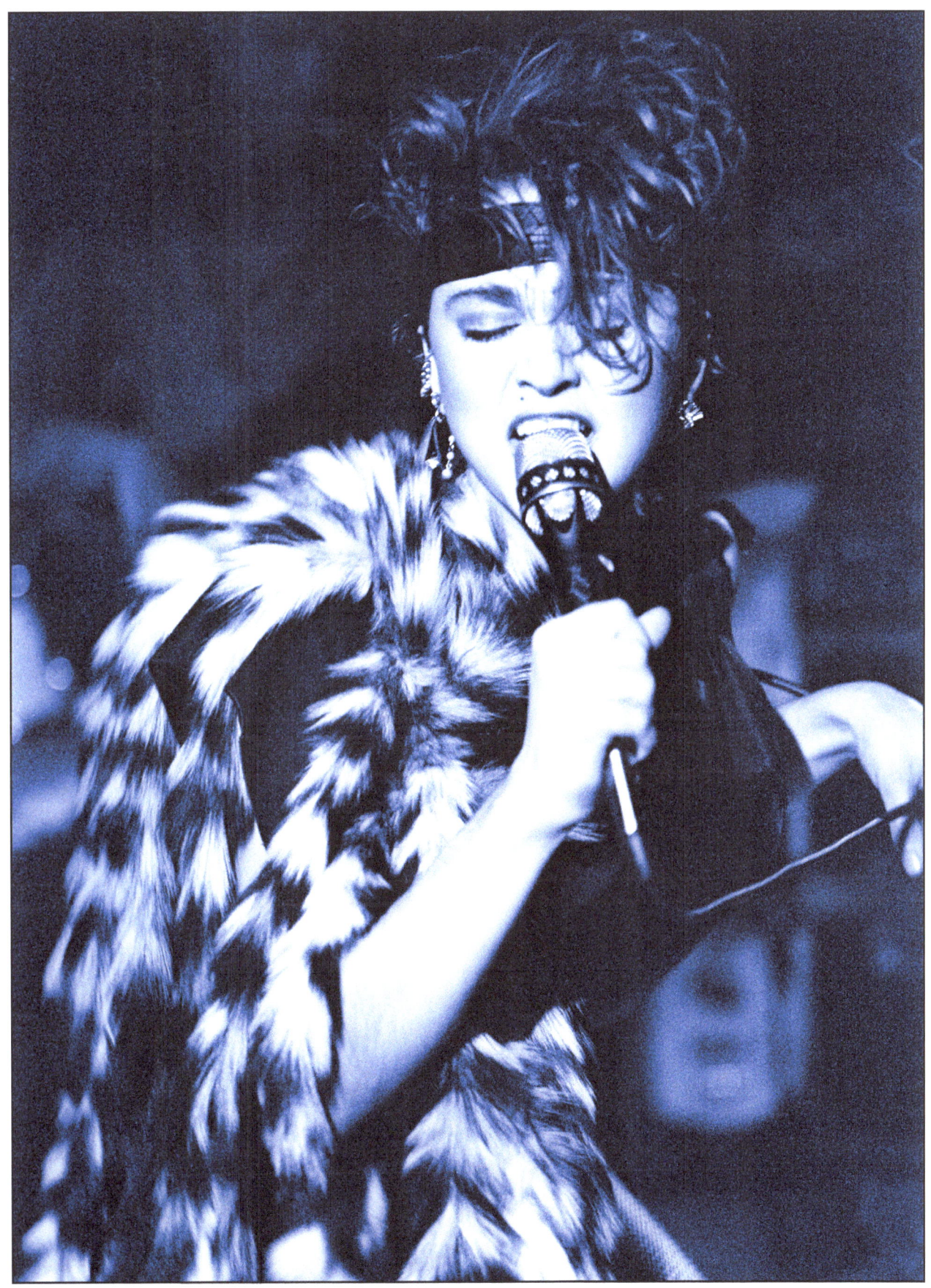

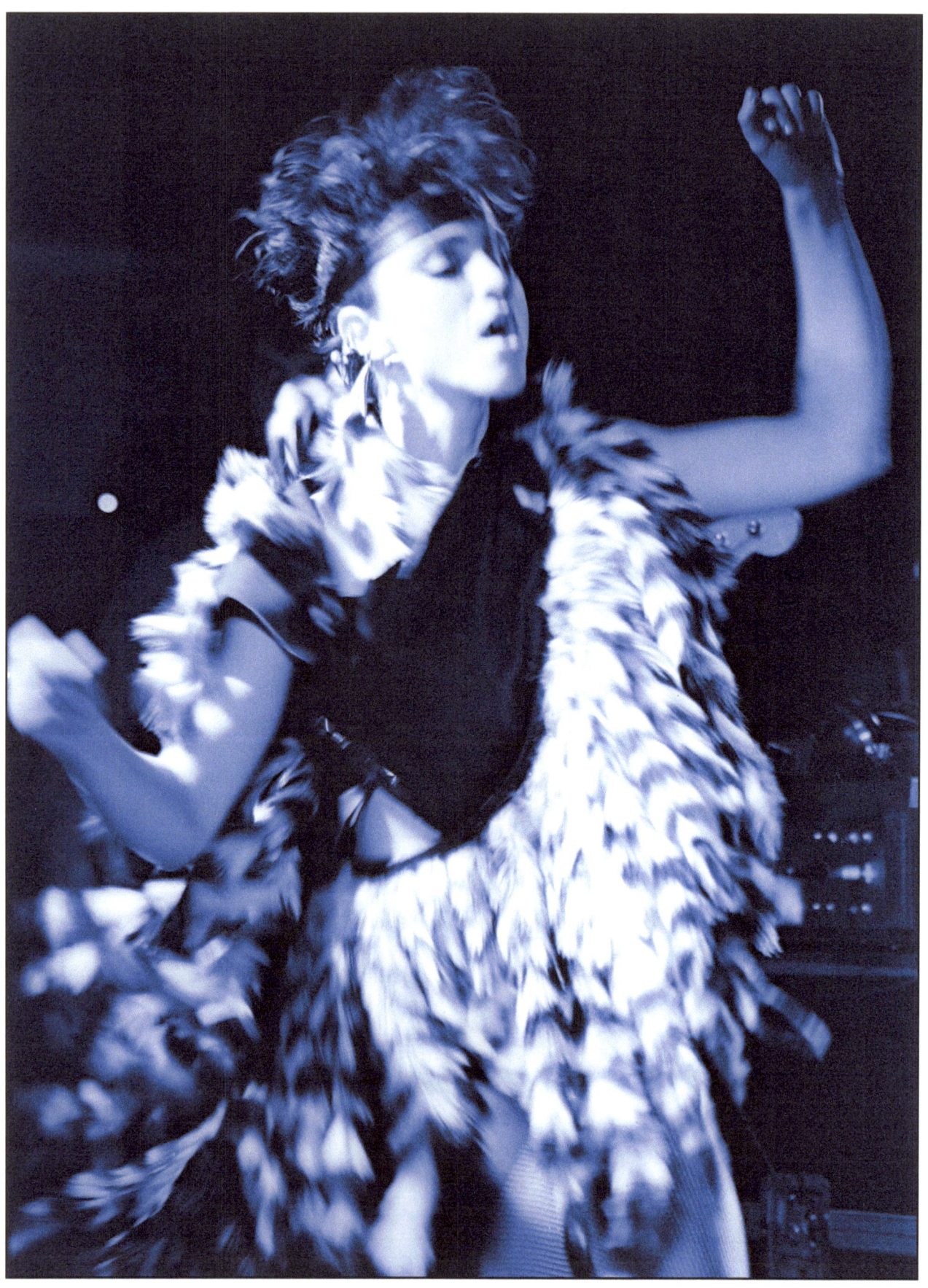

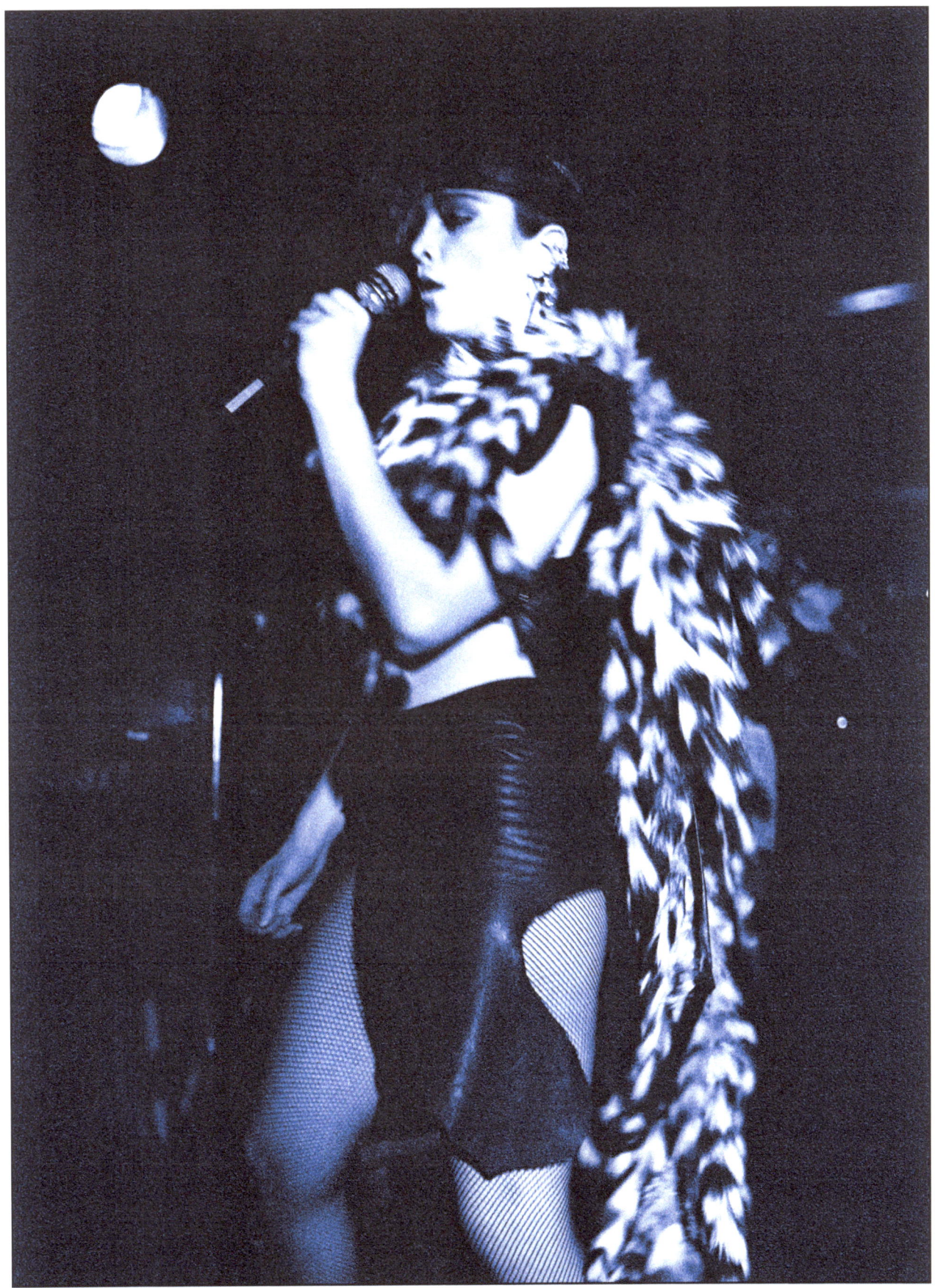

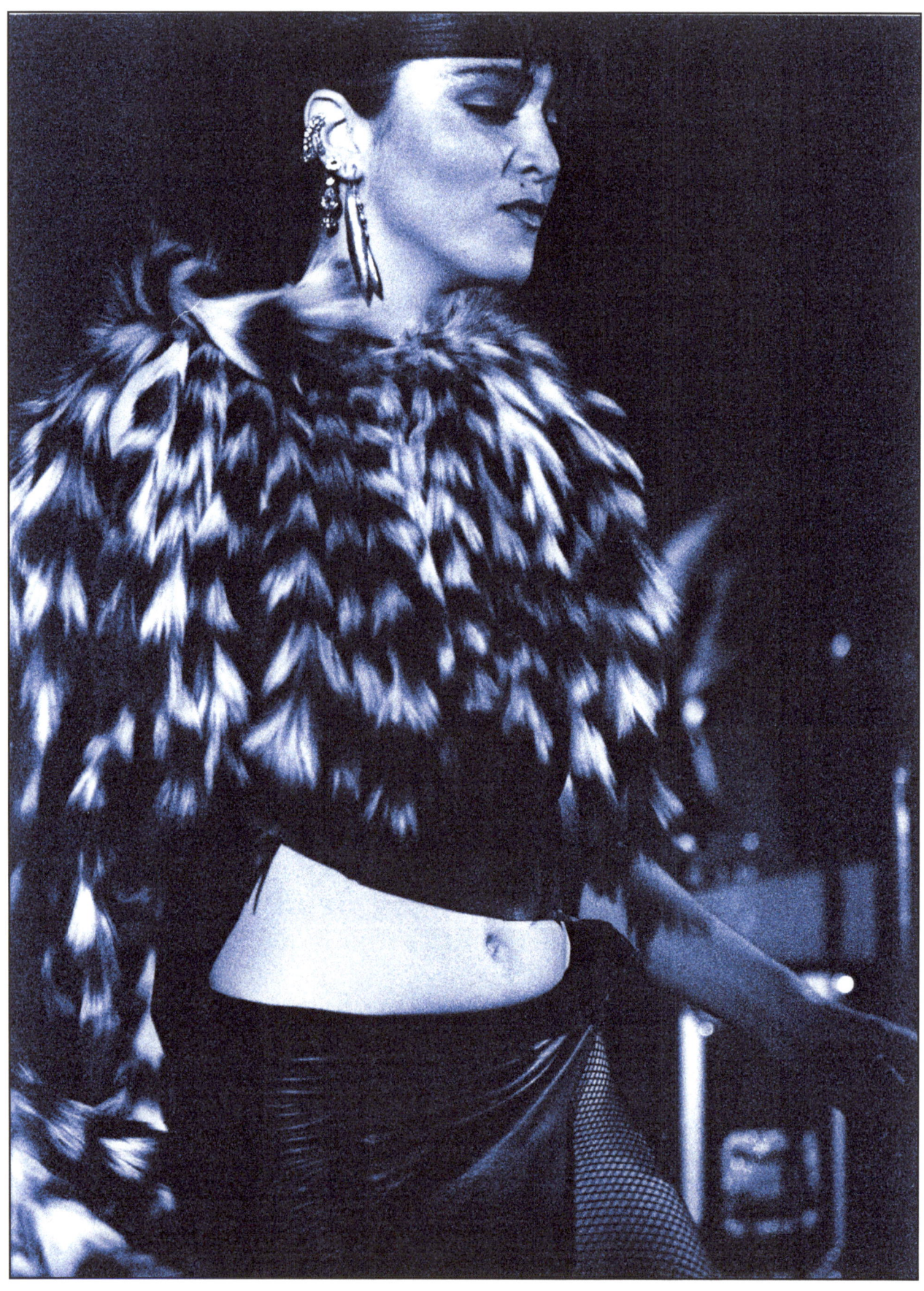

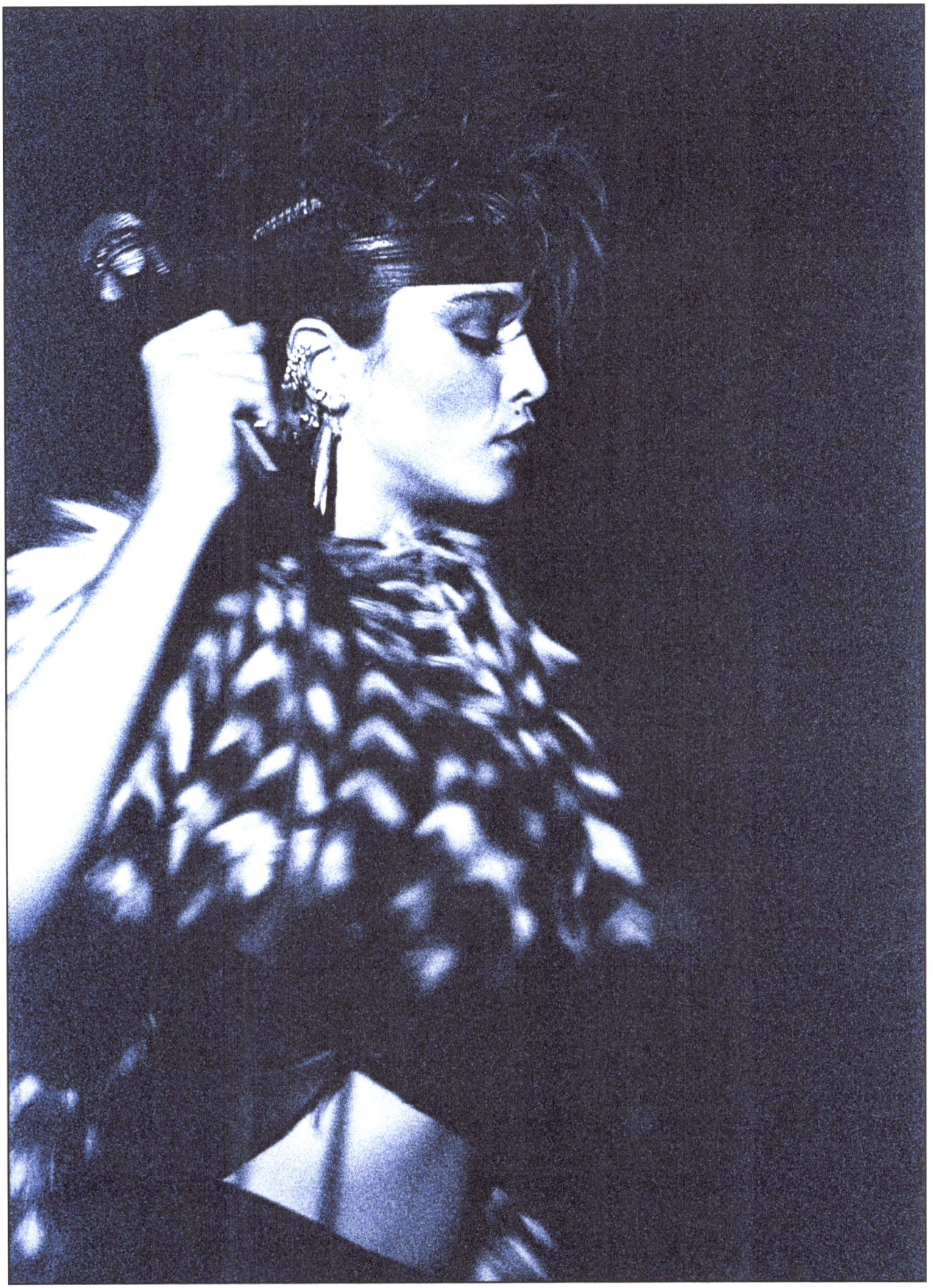

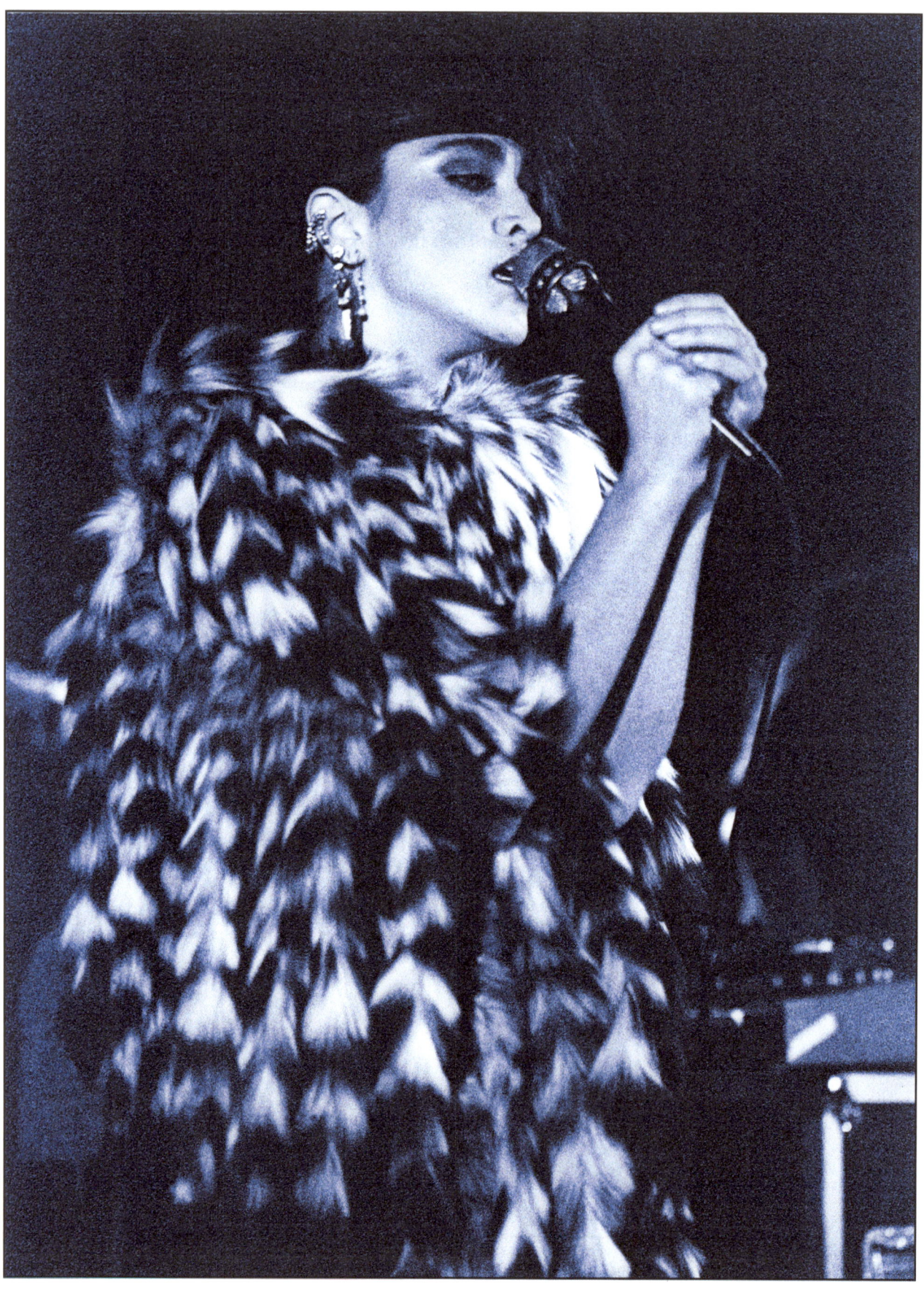

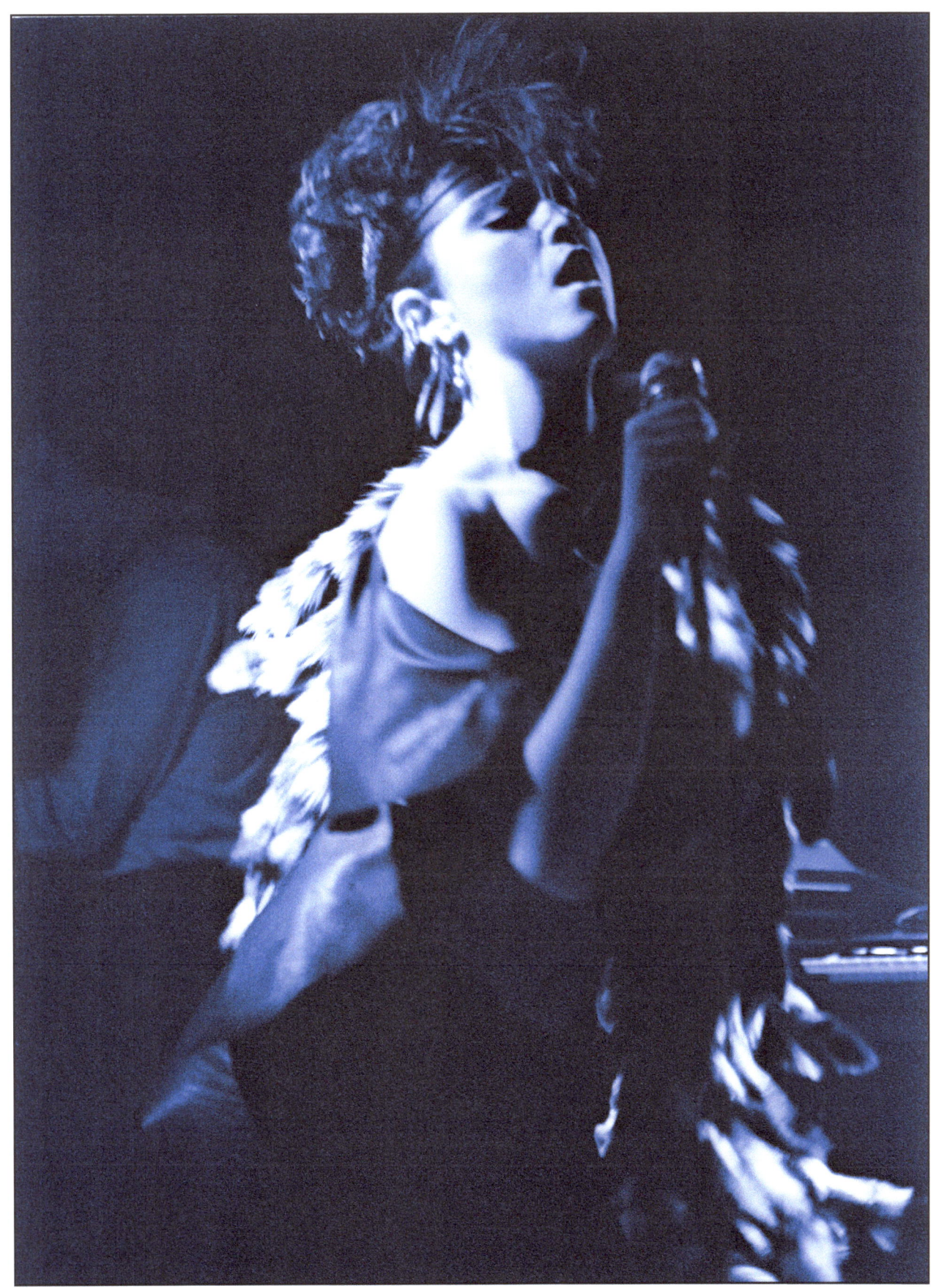

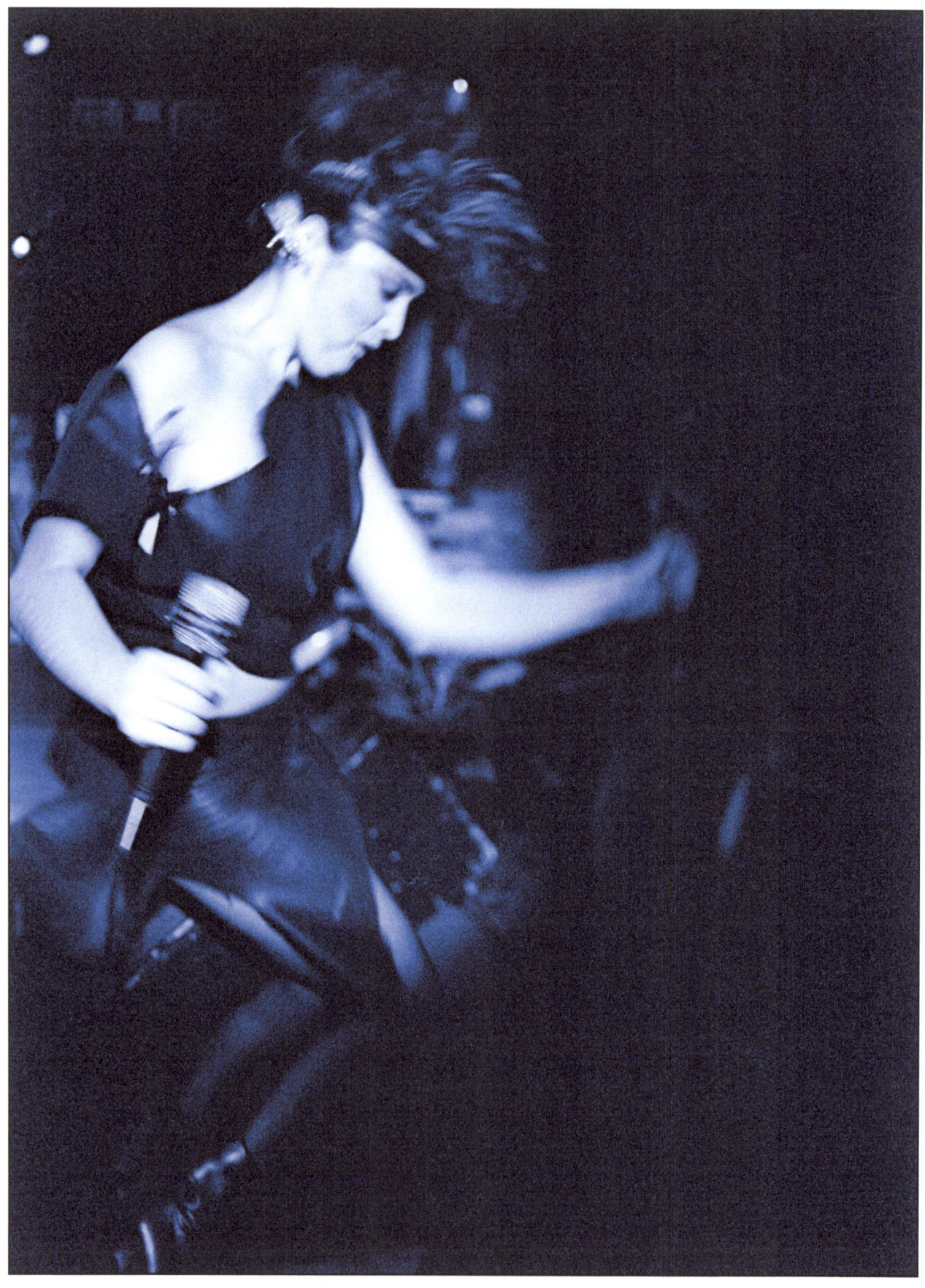

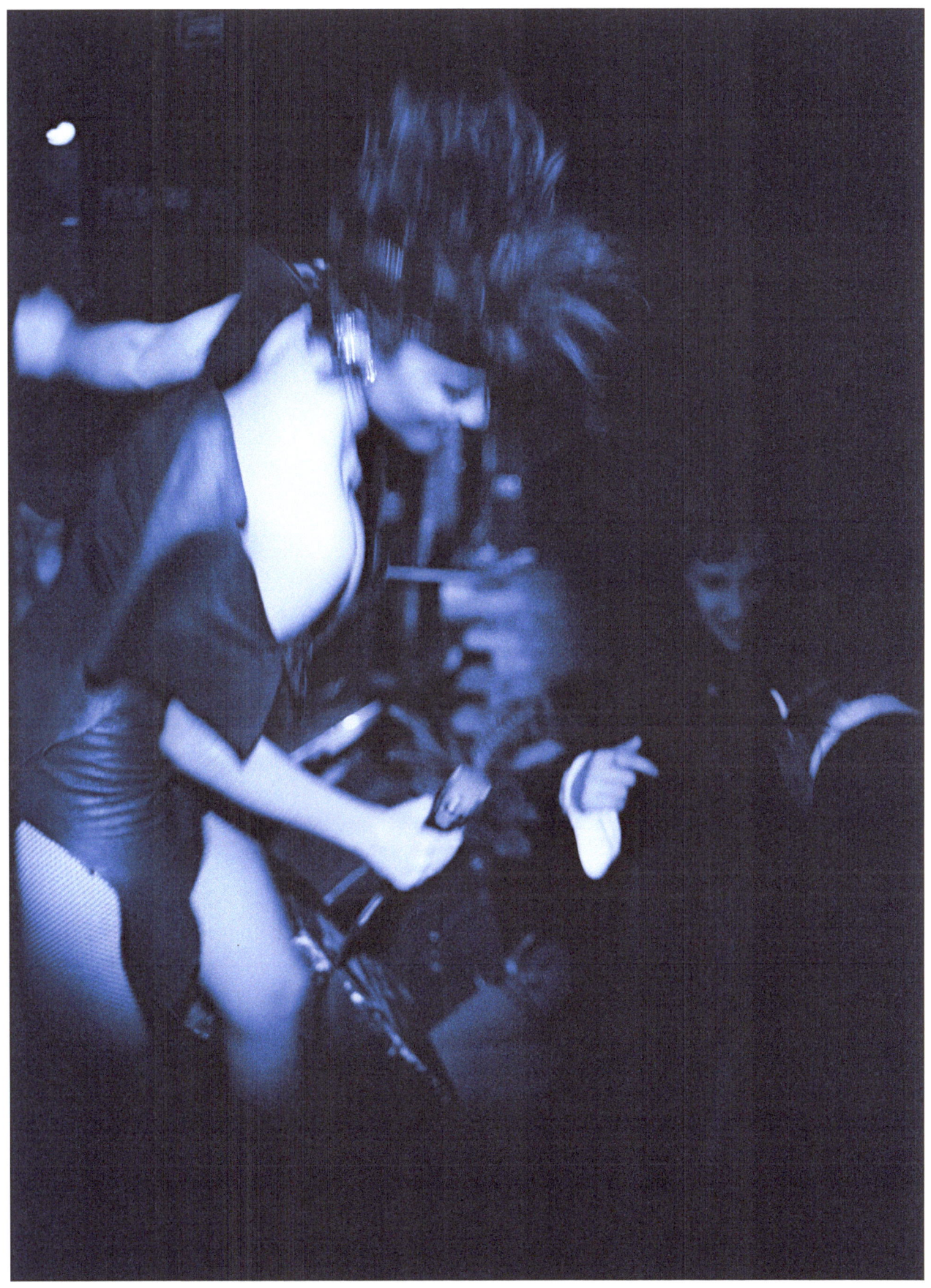

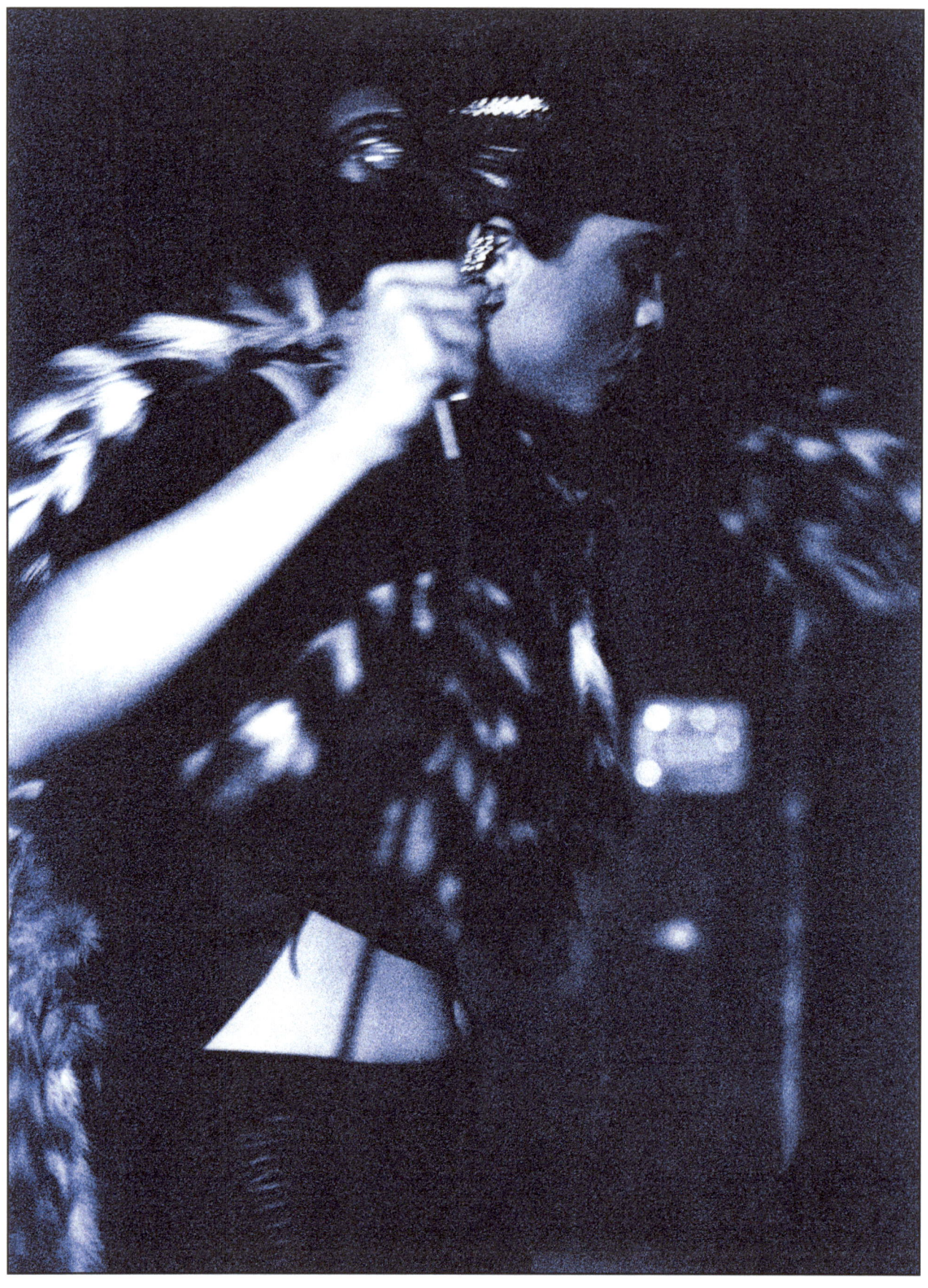

44

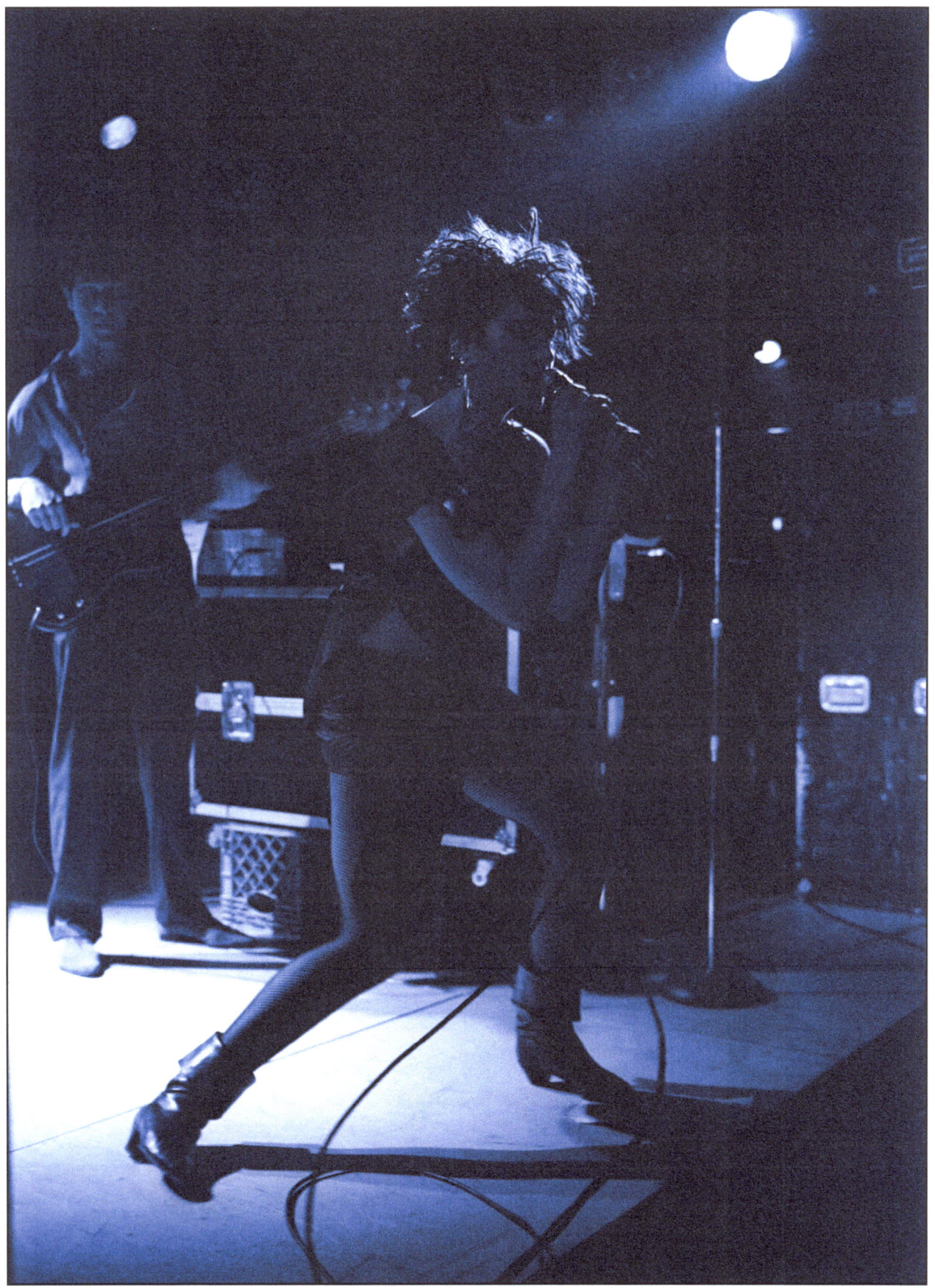

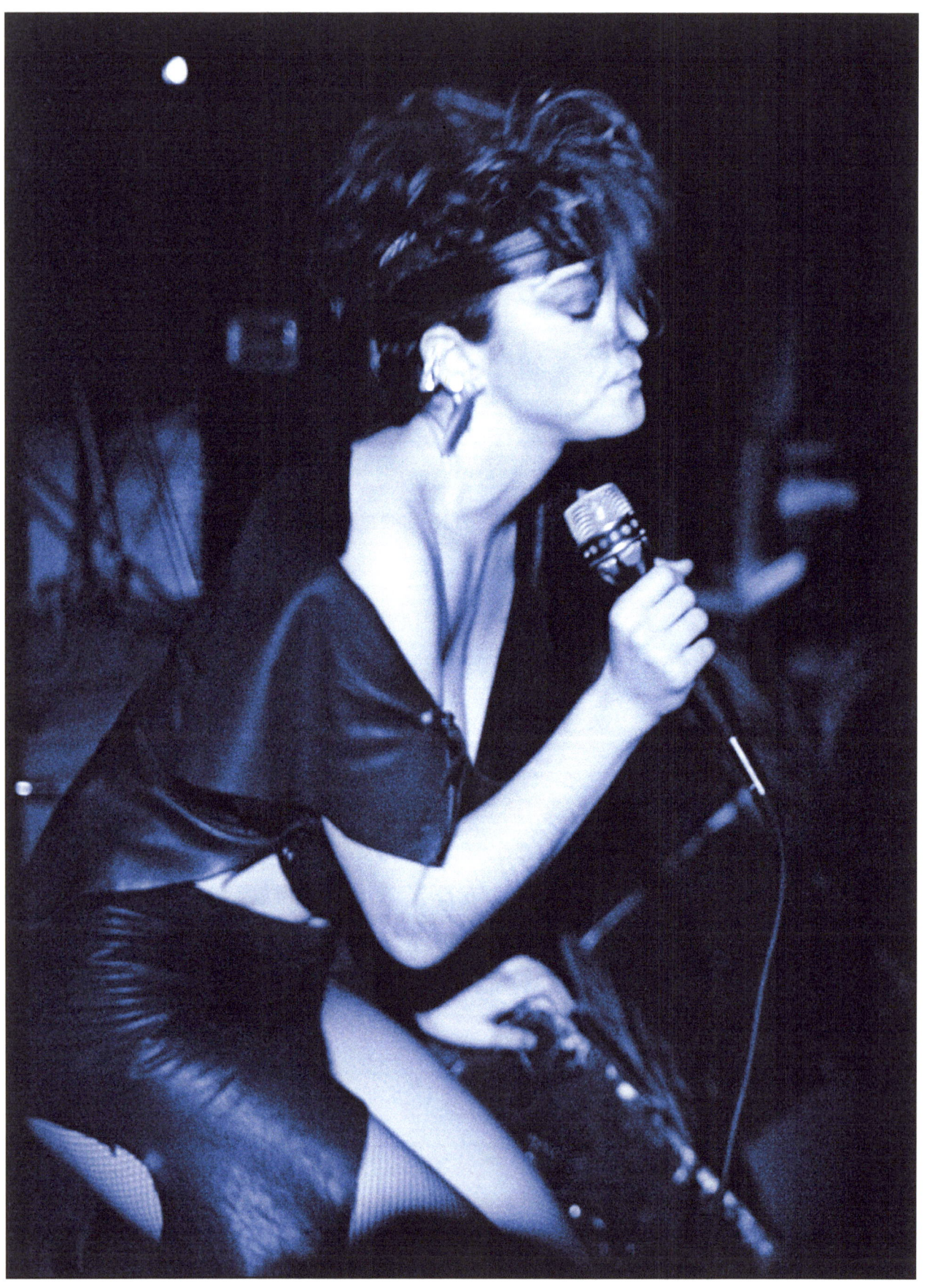

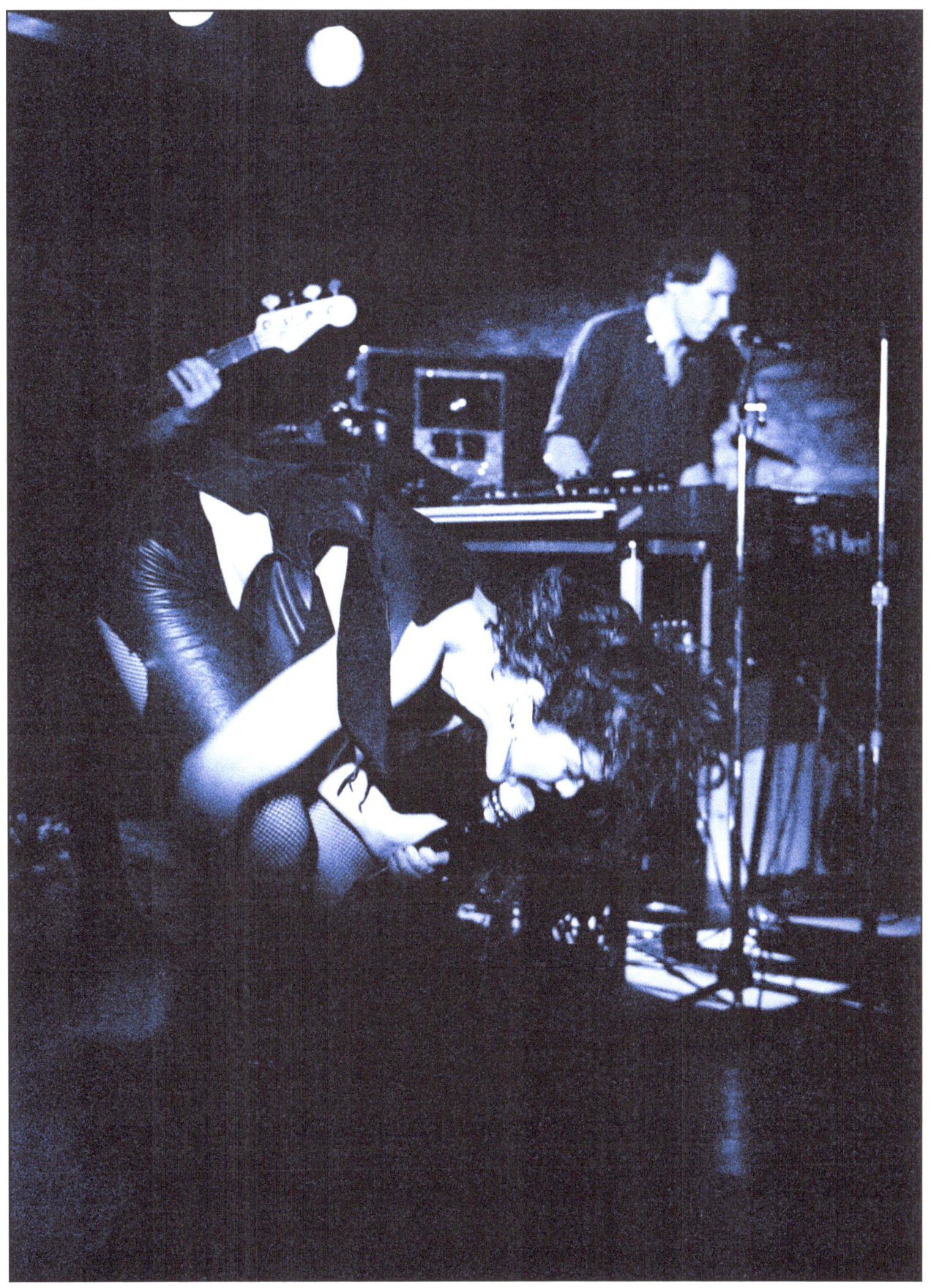

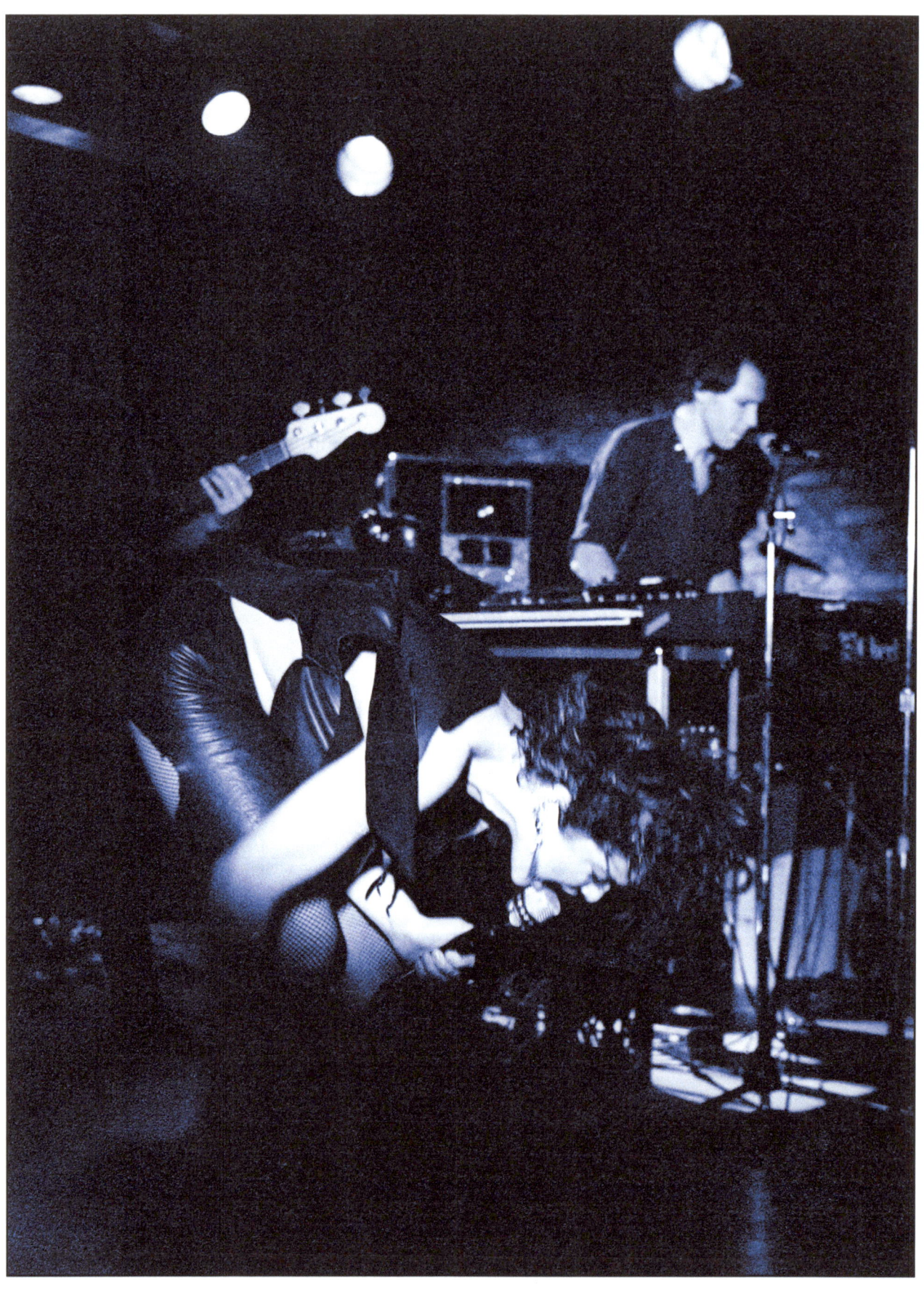

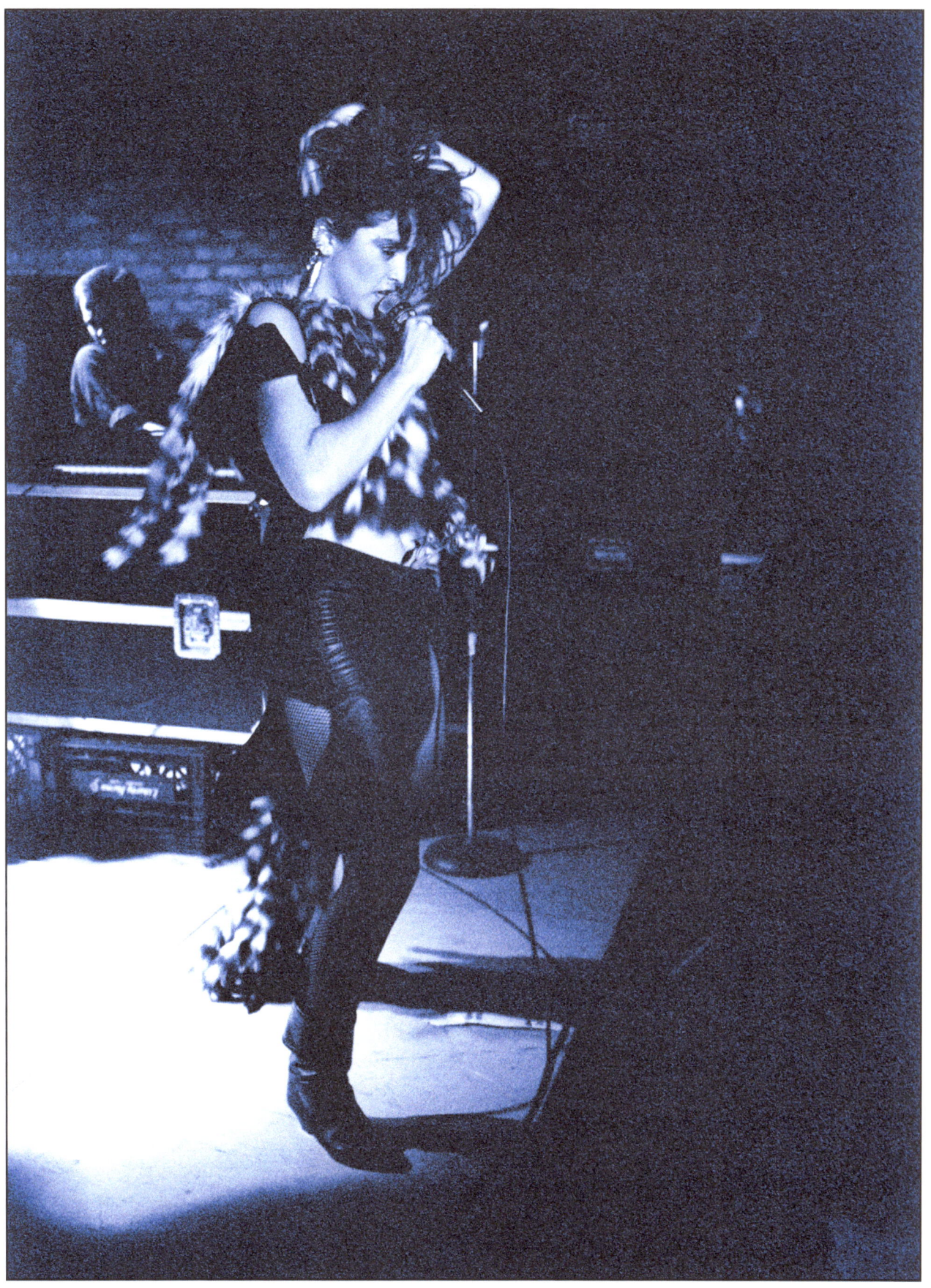

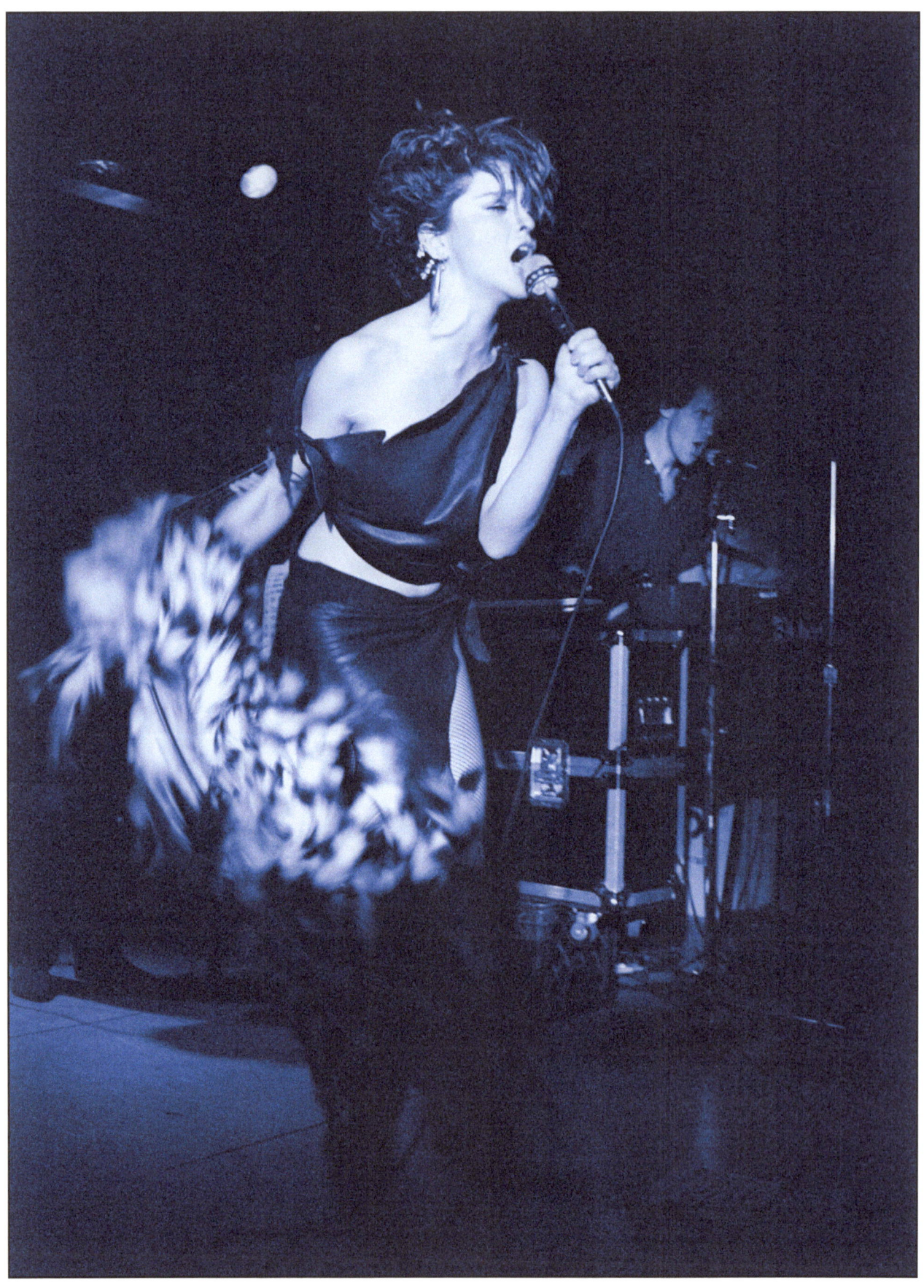

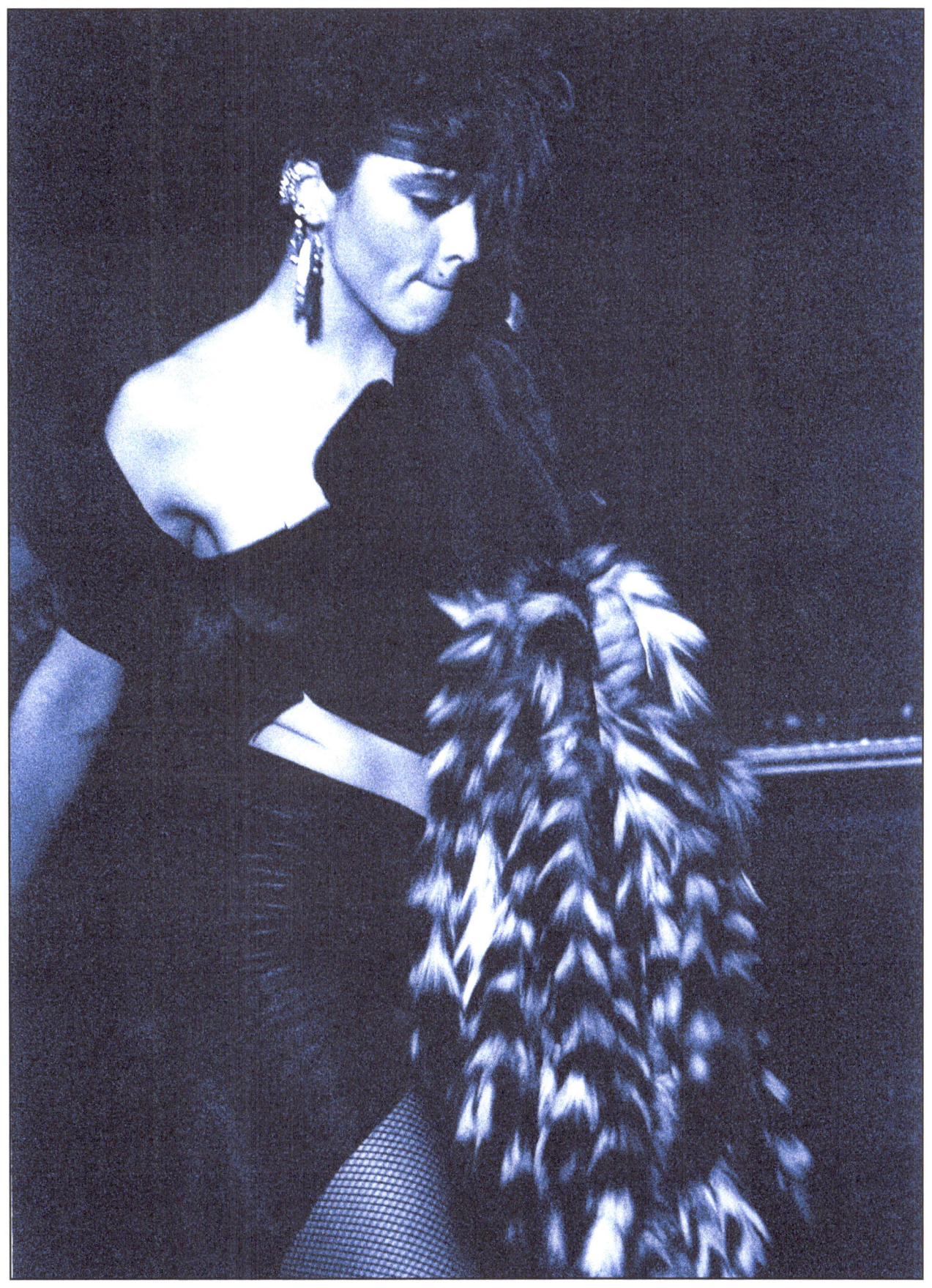

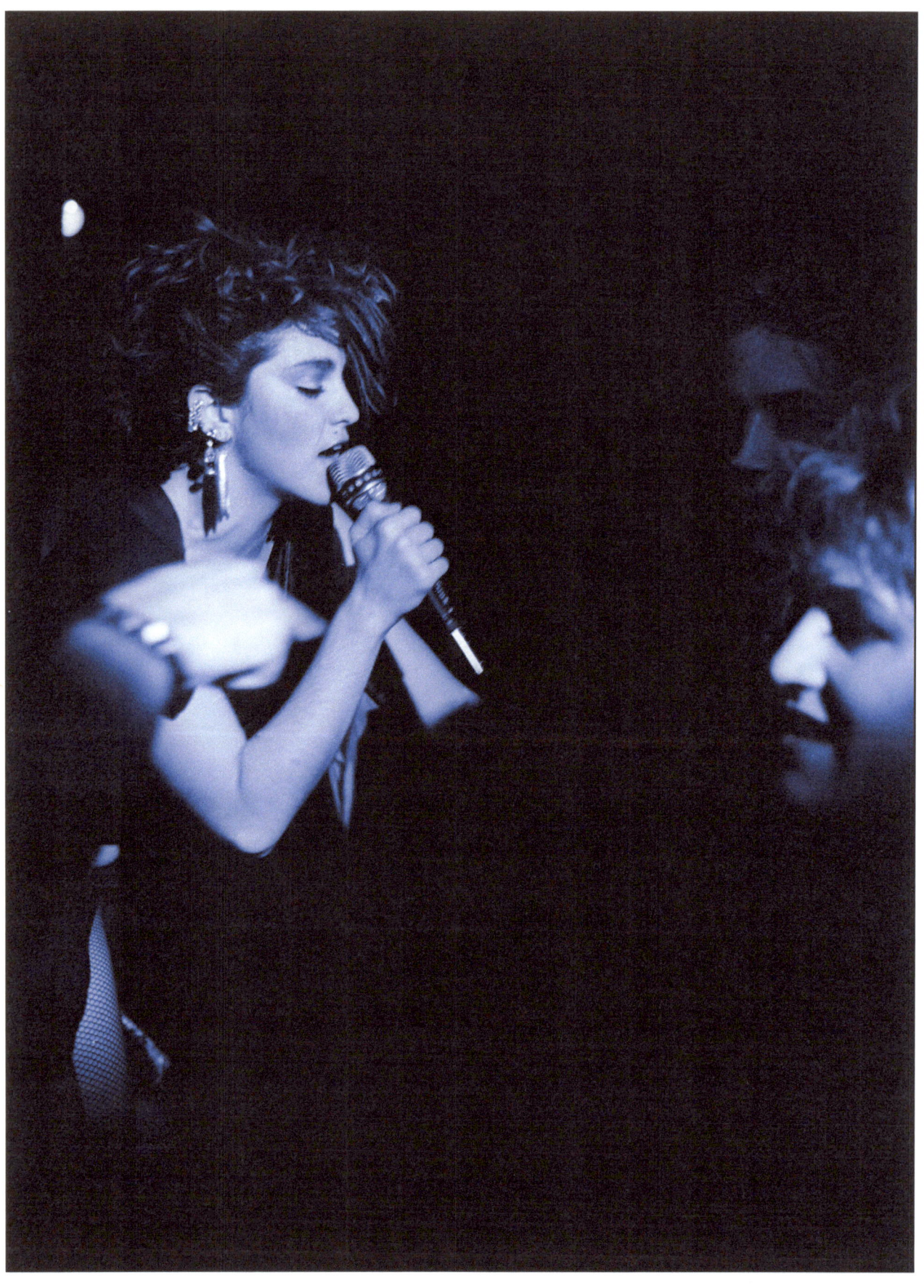

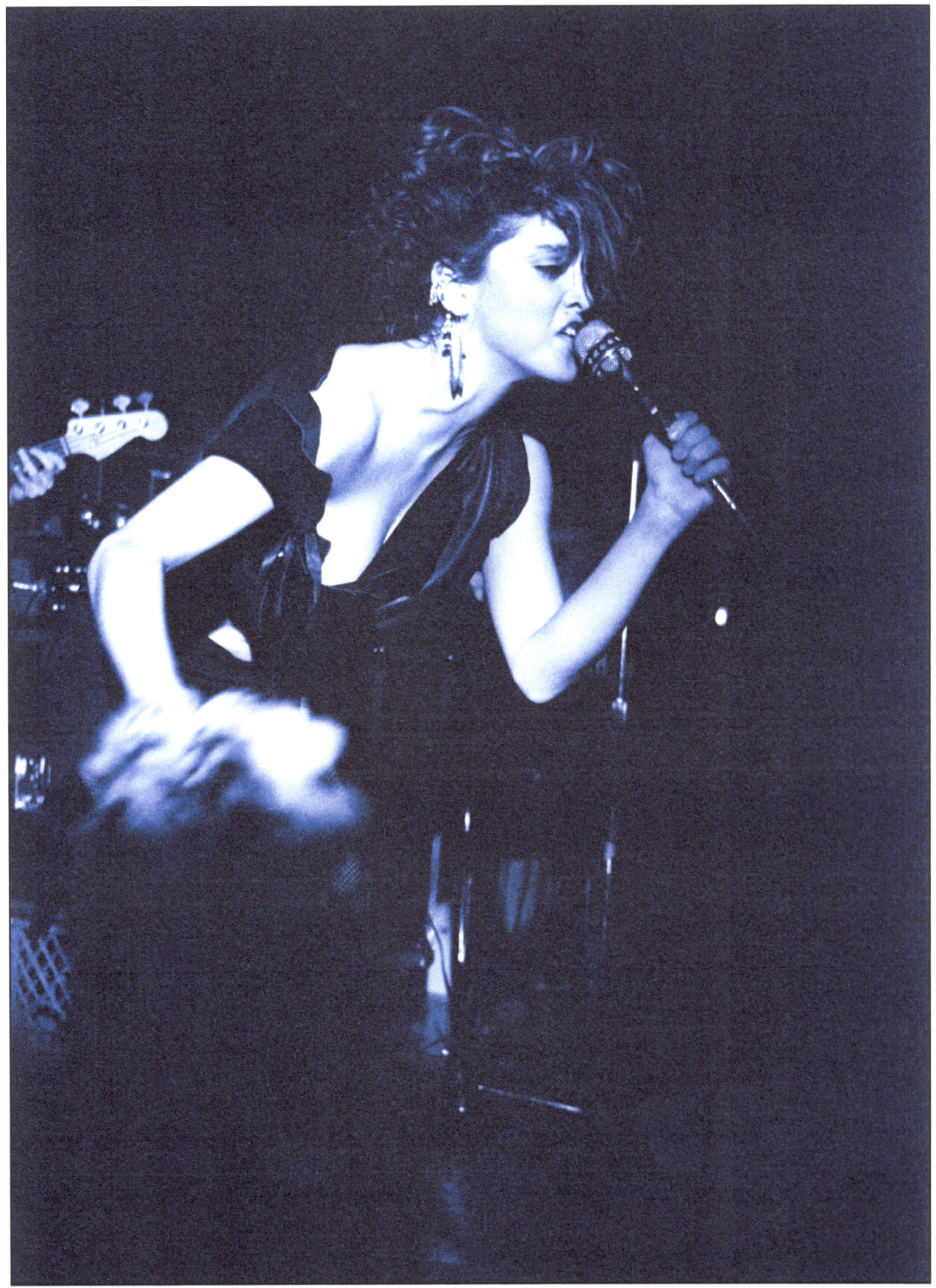

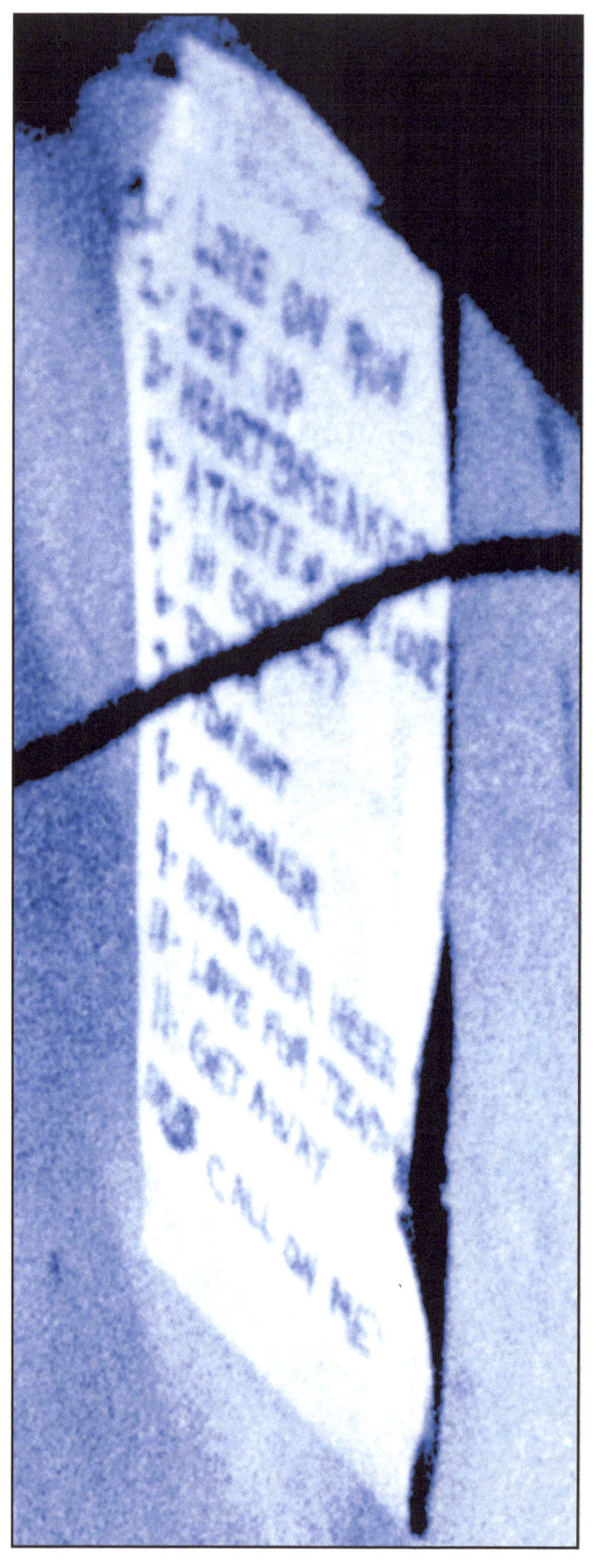

54

The following photos are what I would normally not show to anyone.

In the interest of Freedom of Information and to answer the question "Are there any more shots?

I am including every picture it took that memorable evening.

Warts and all...

My warts, not Madonna's

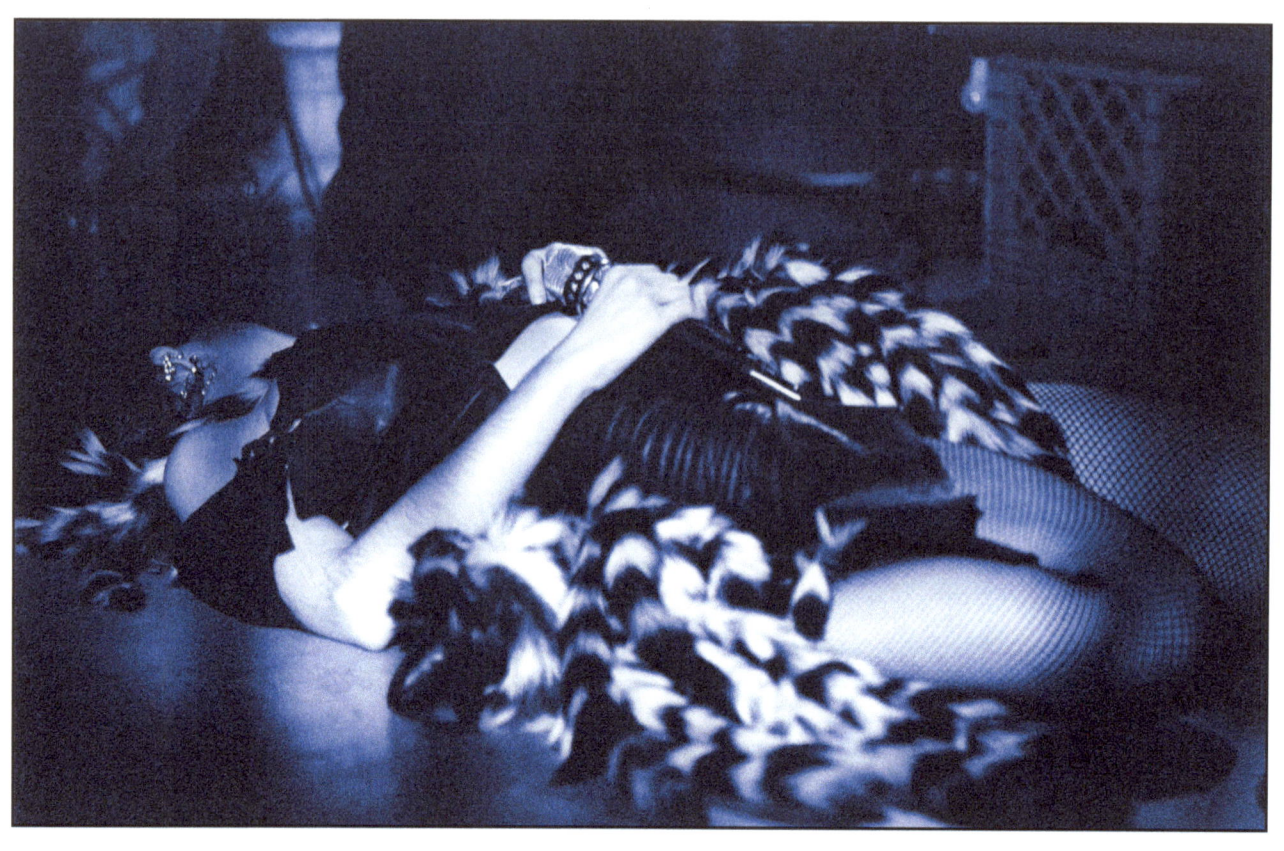

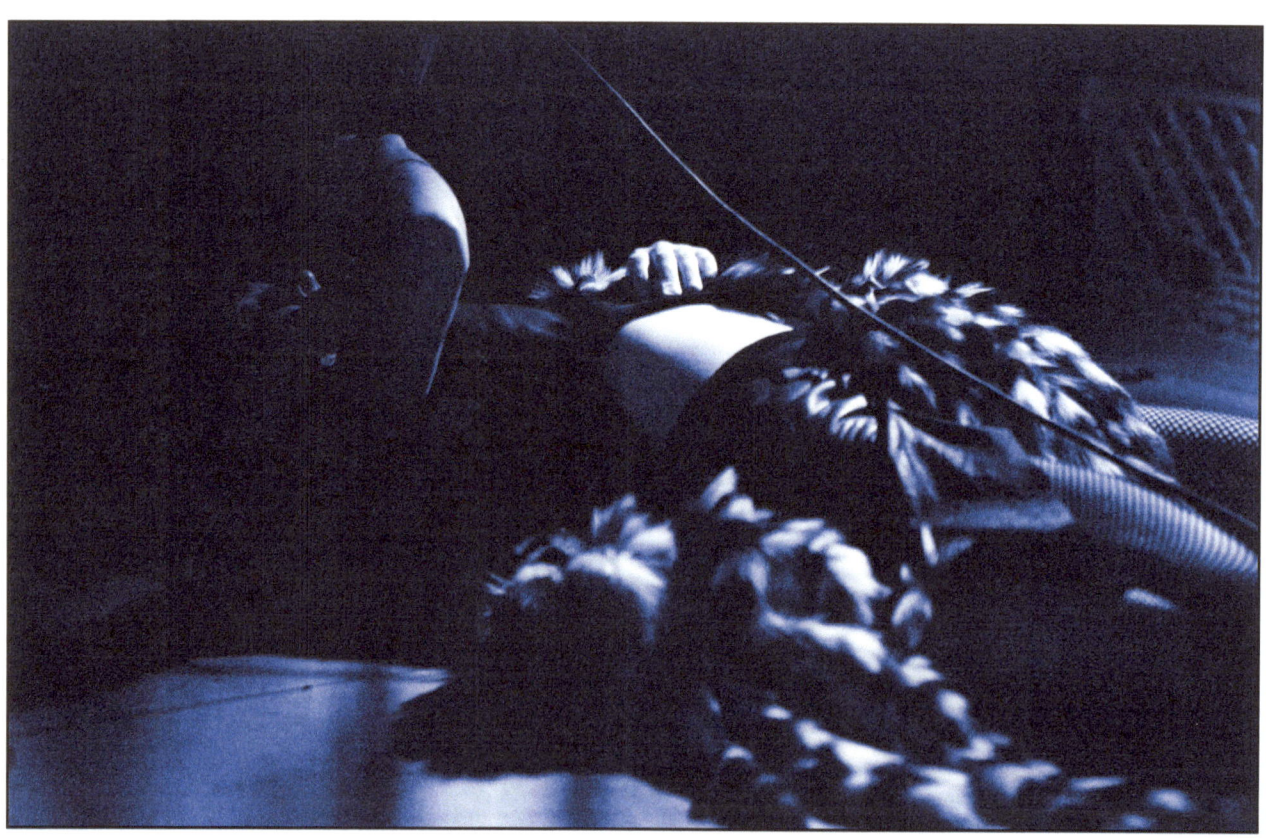

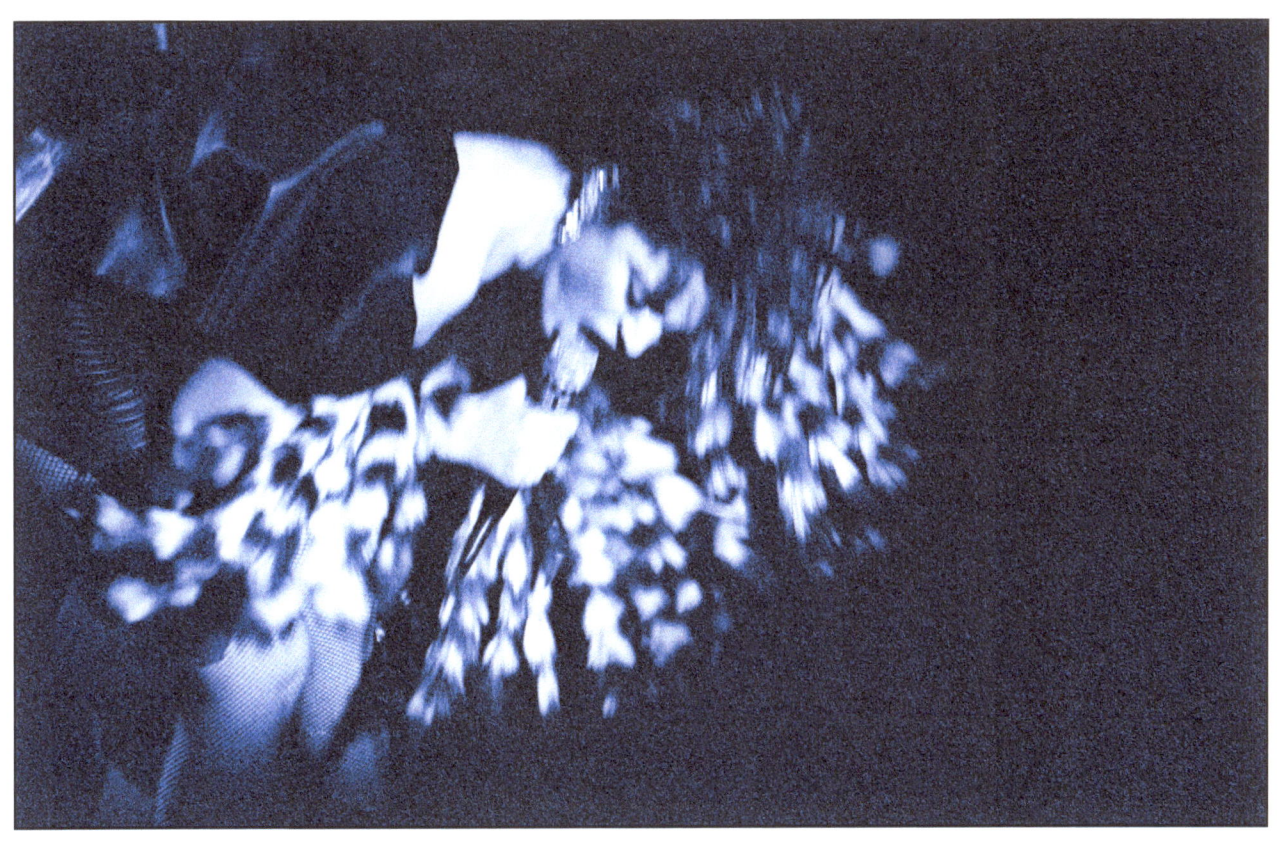

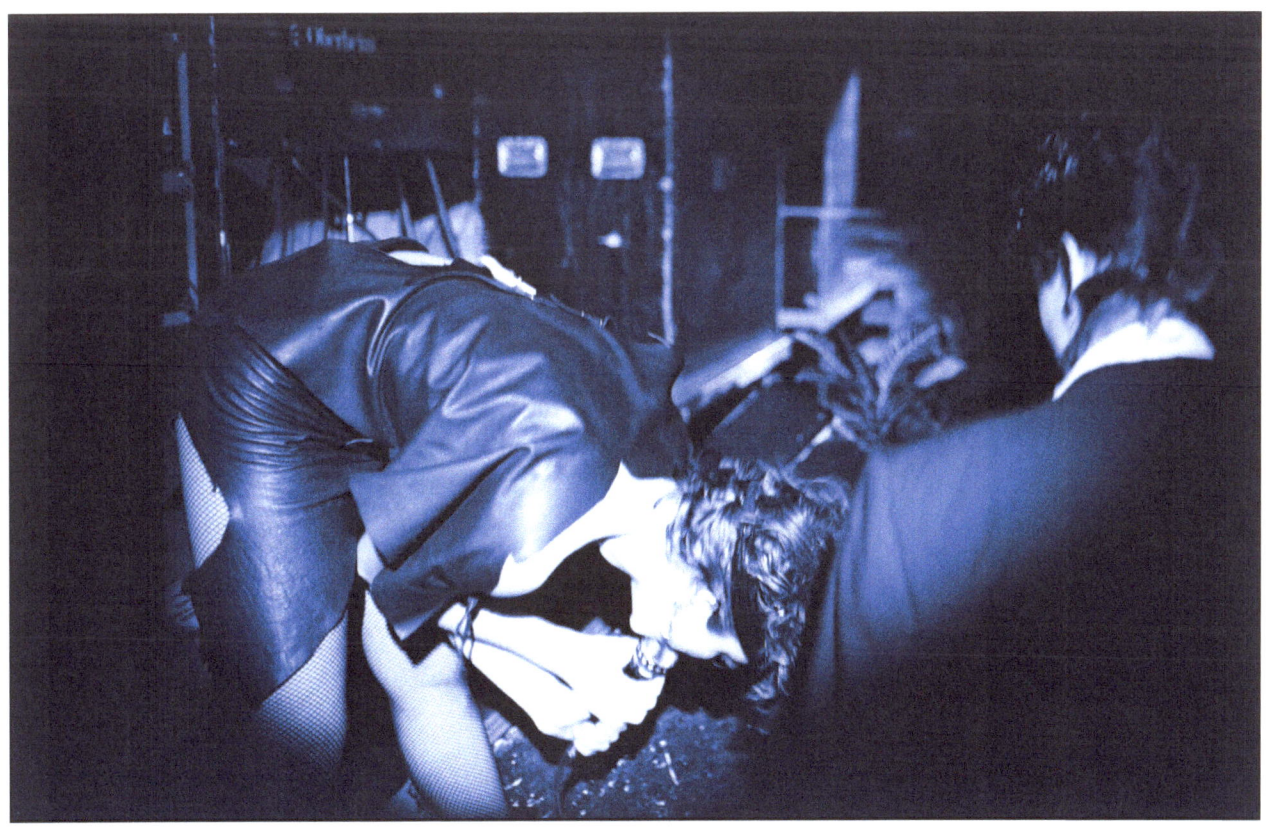

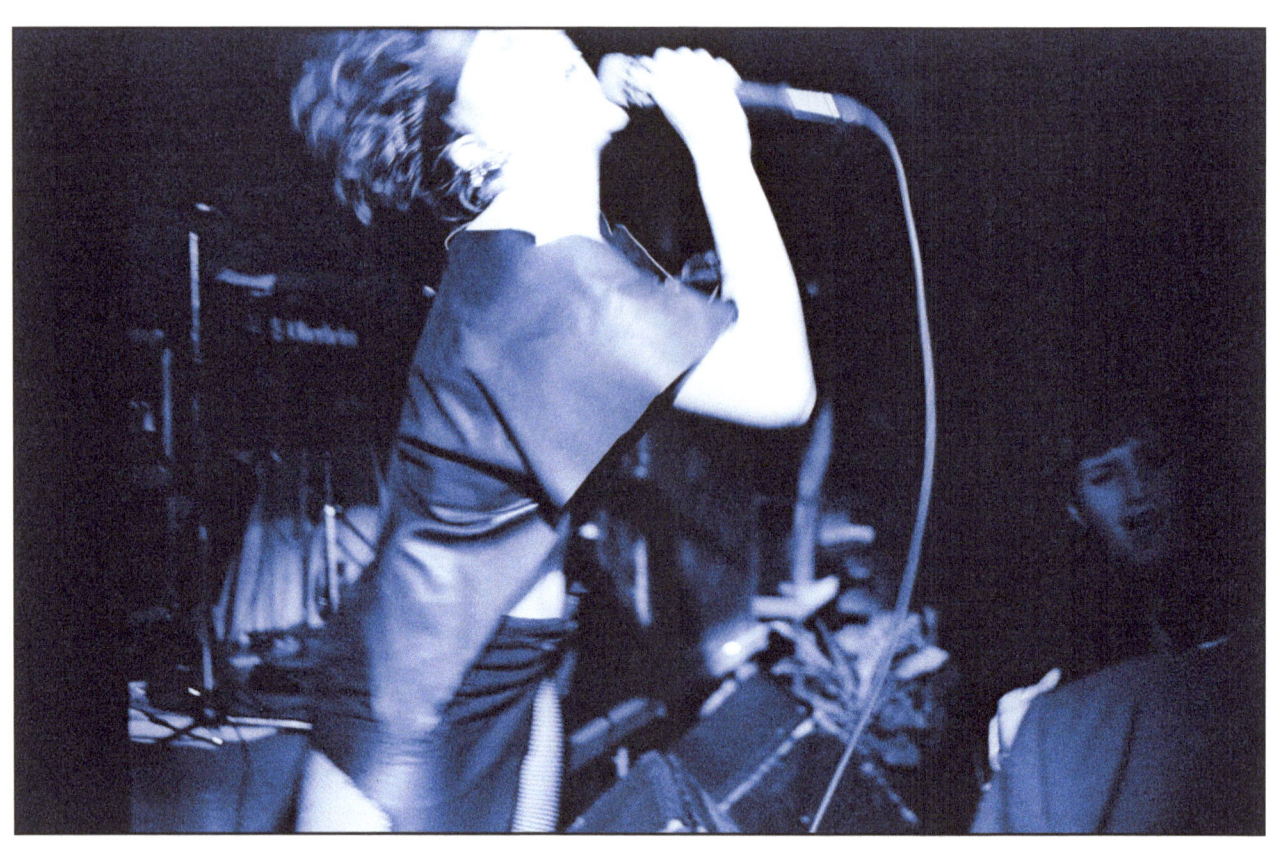

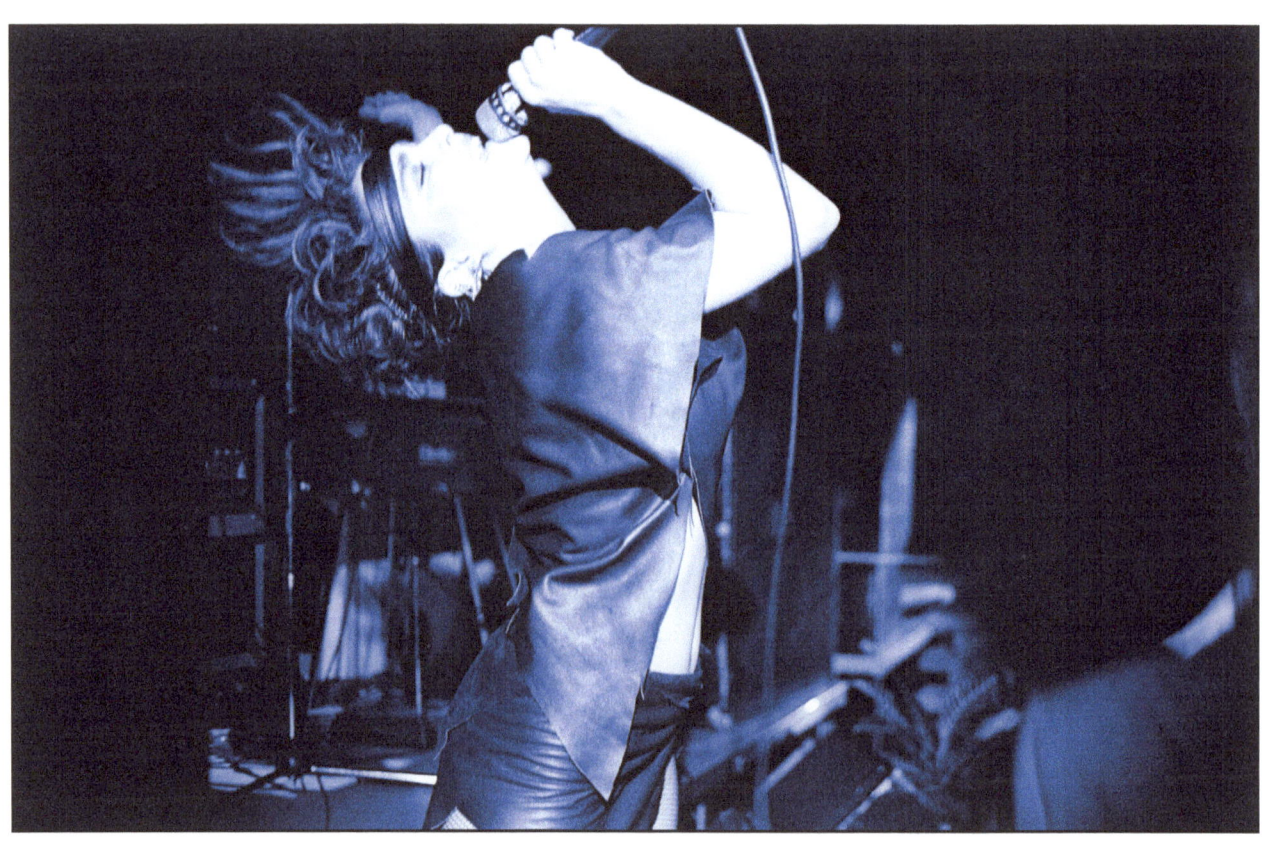

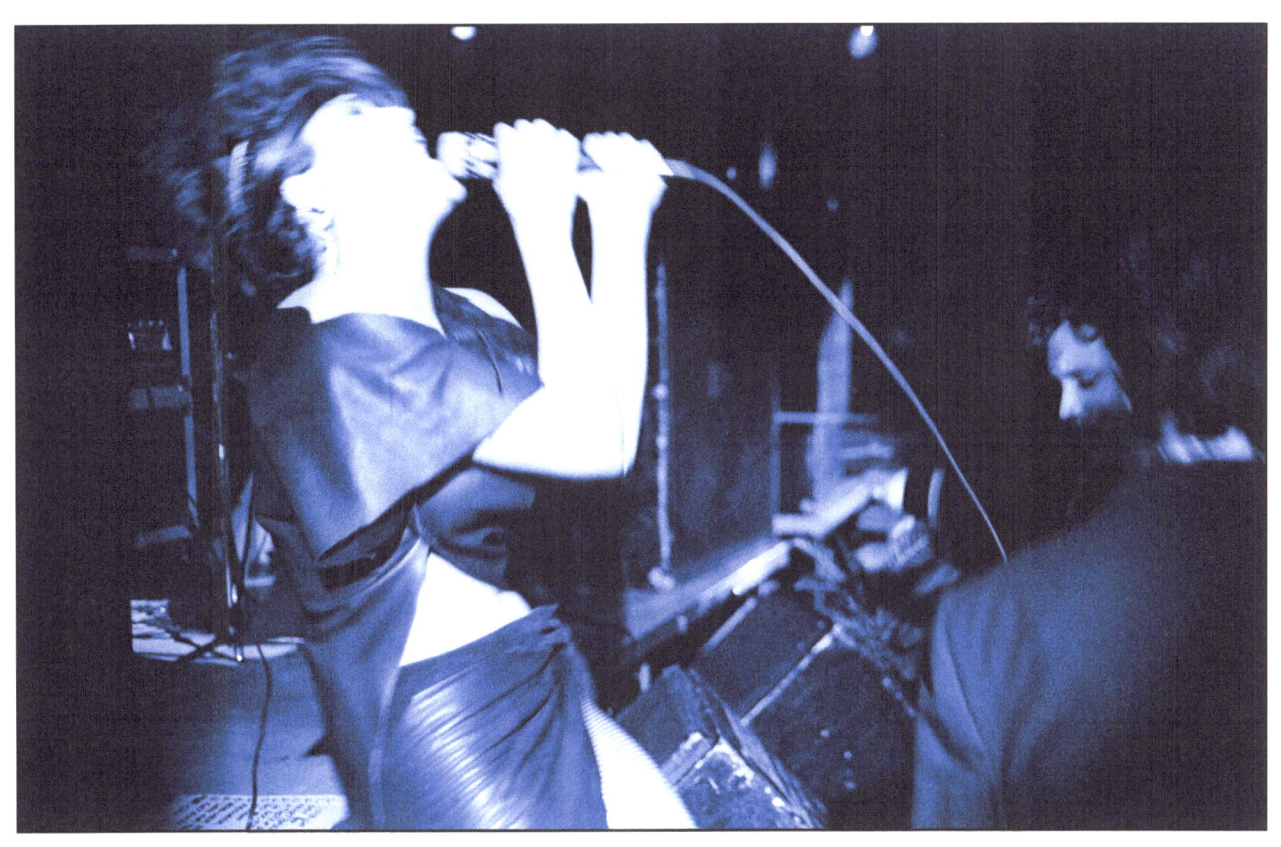

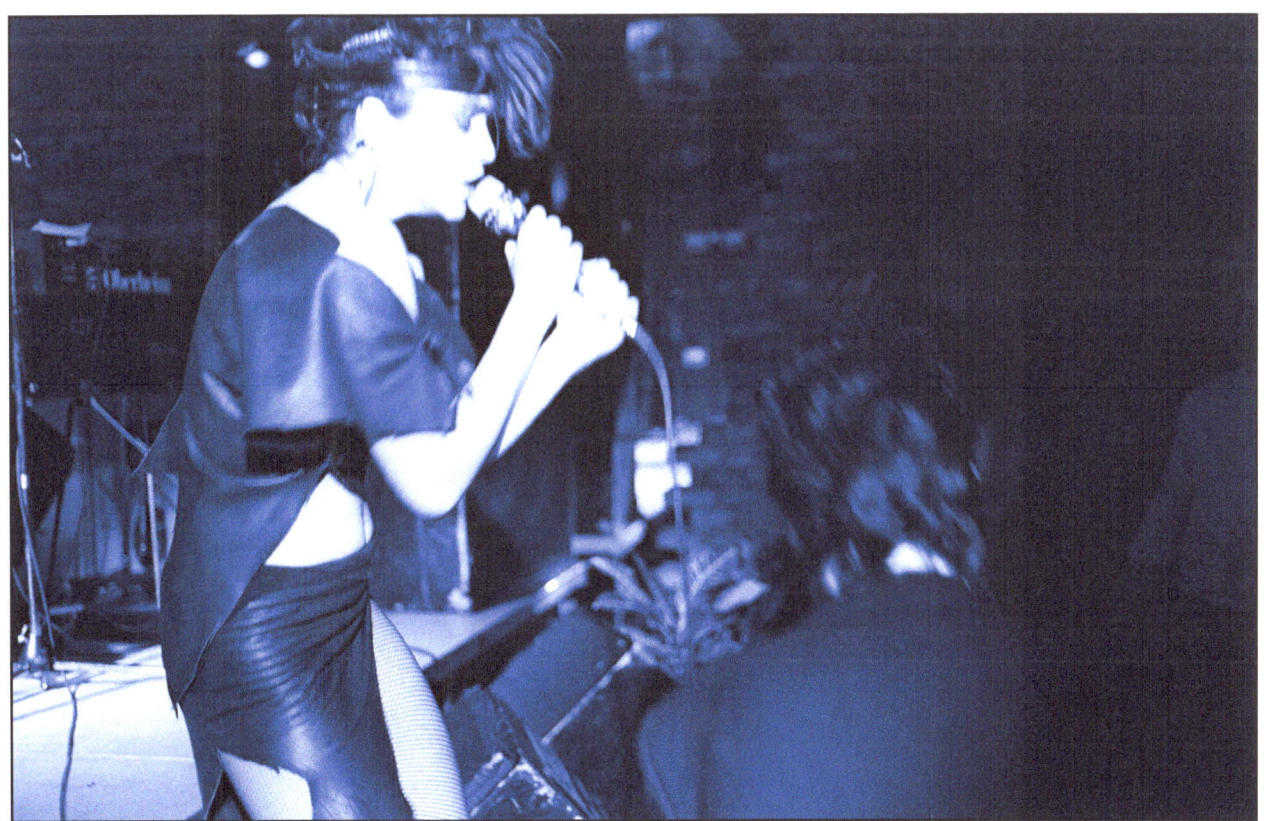

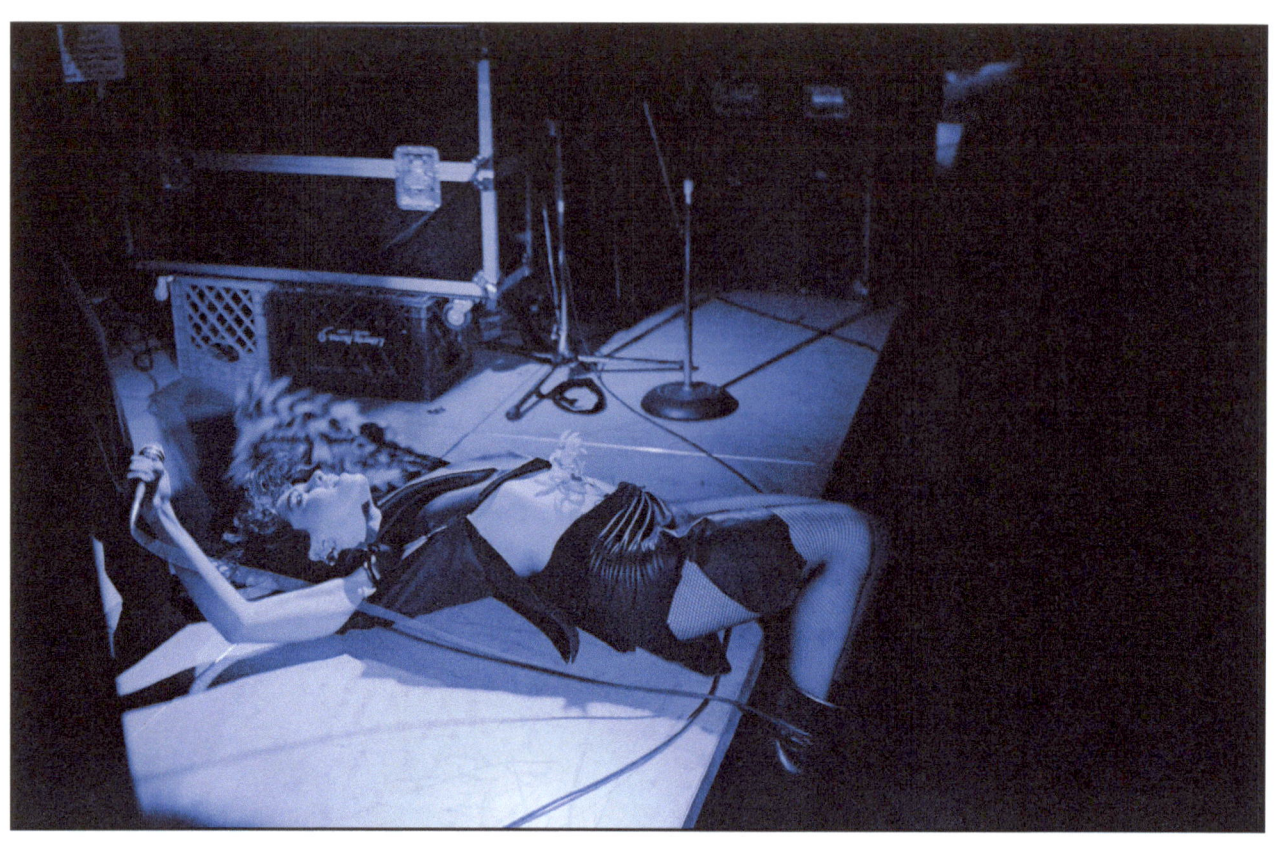

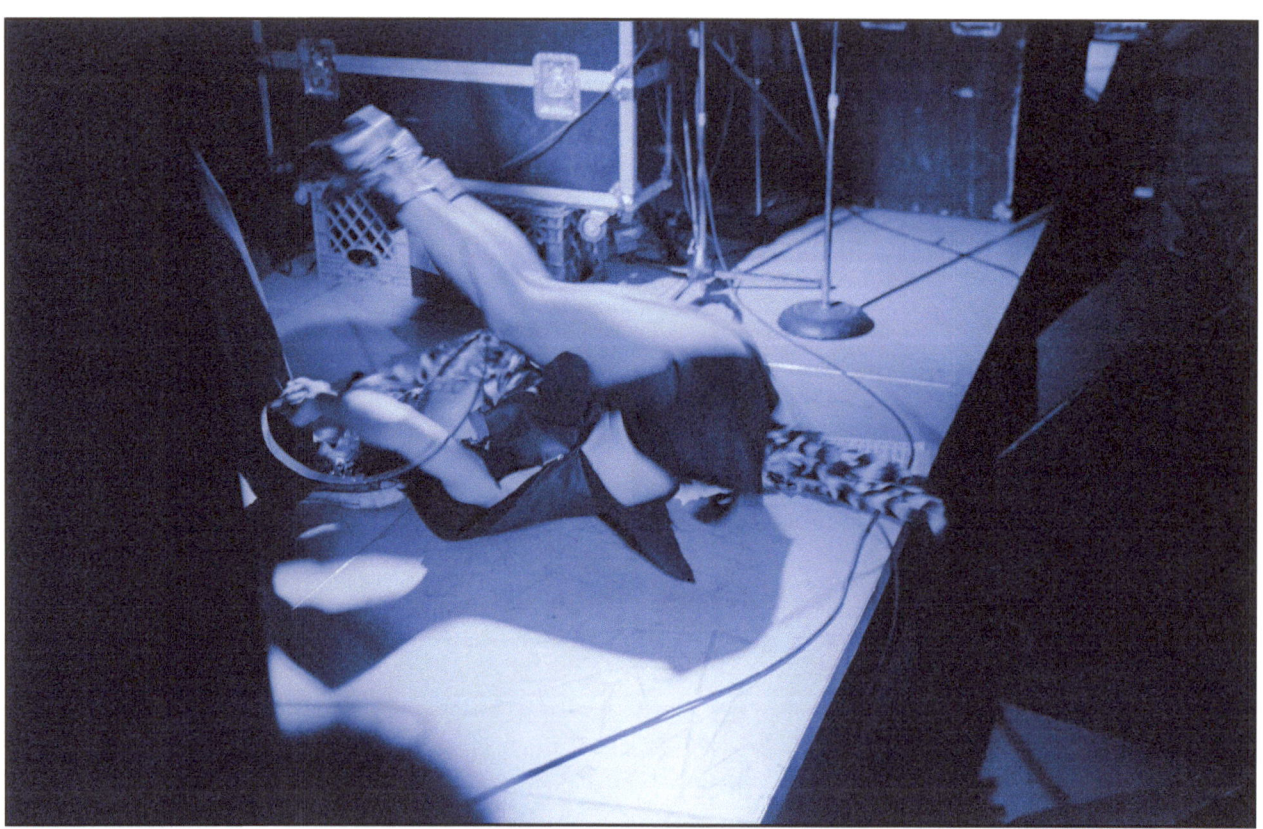

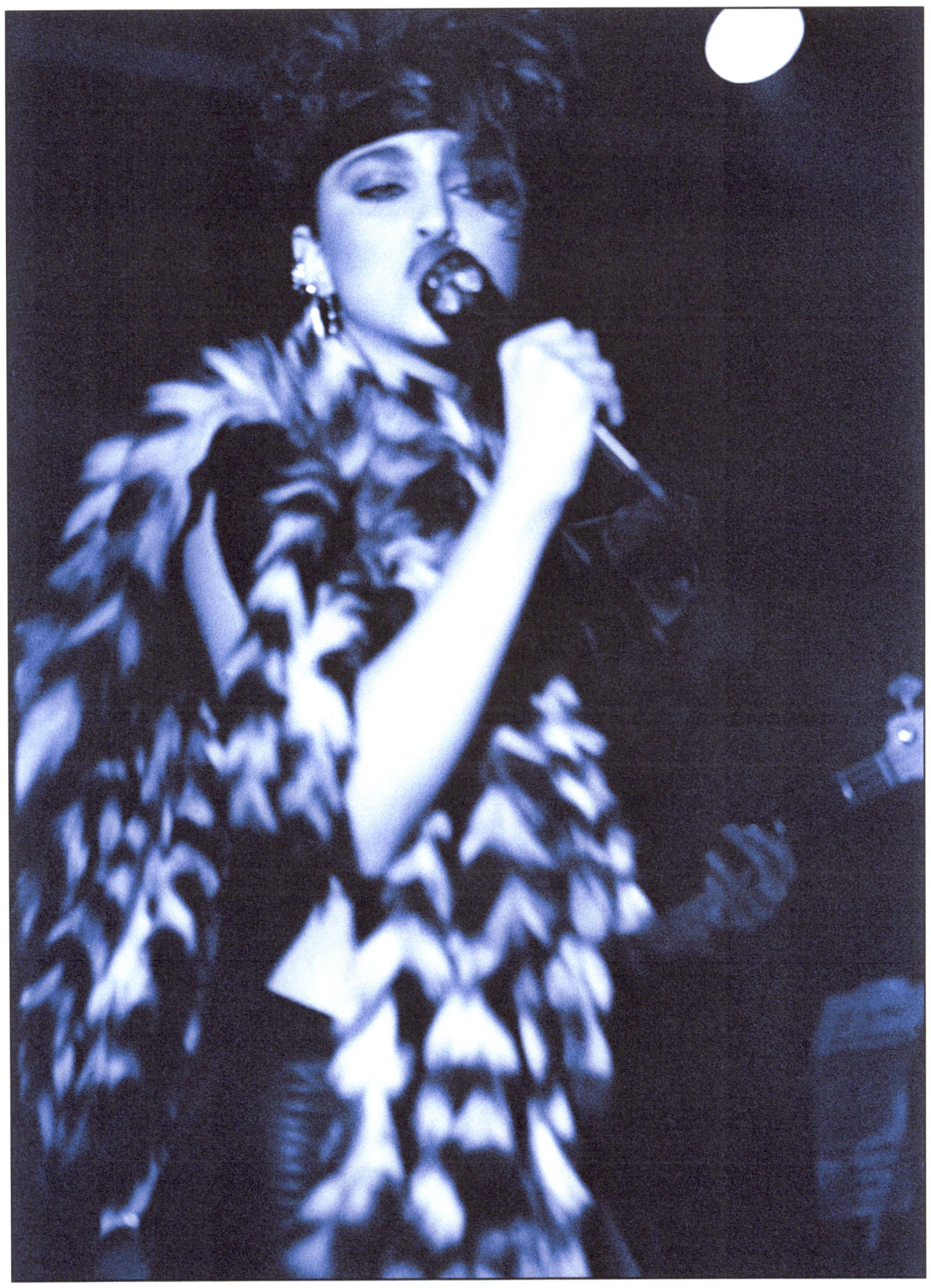

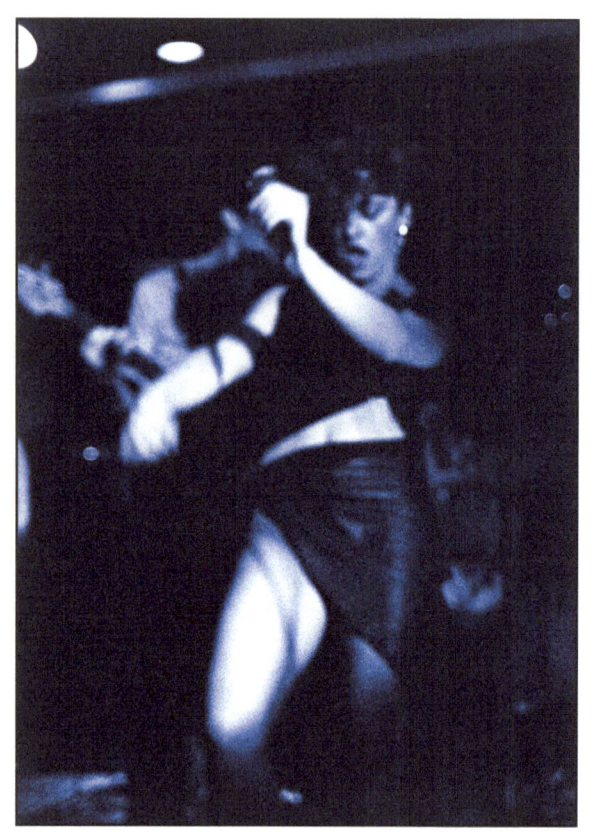 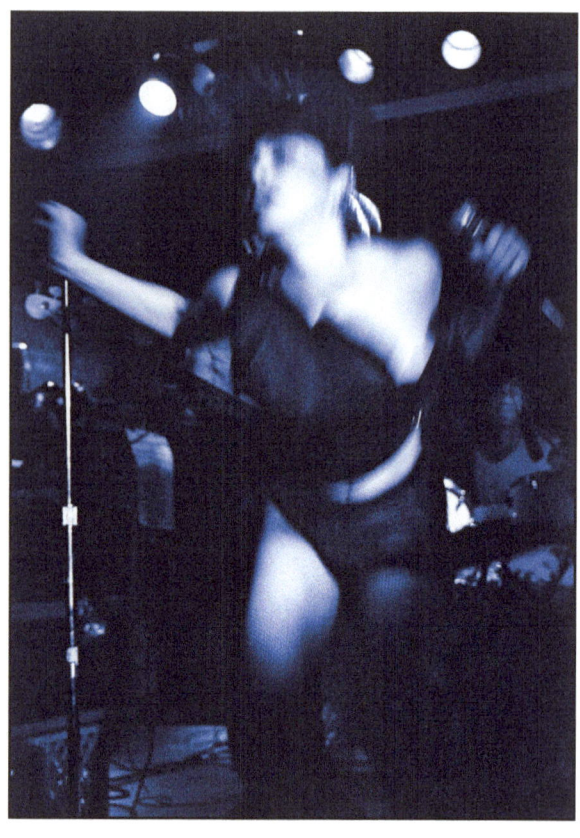

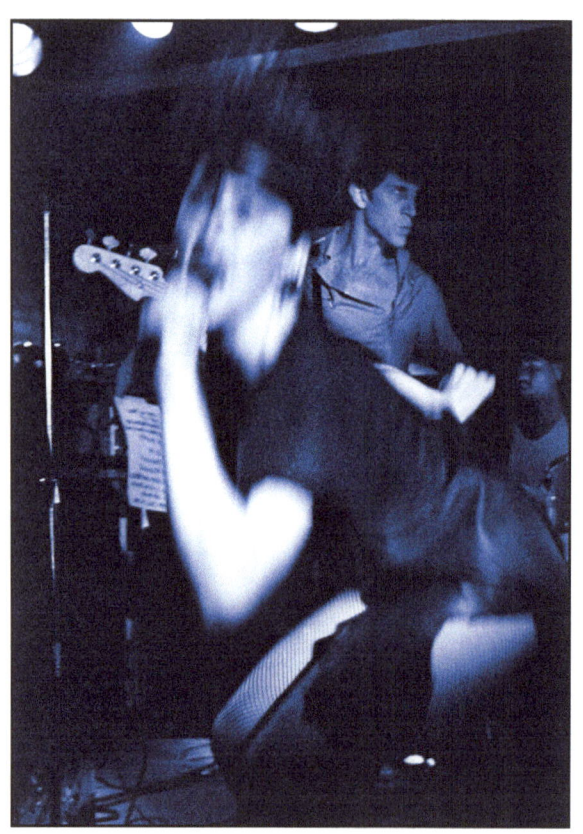 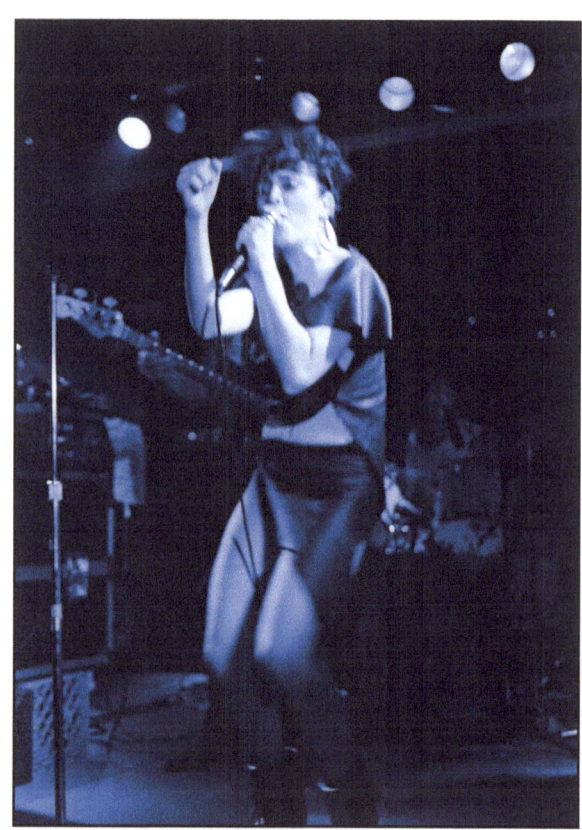

62

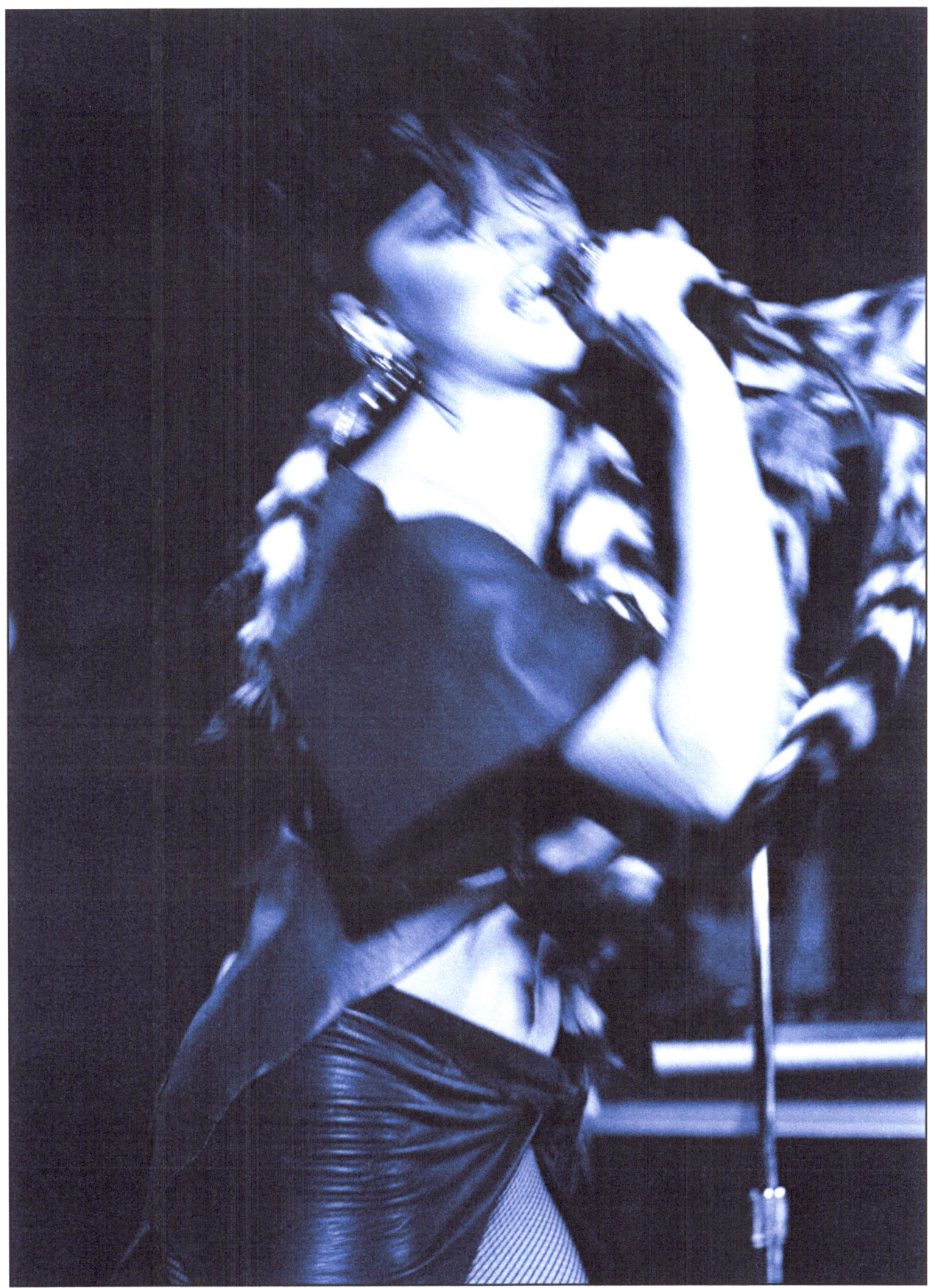

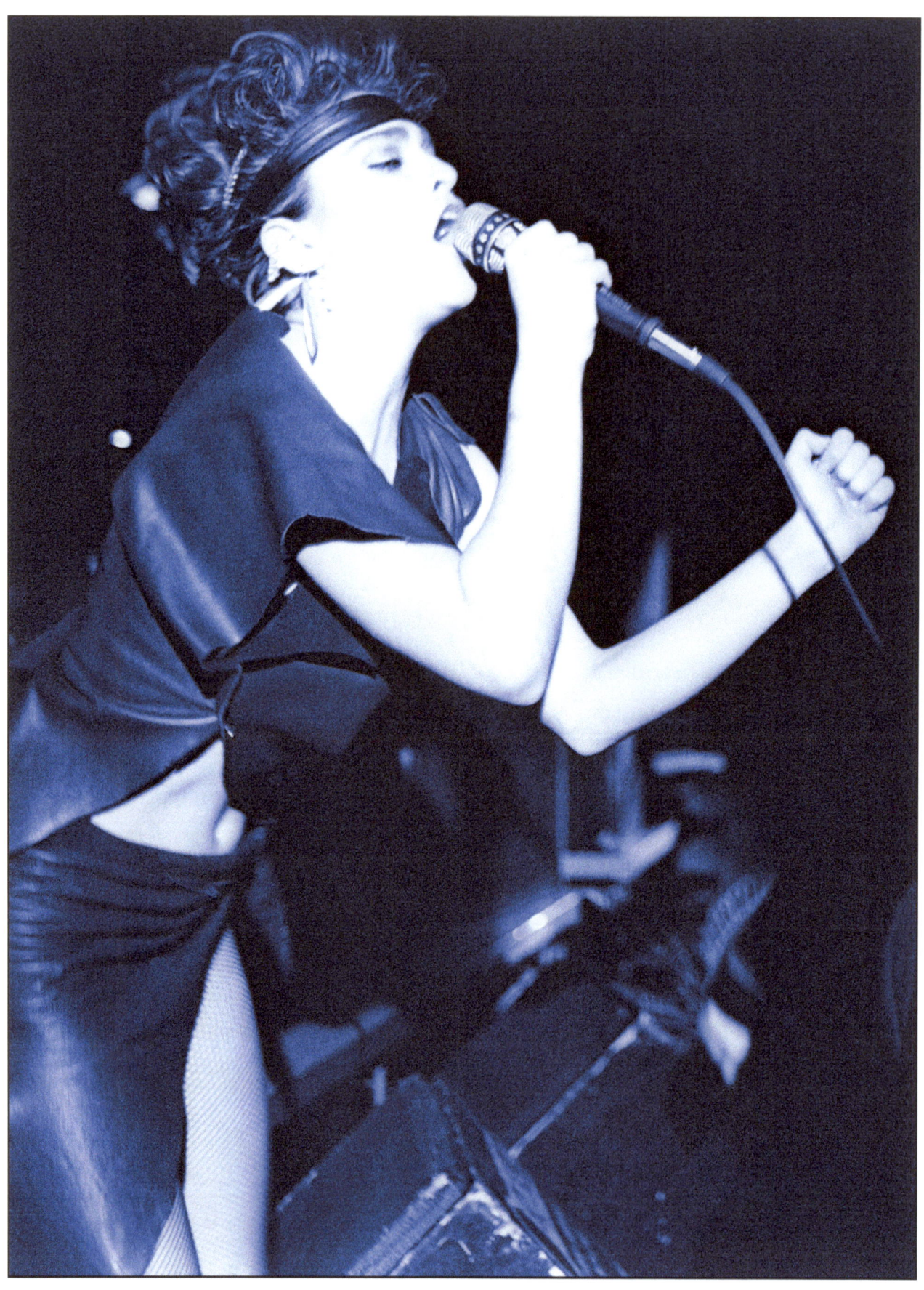

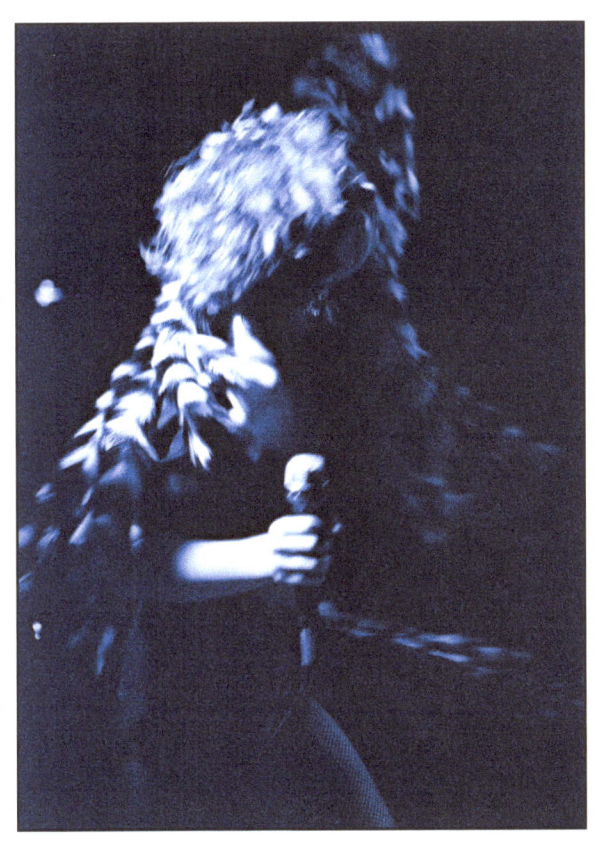 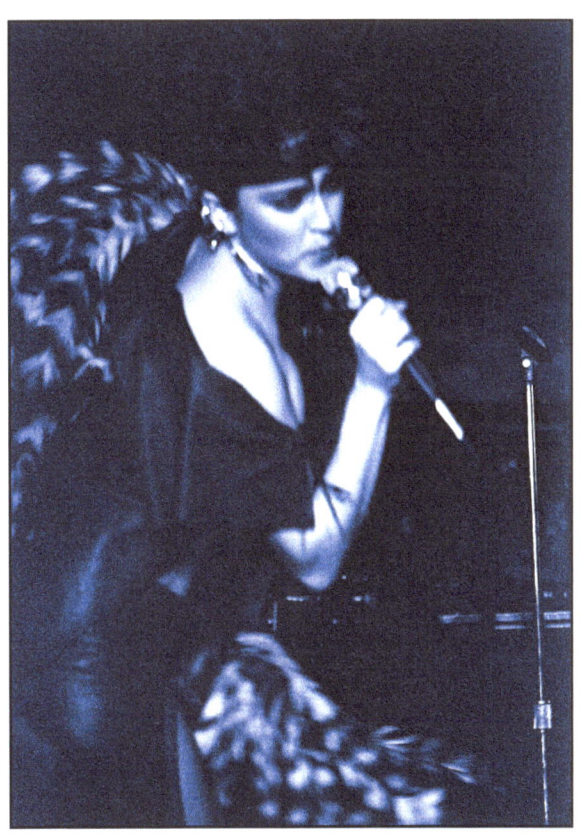

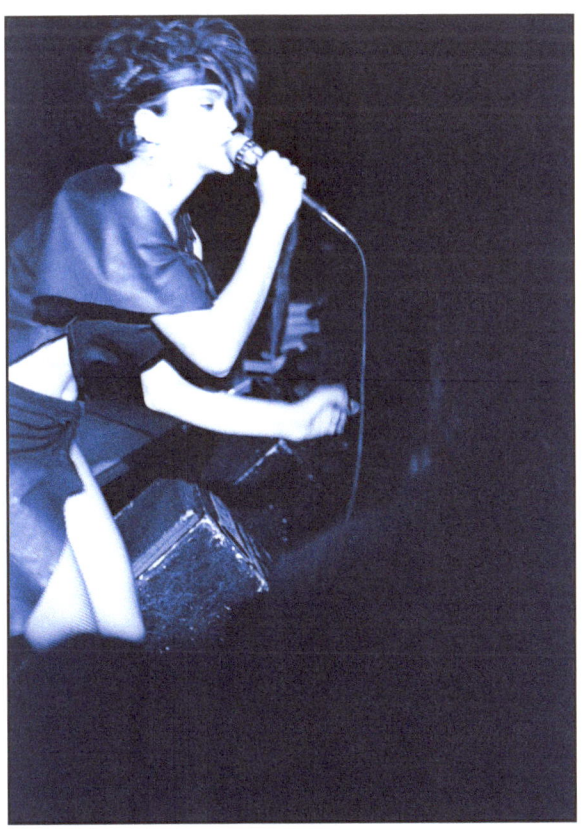 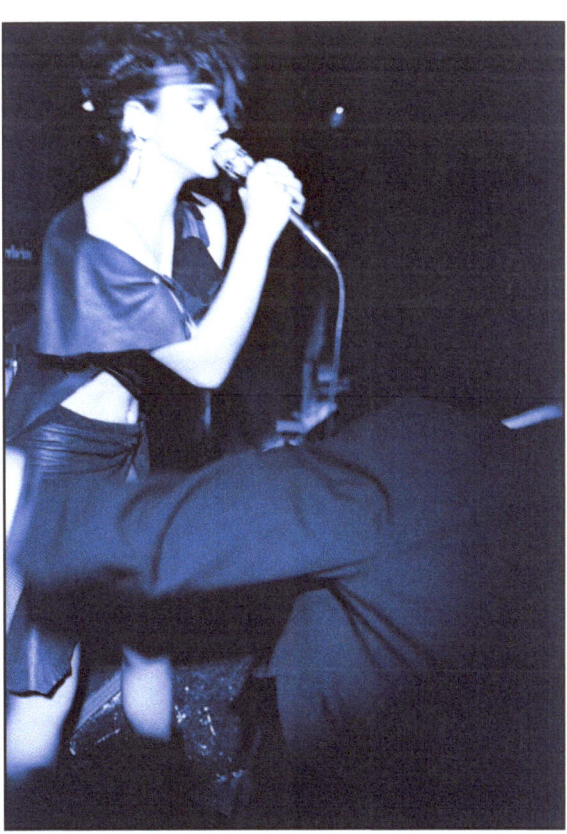

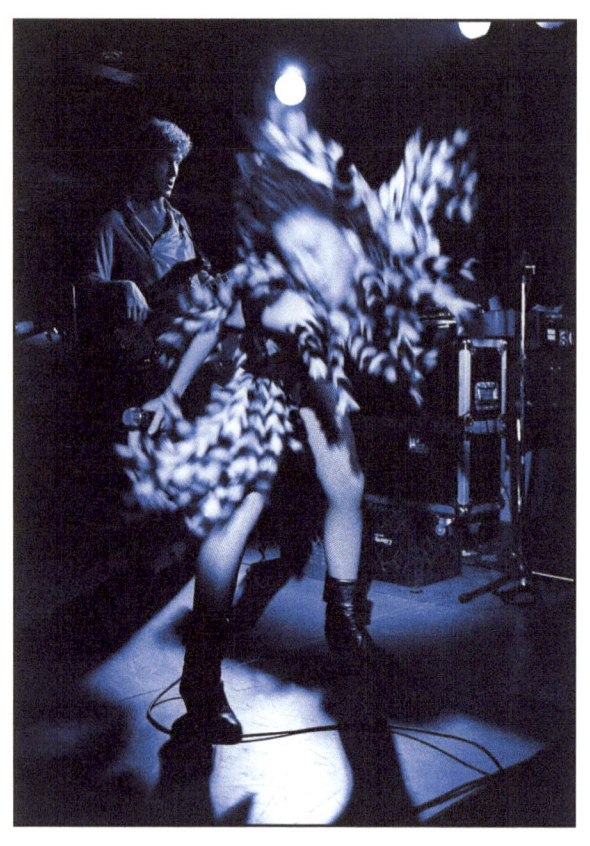
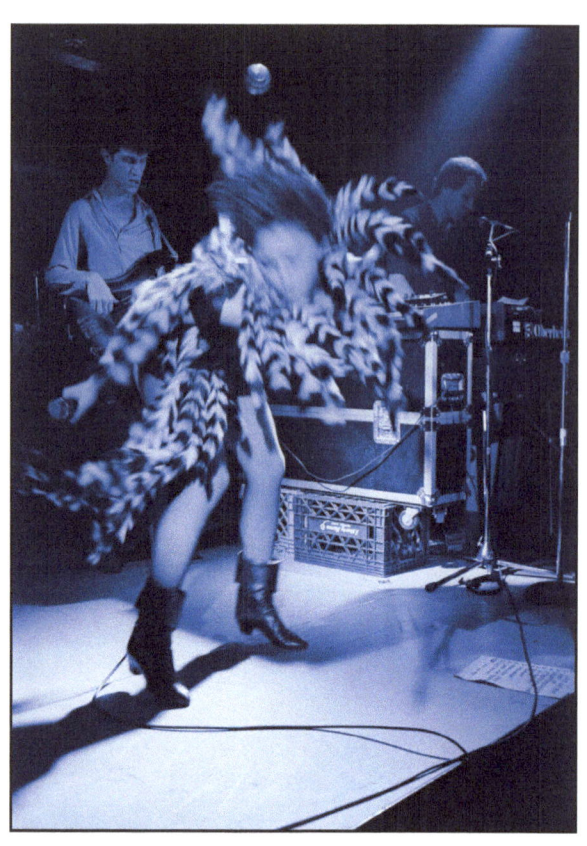
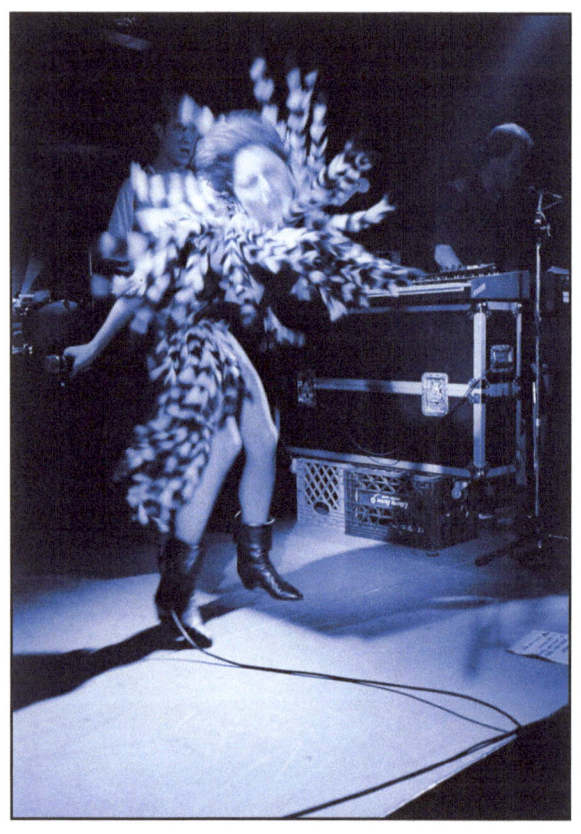
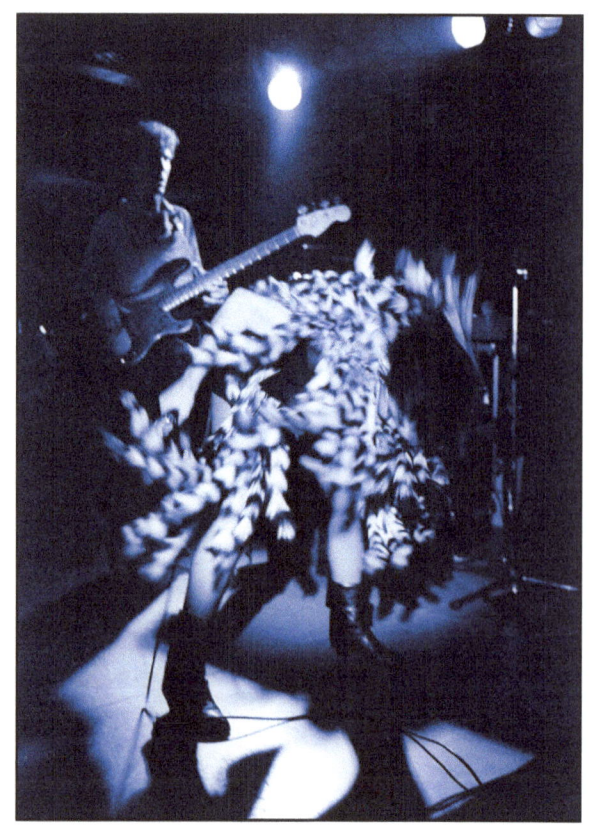

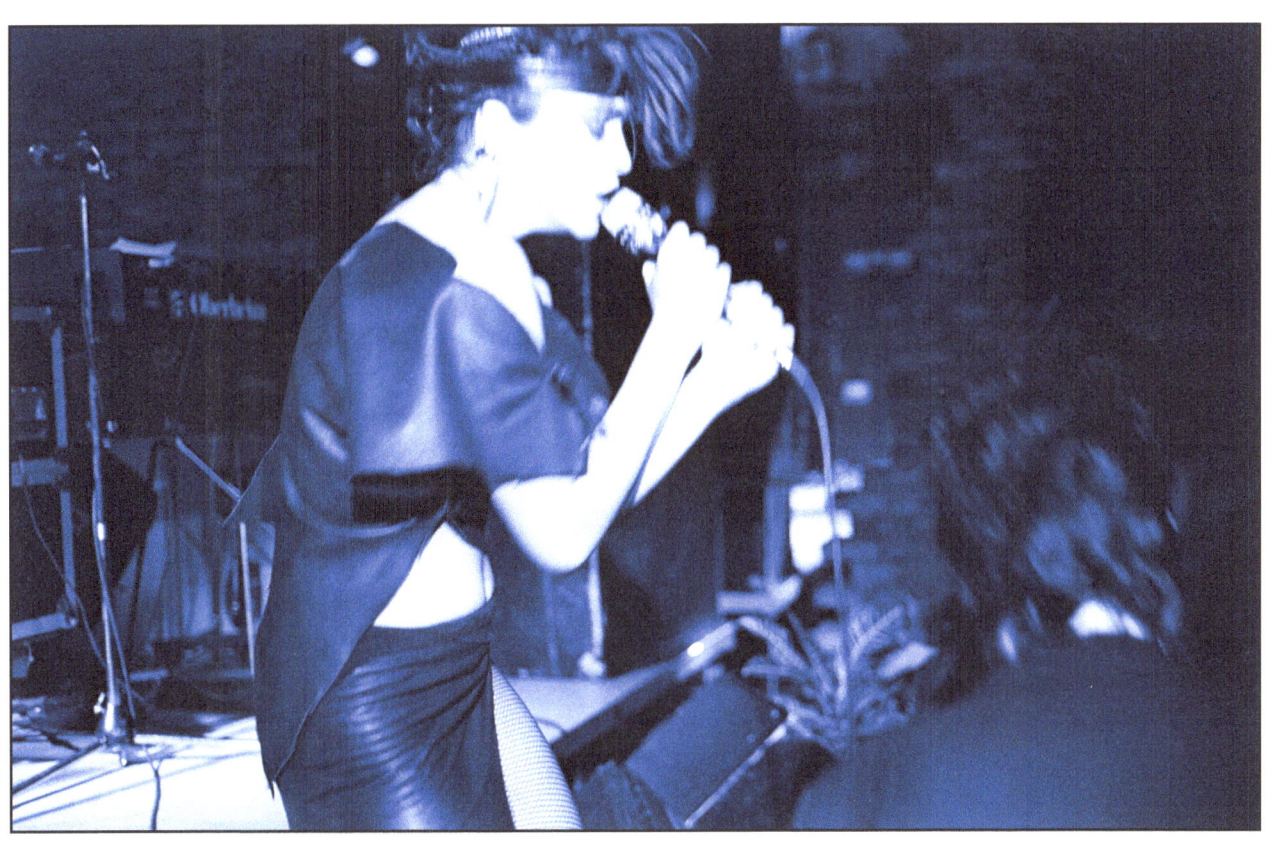

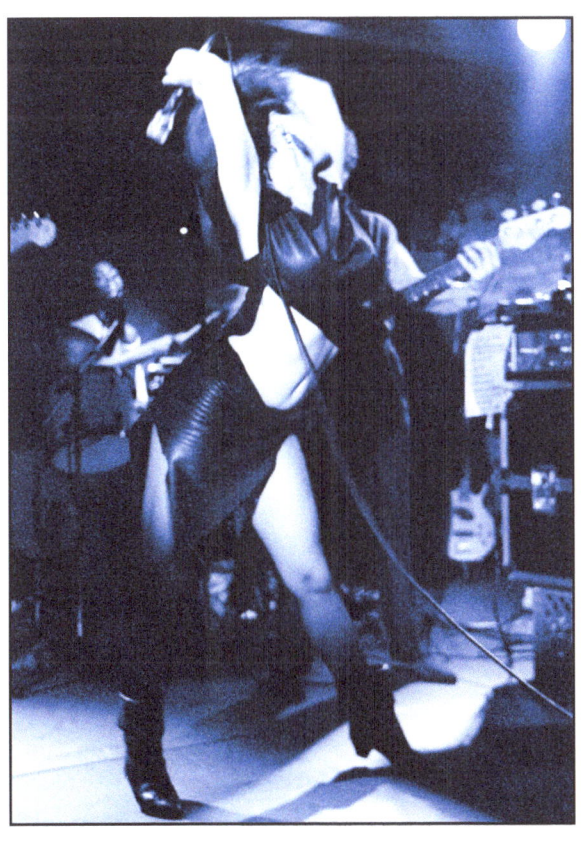

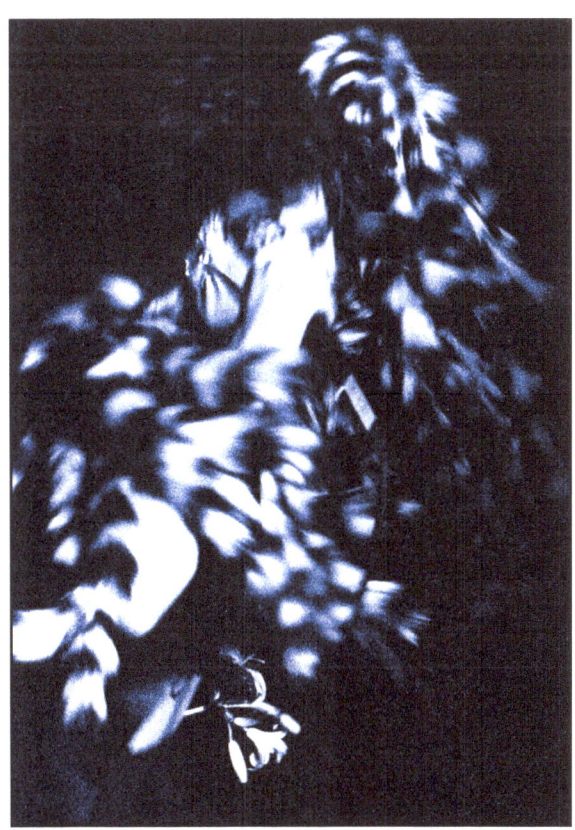

After ingloriously getting myself ejected from Madonna's dressing room for trying to give her some encouraging words, between the two sets of her show, I went back to the main room of the club and waited for Madonna's performance to continue.

She came back to the stage with a completely different wardrobe and proceded to shed layers of her costume as the second set progressed.

I liked the University of Michigan letter sweater. The large "M" could stand for Michigan, where Madonna was originally from or it could stand for Madonna.

Although the outfit Madonna wore for her second set of the evening wasn't as sexy as the tribal look from the first set, Madonna made these clothes work.

Her skill as an entertainer was clear. She was just looking for her stagewear and that new look would soon come after this show in Roslyn.

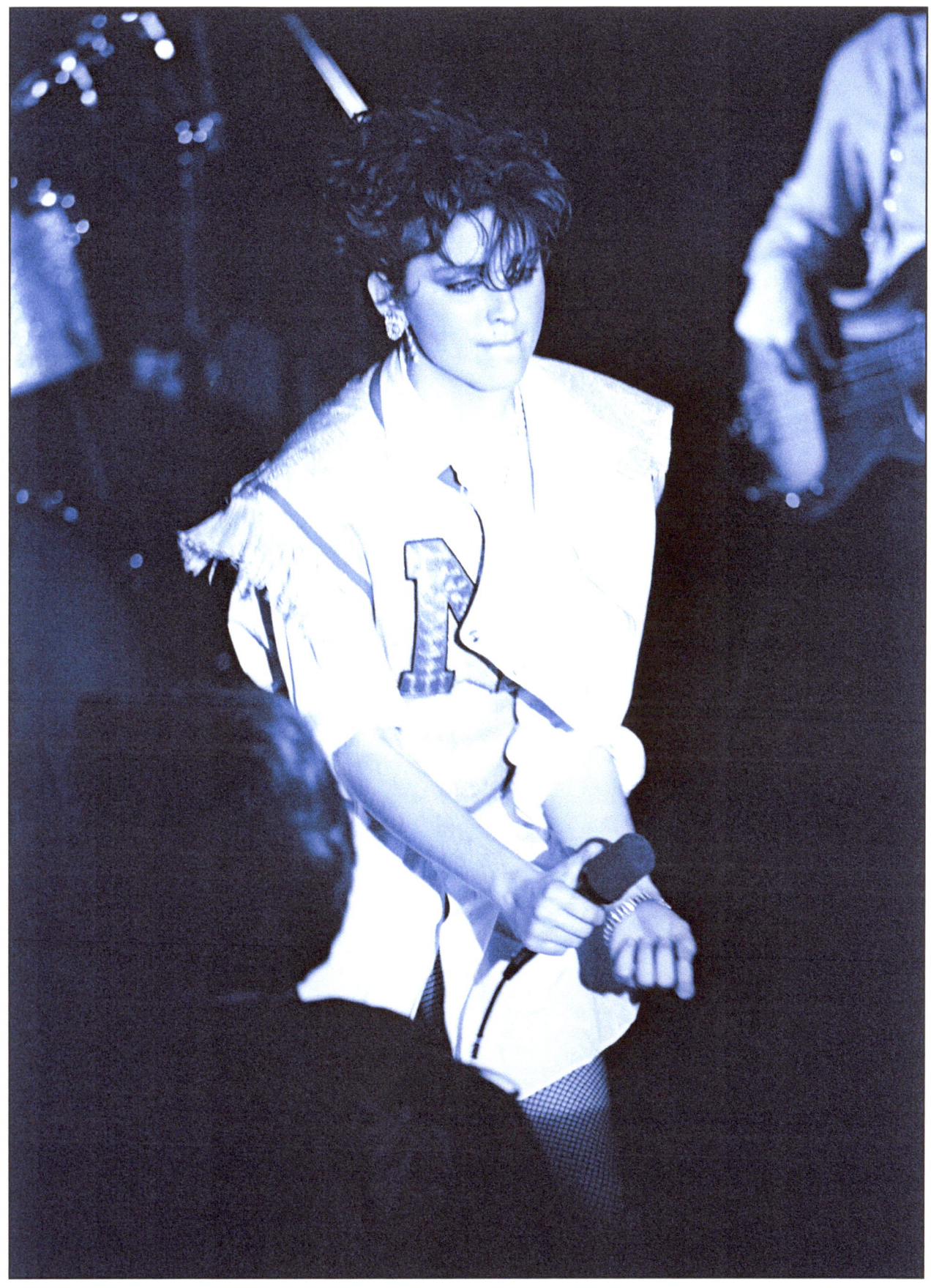

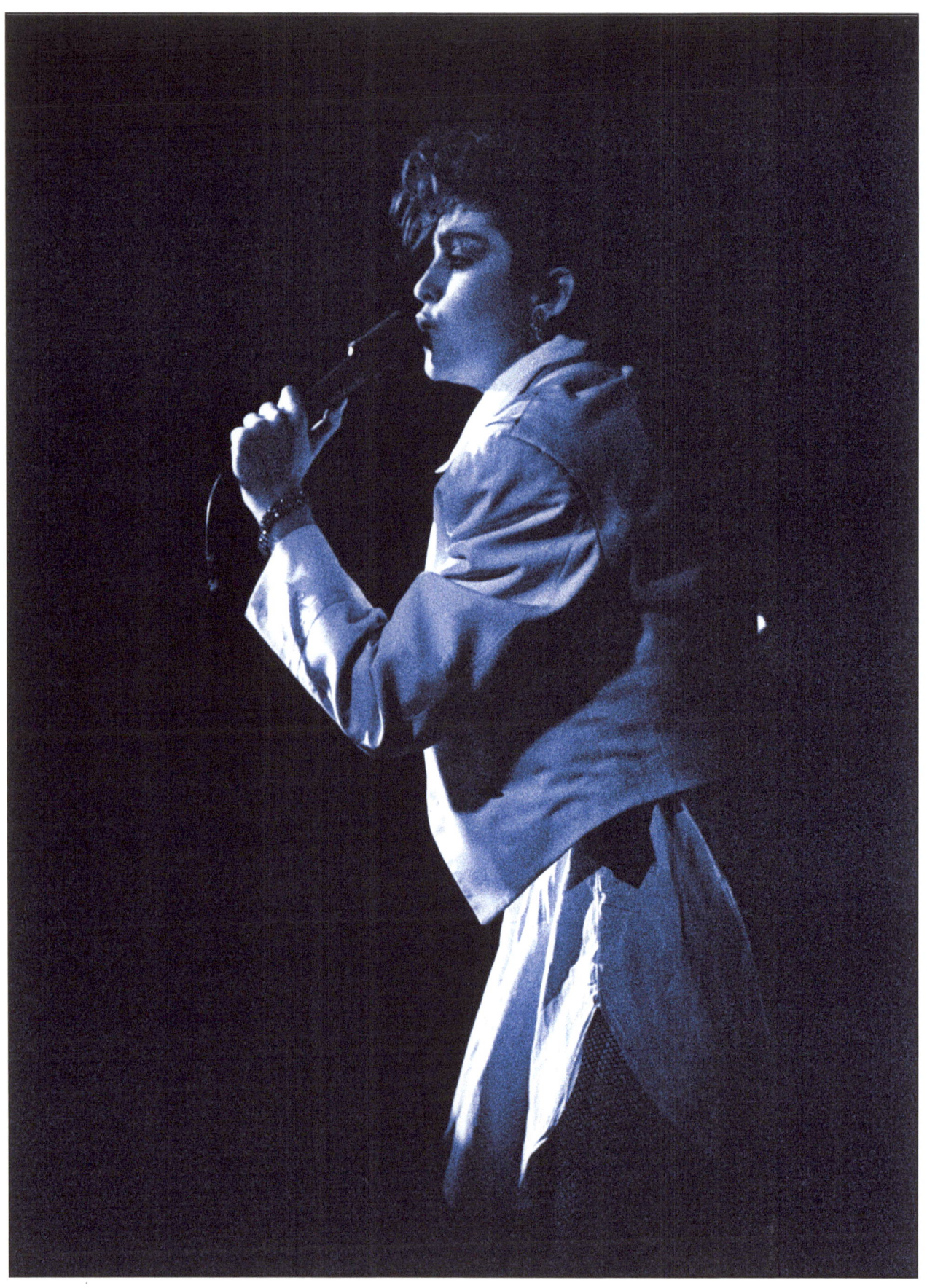

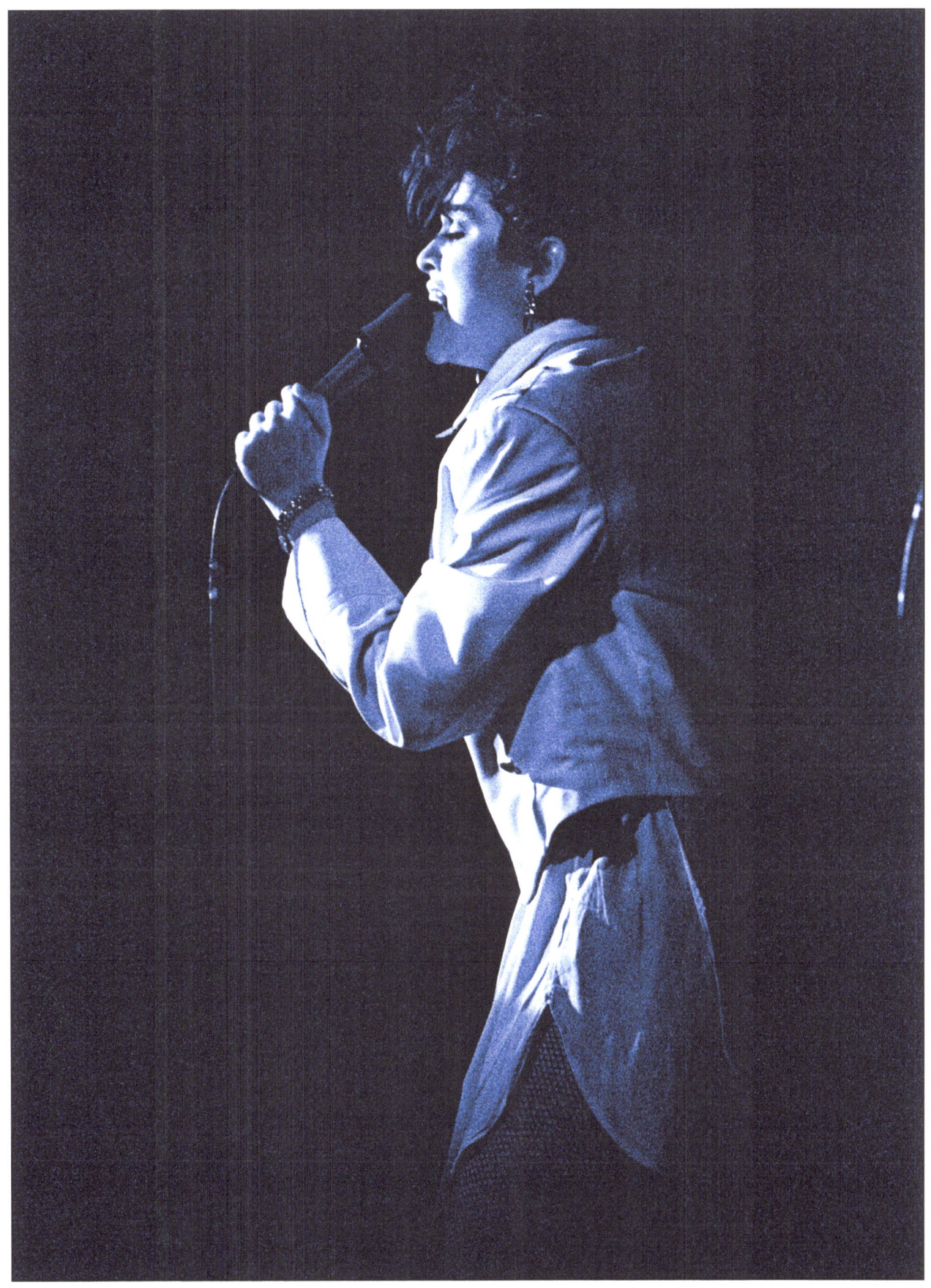

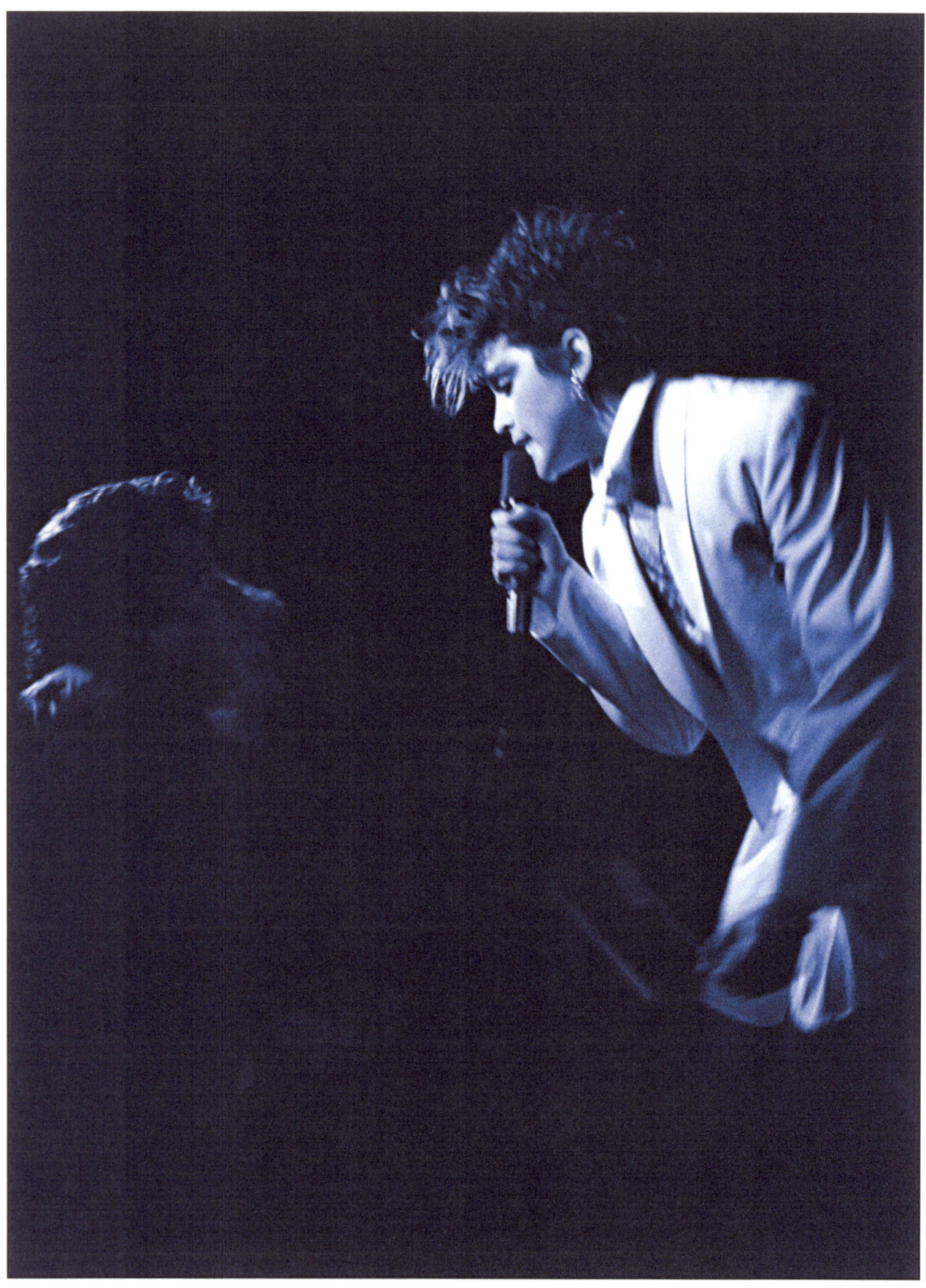

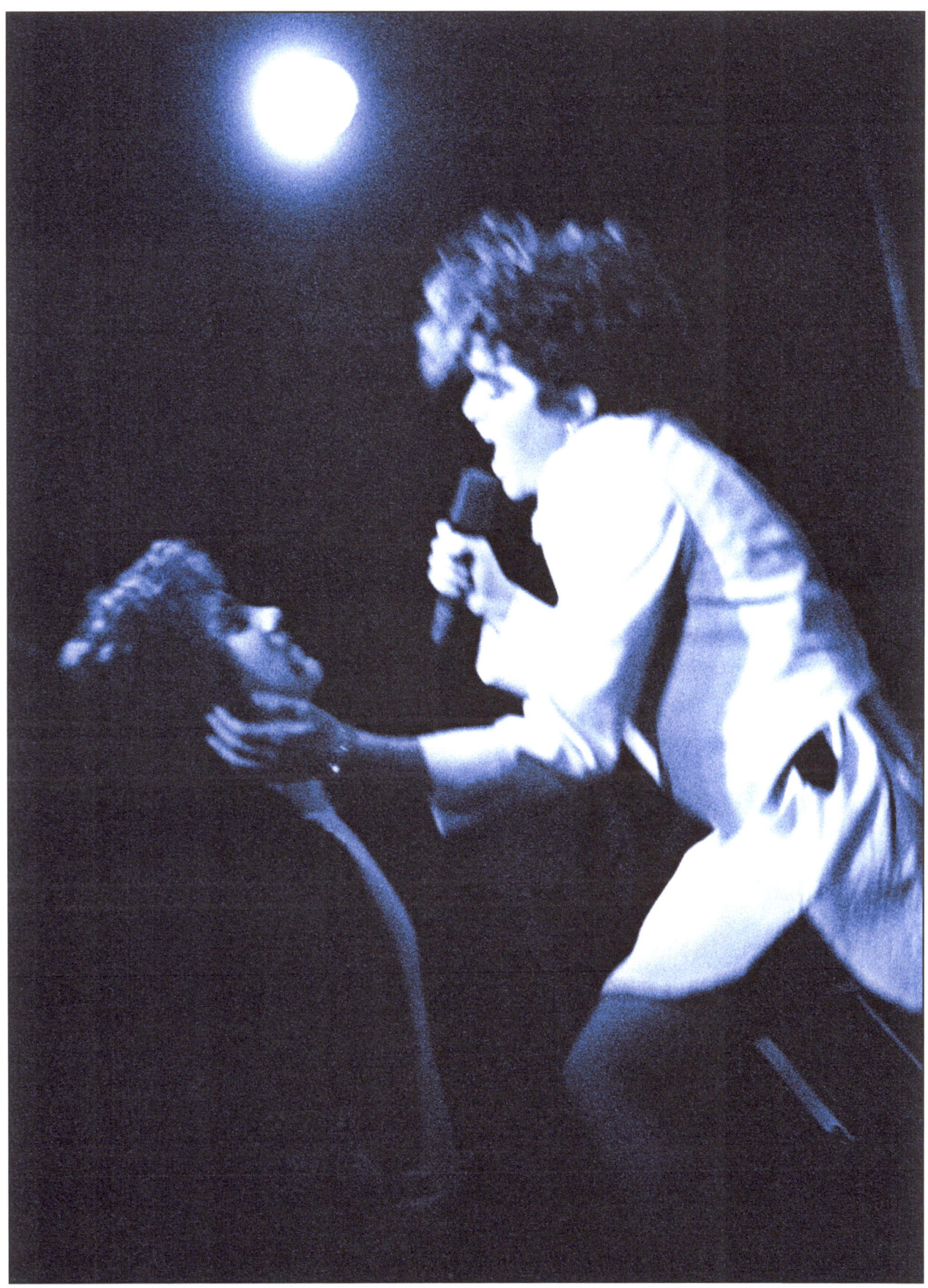

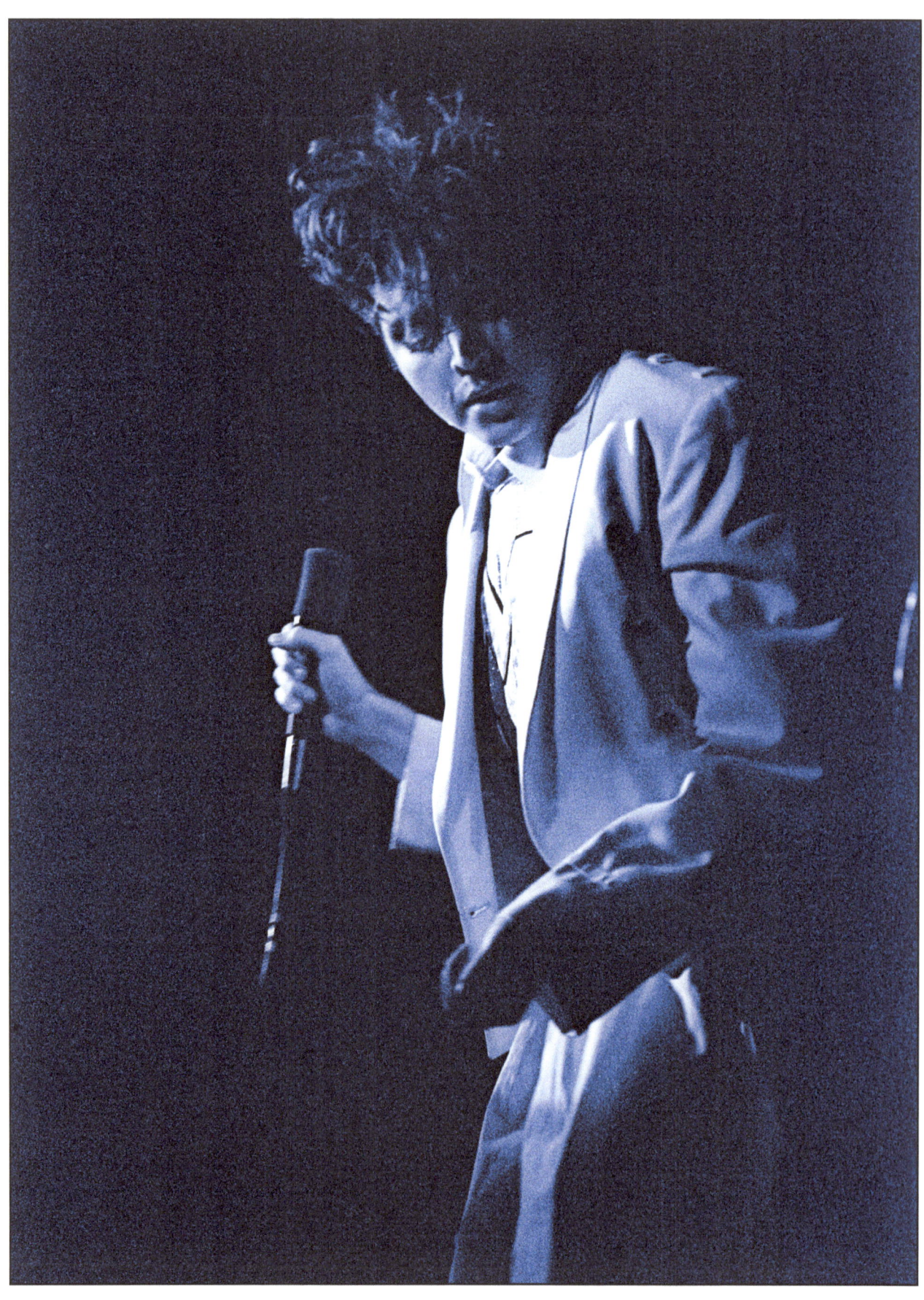

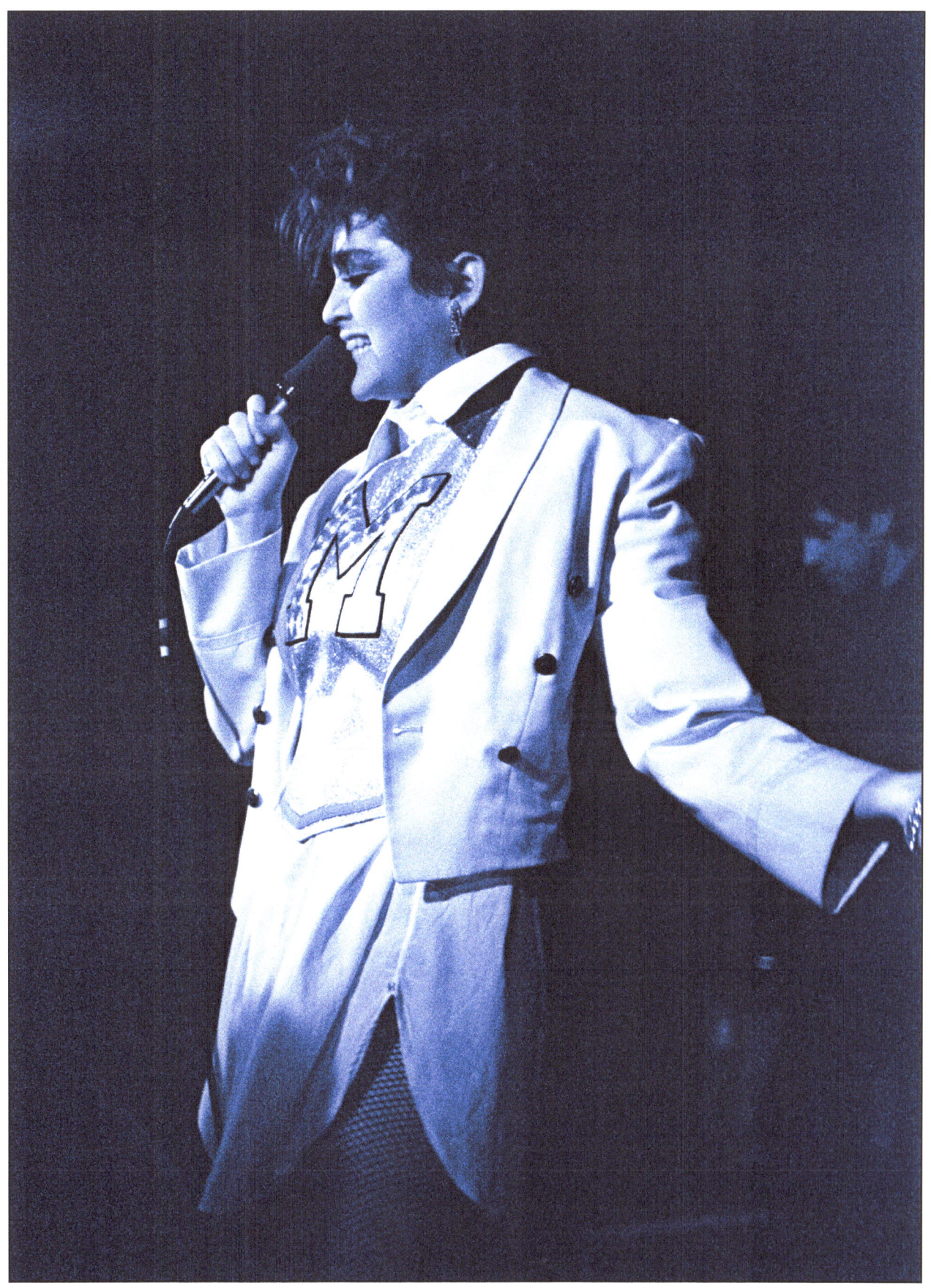

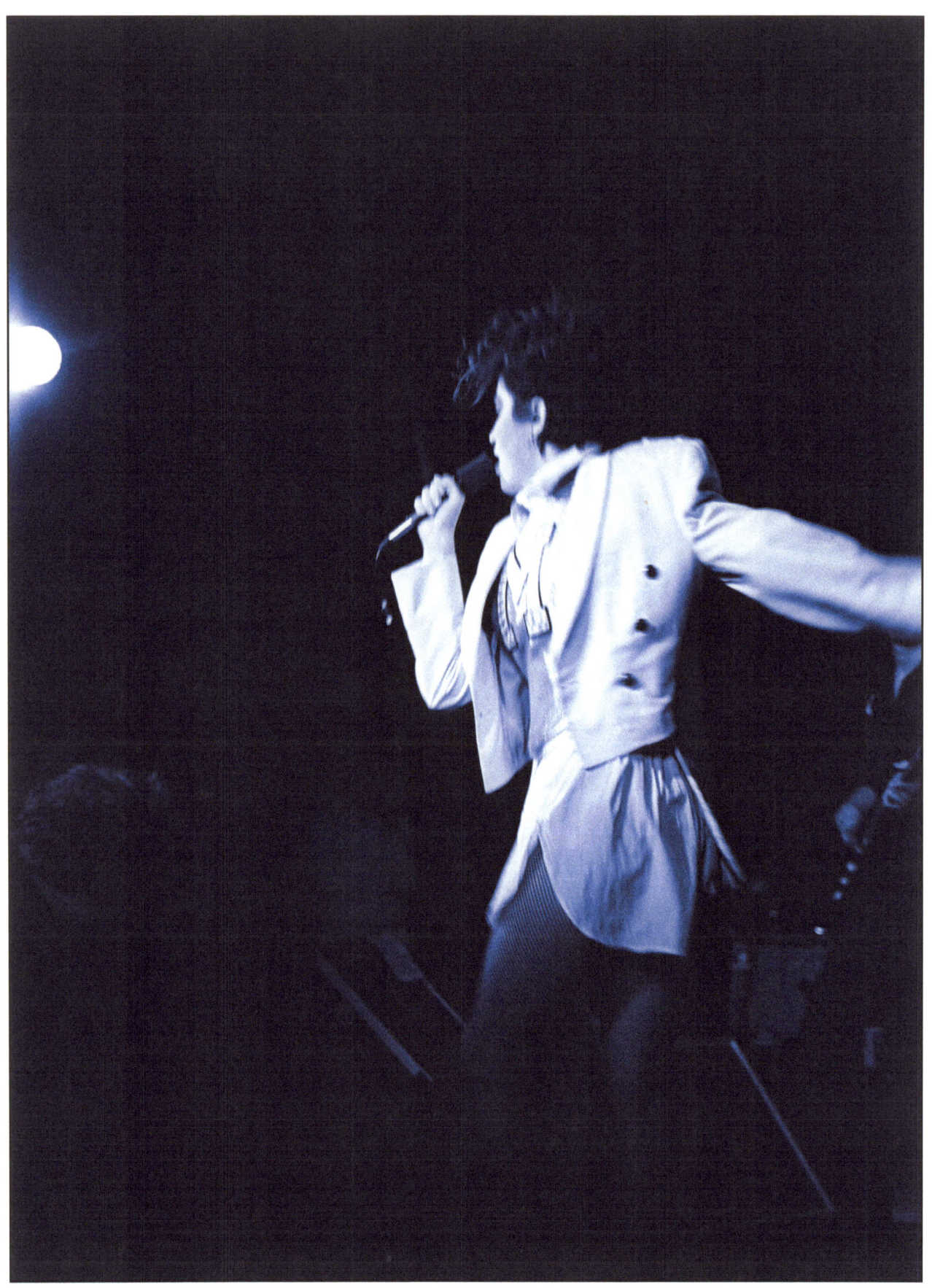

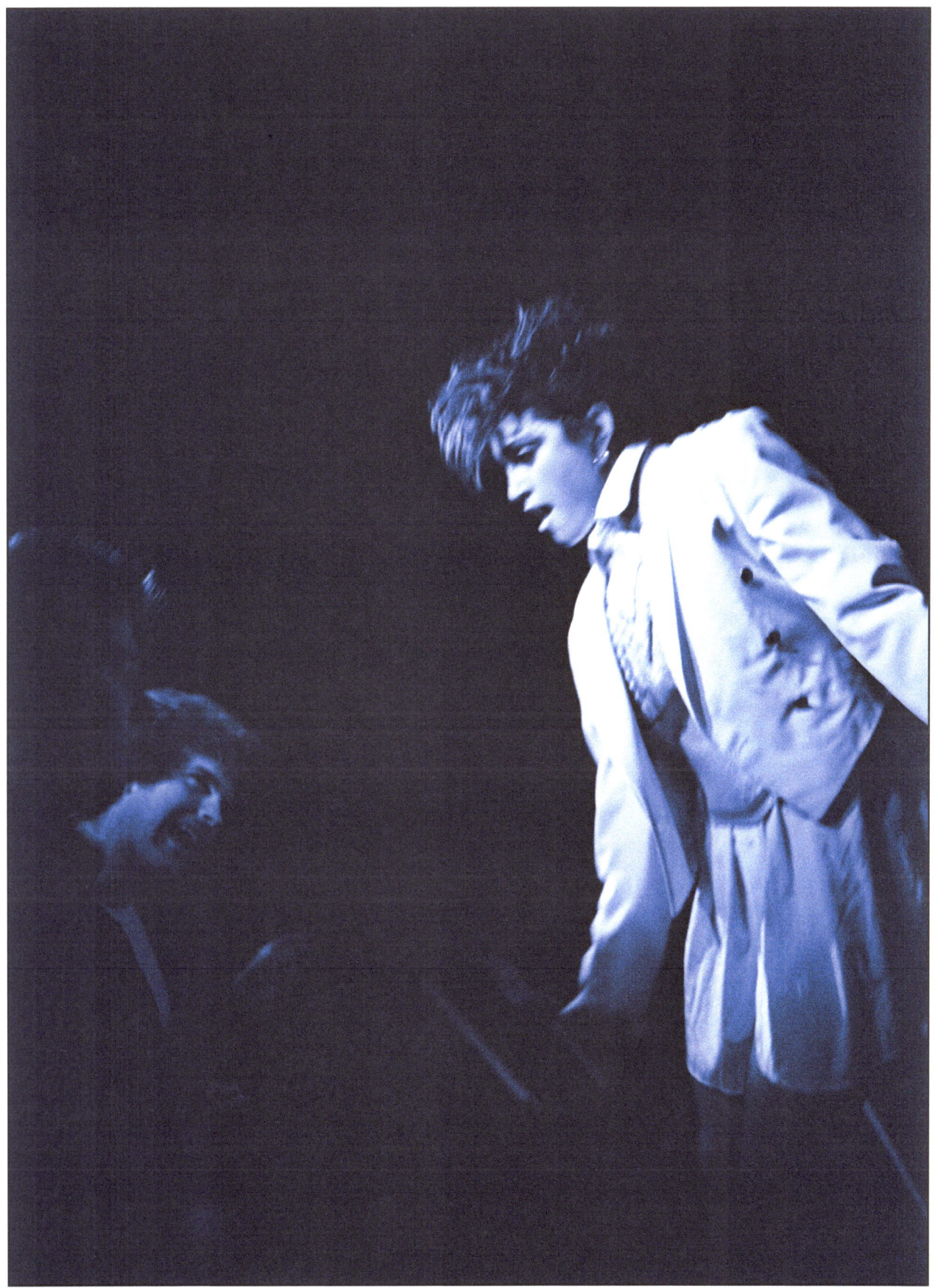

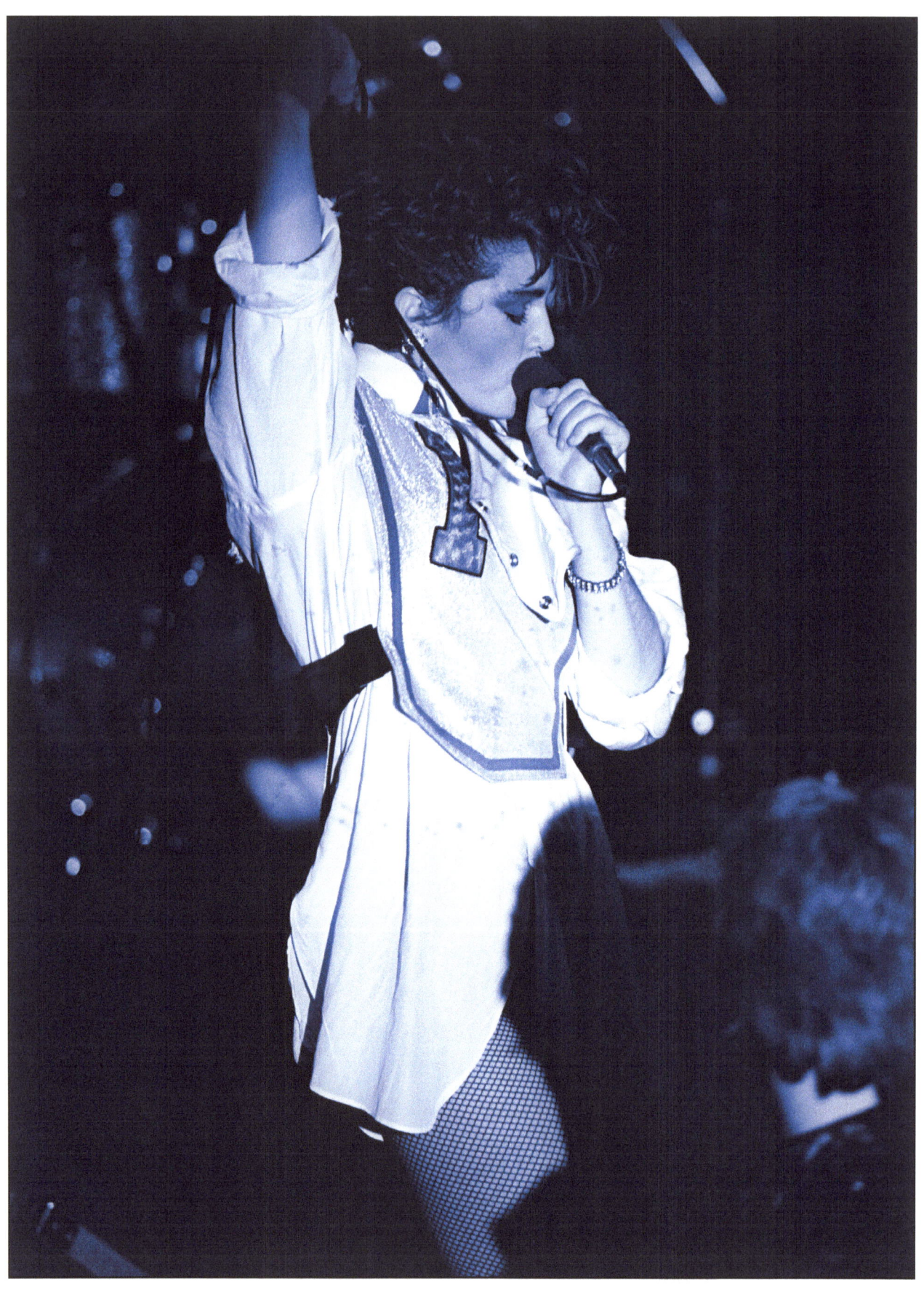

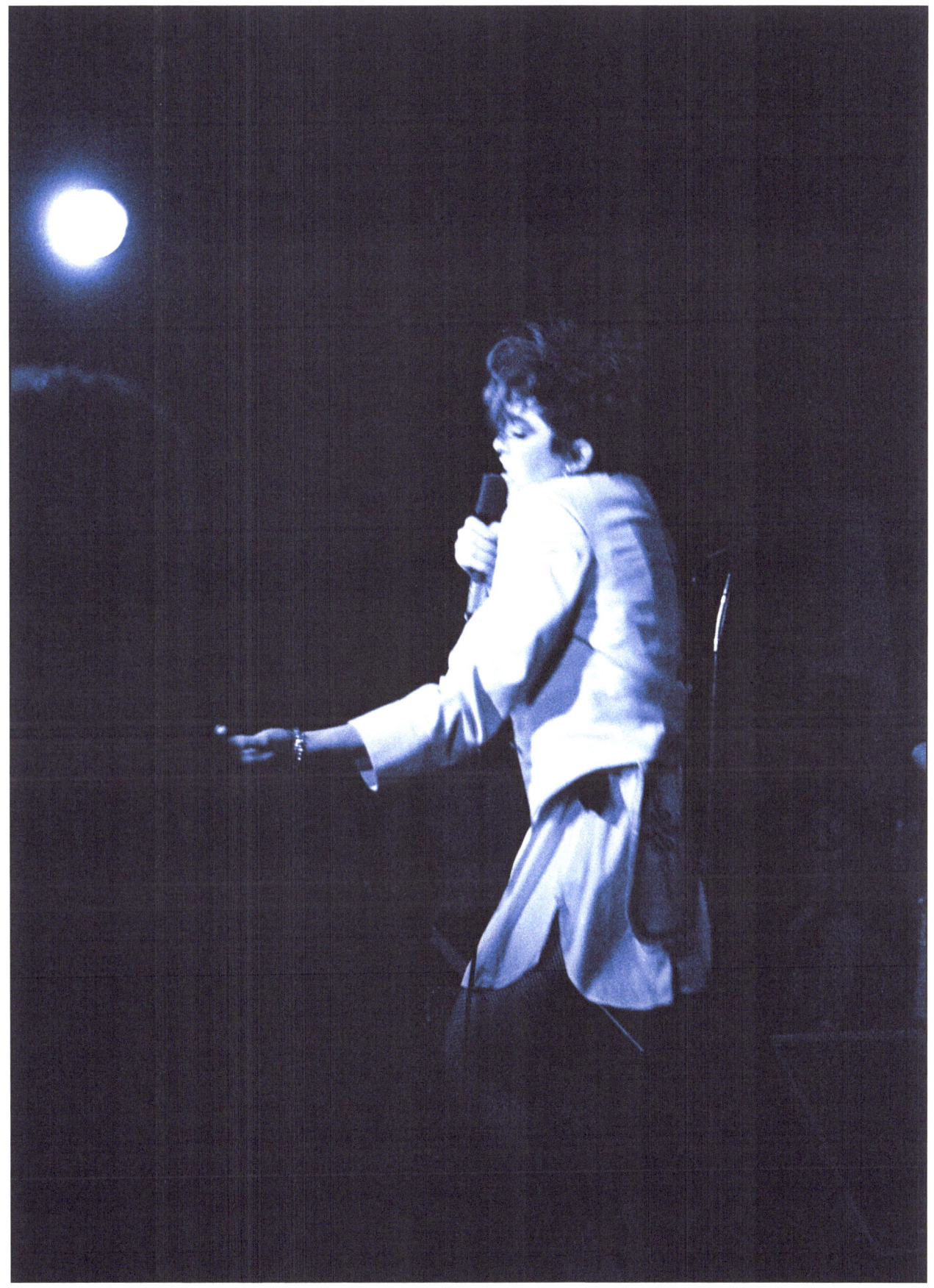

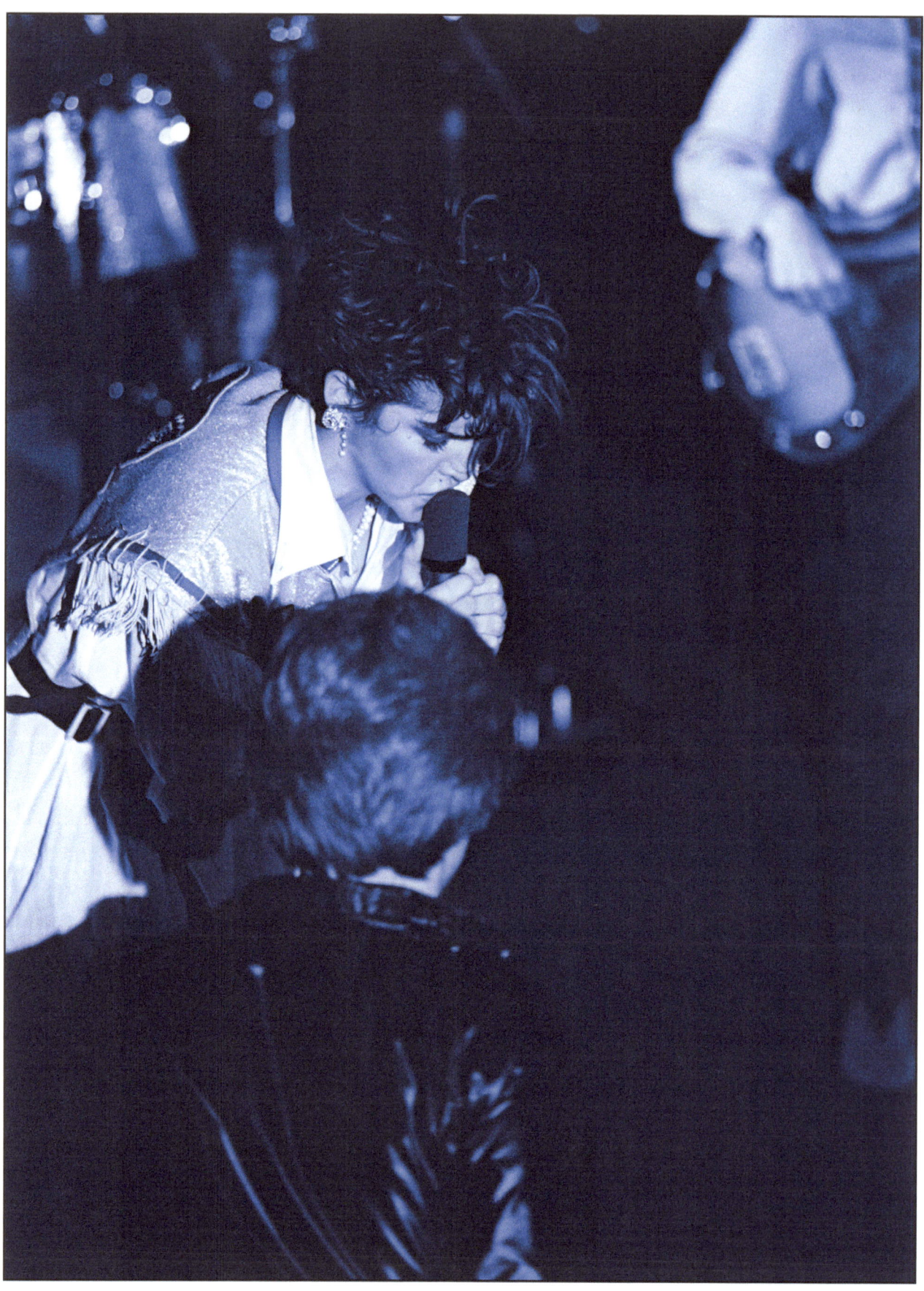

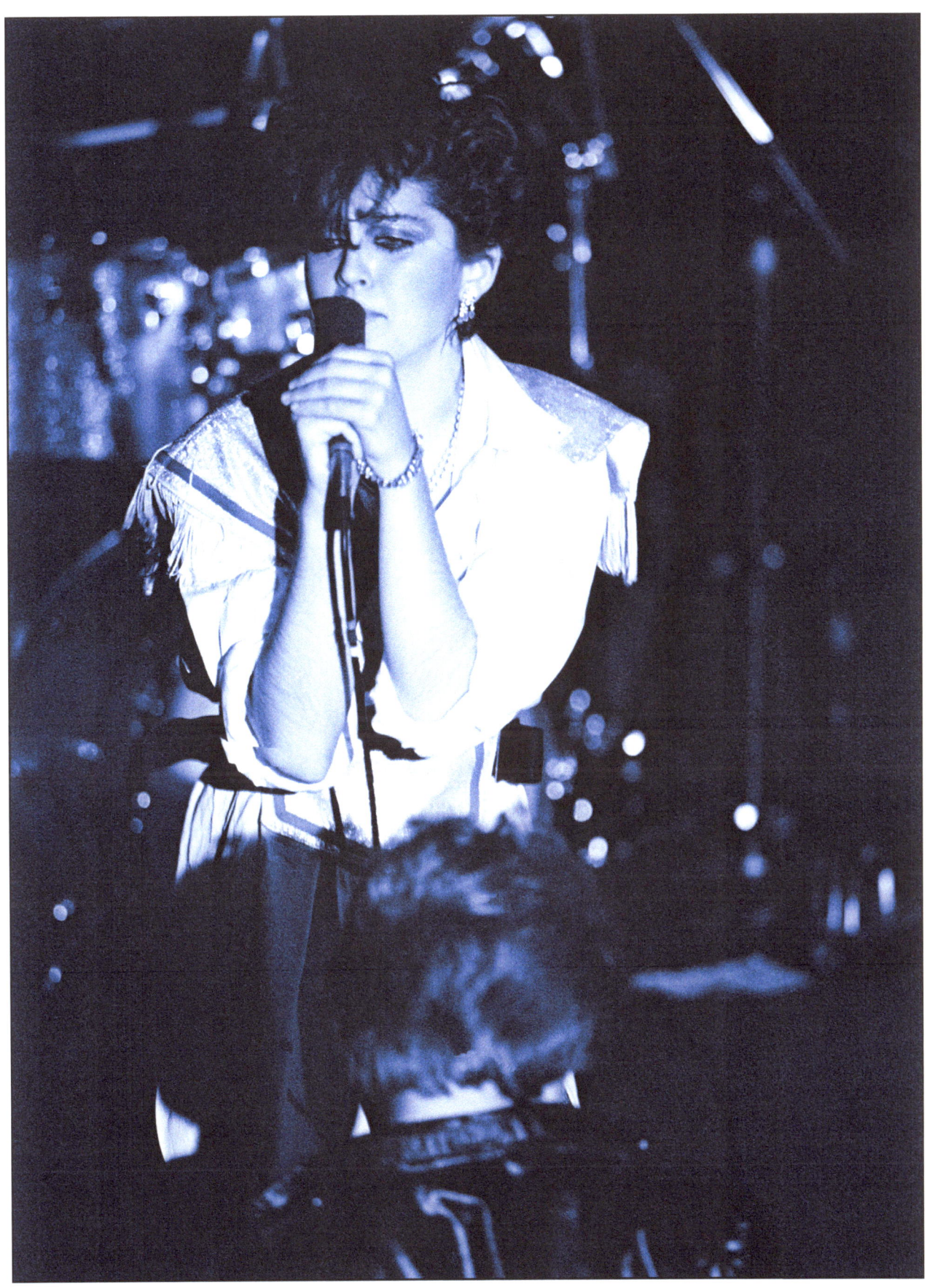

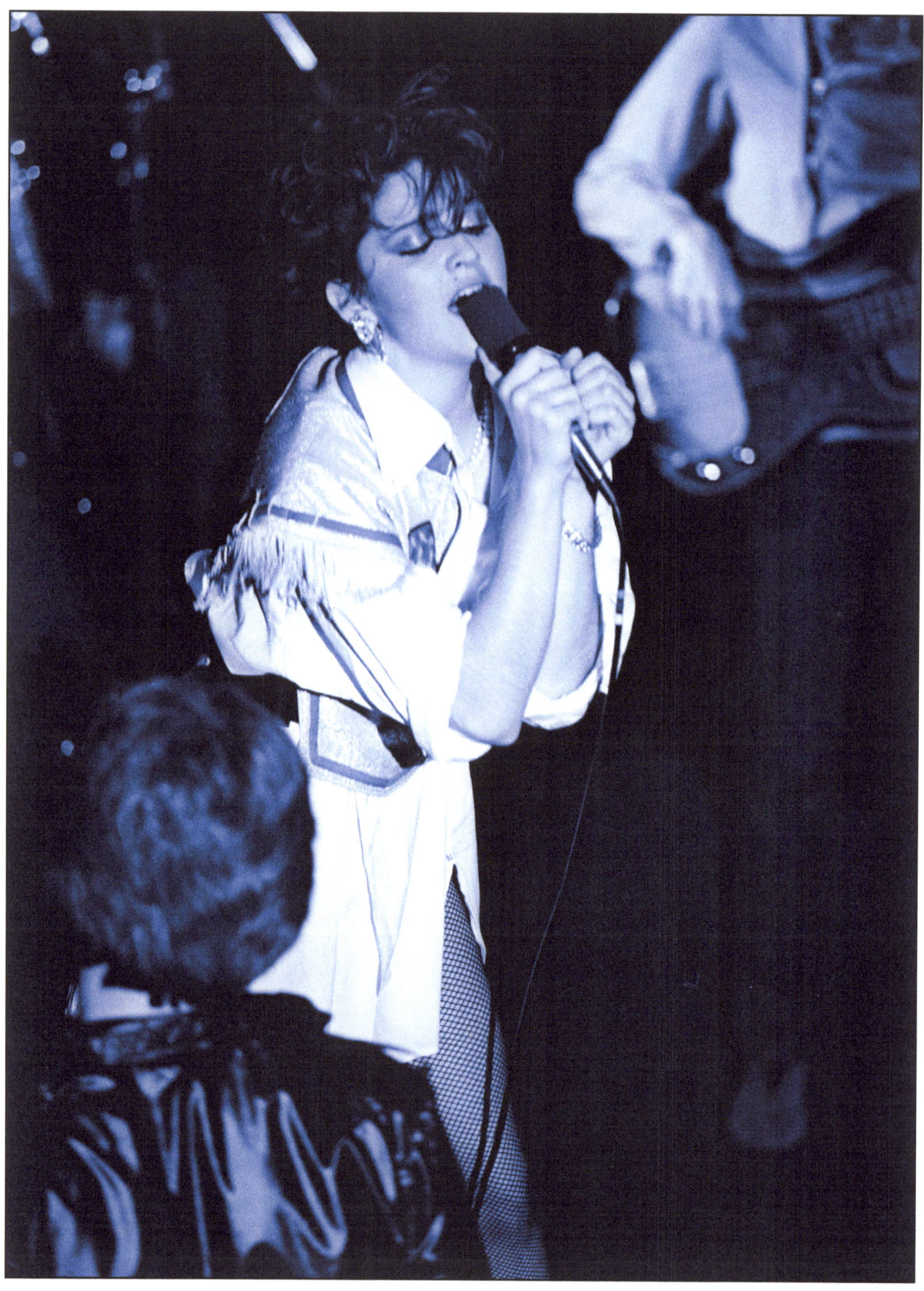

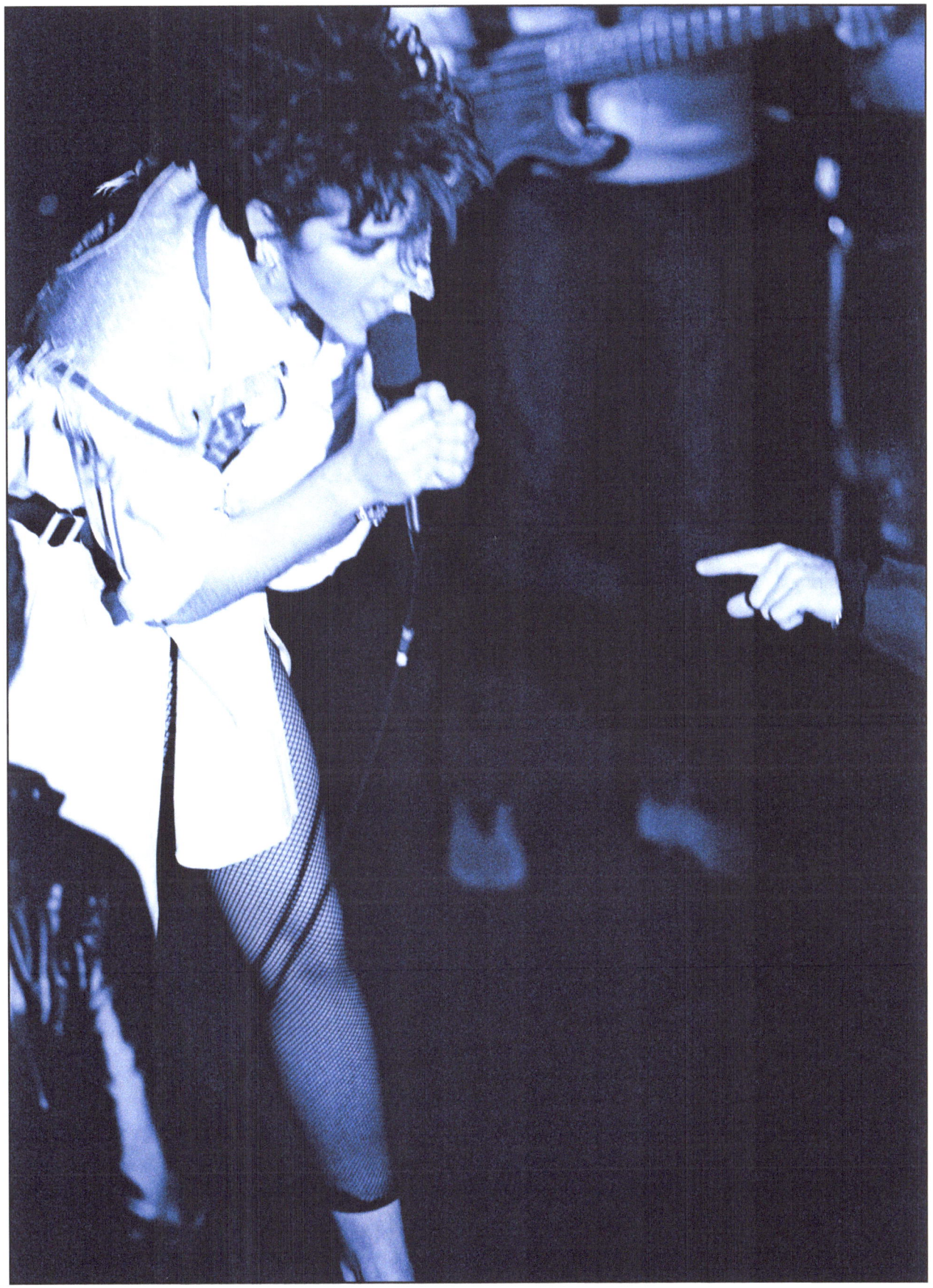

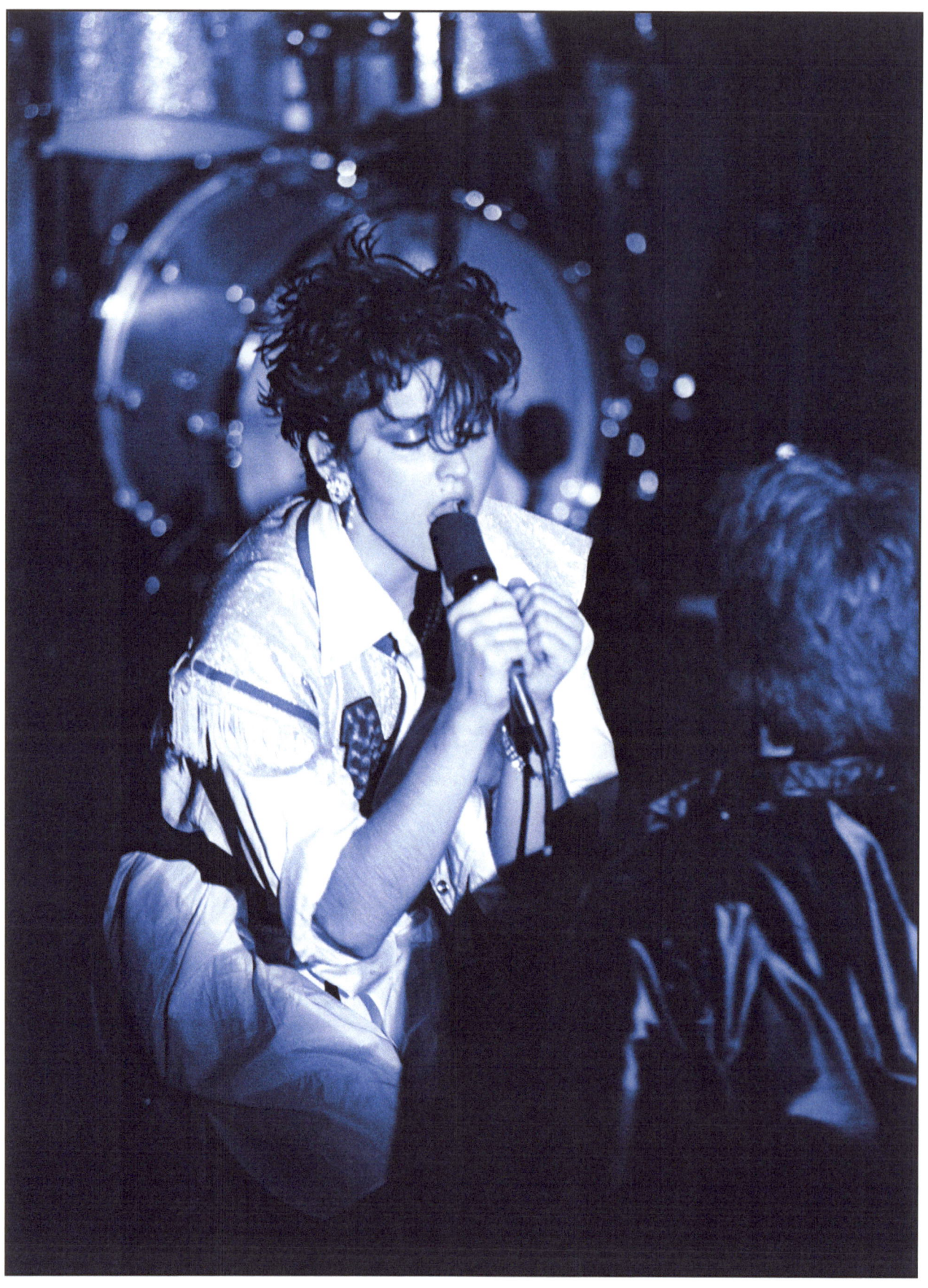

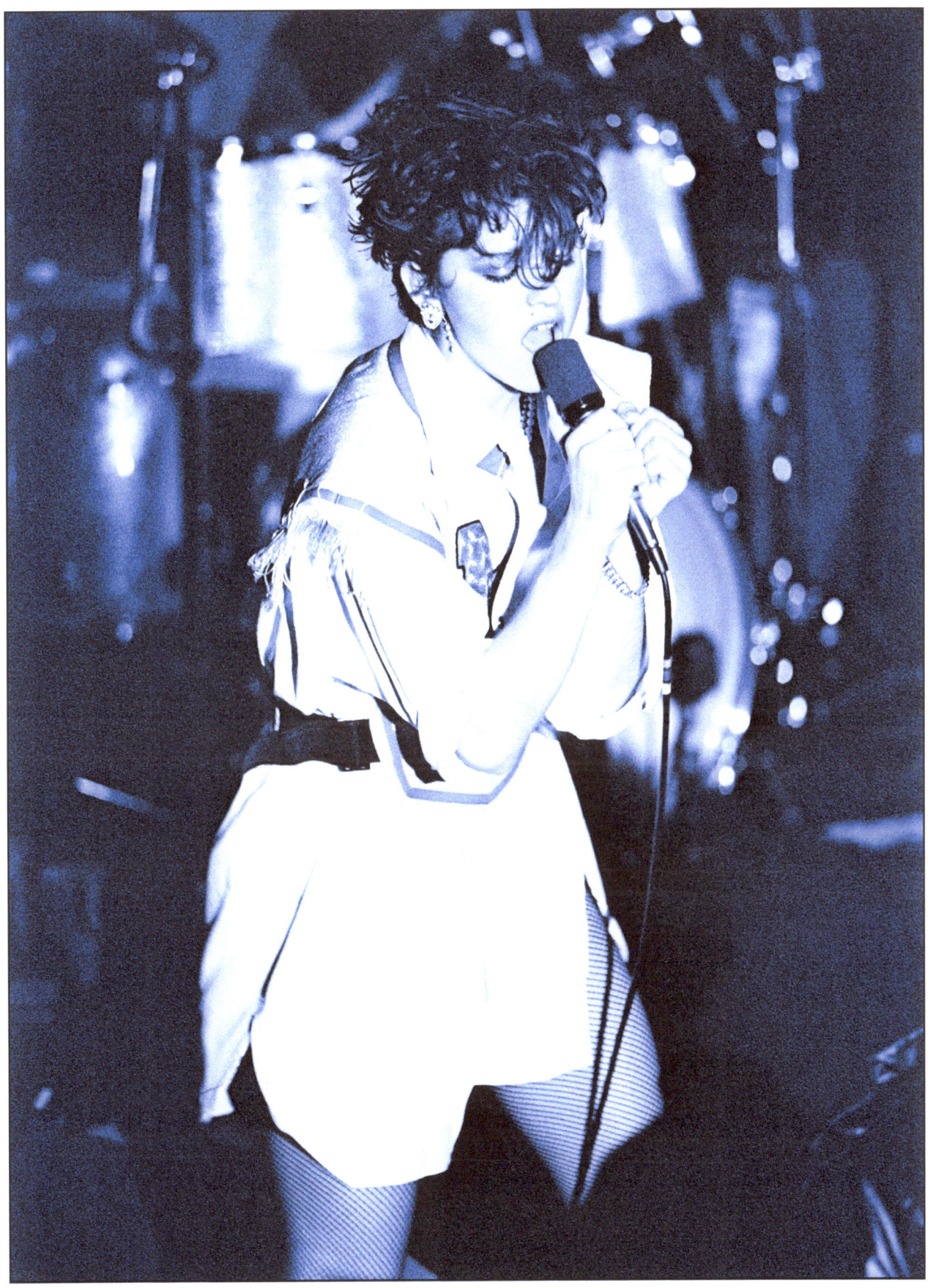

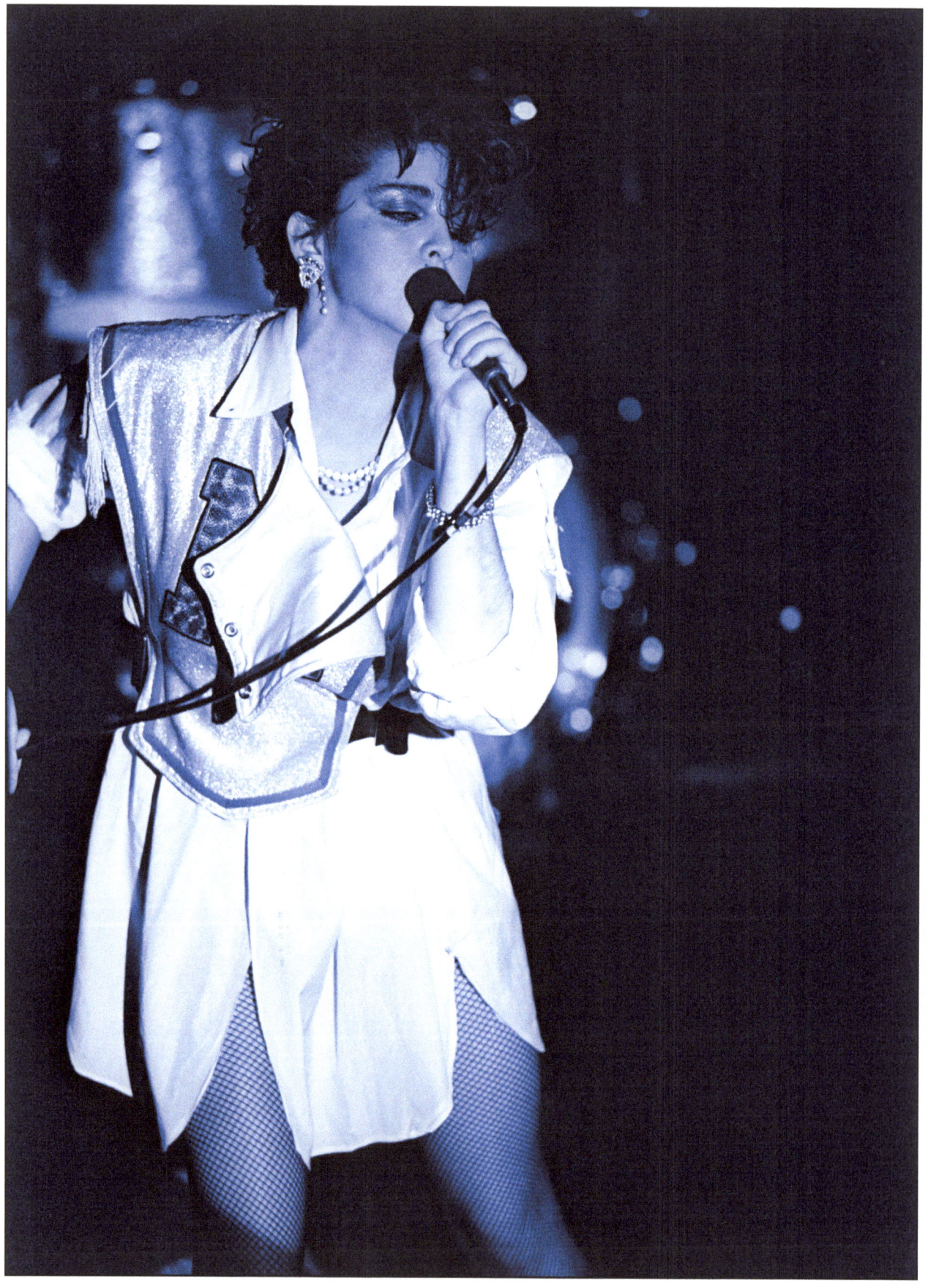

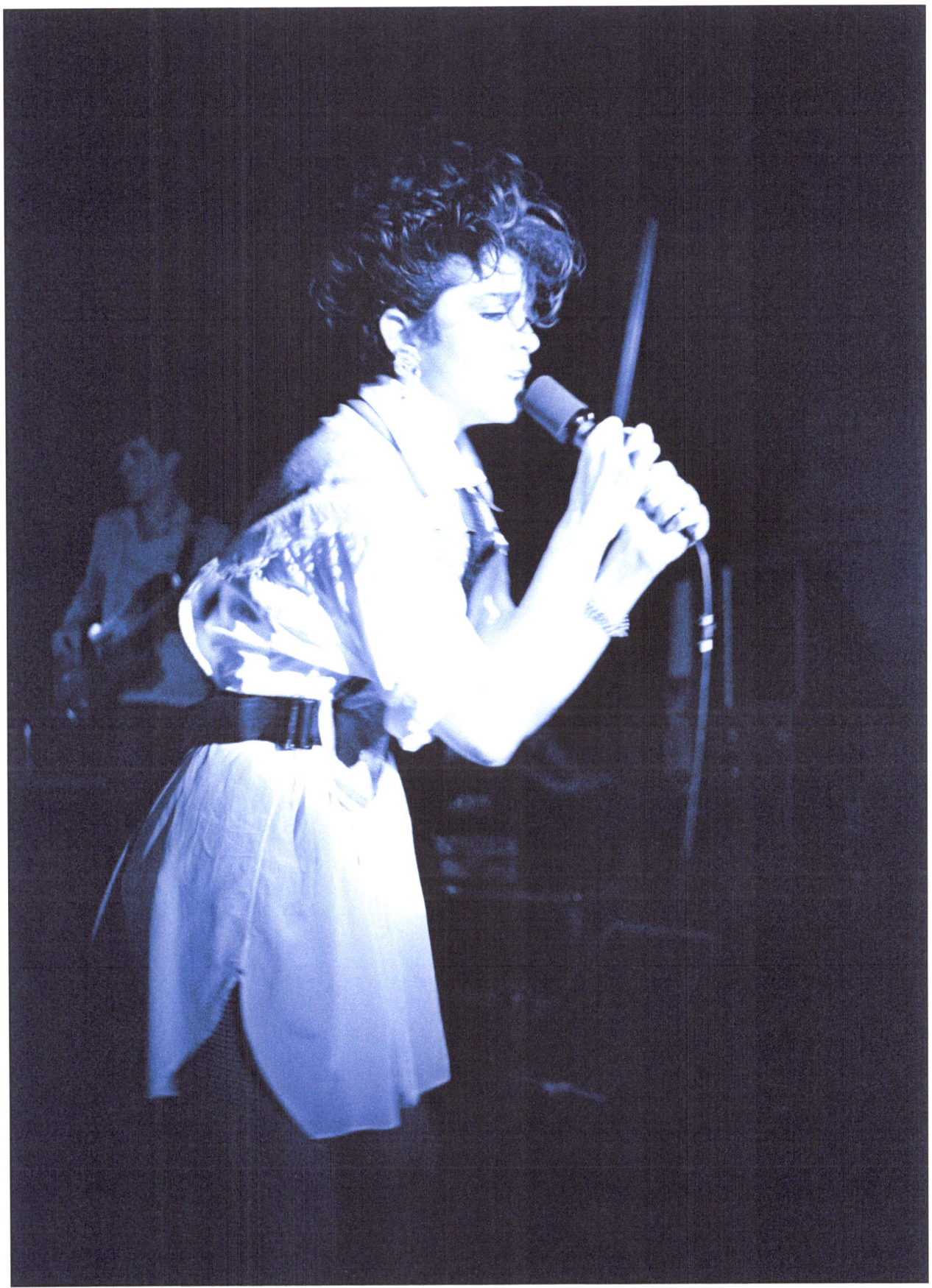

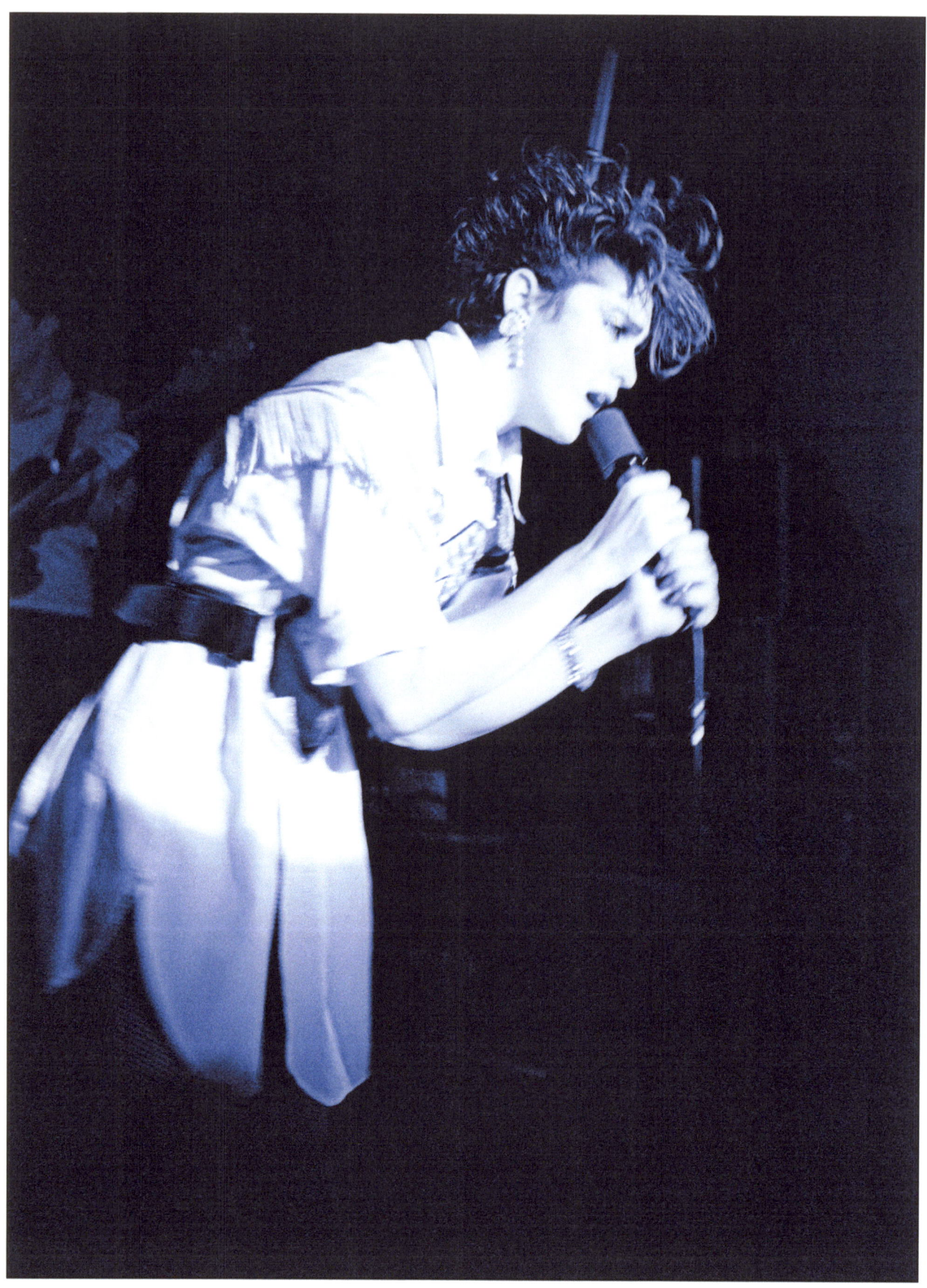

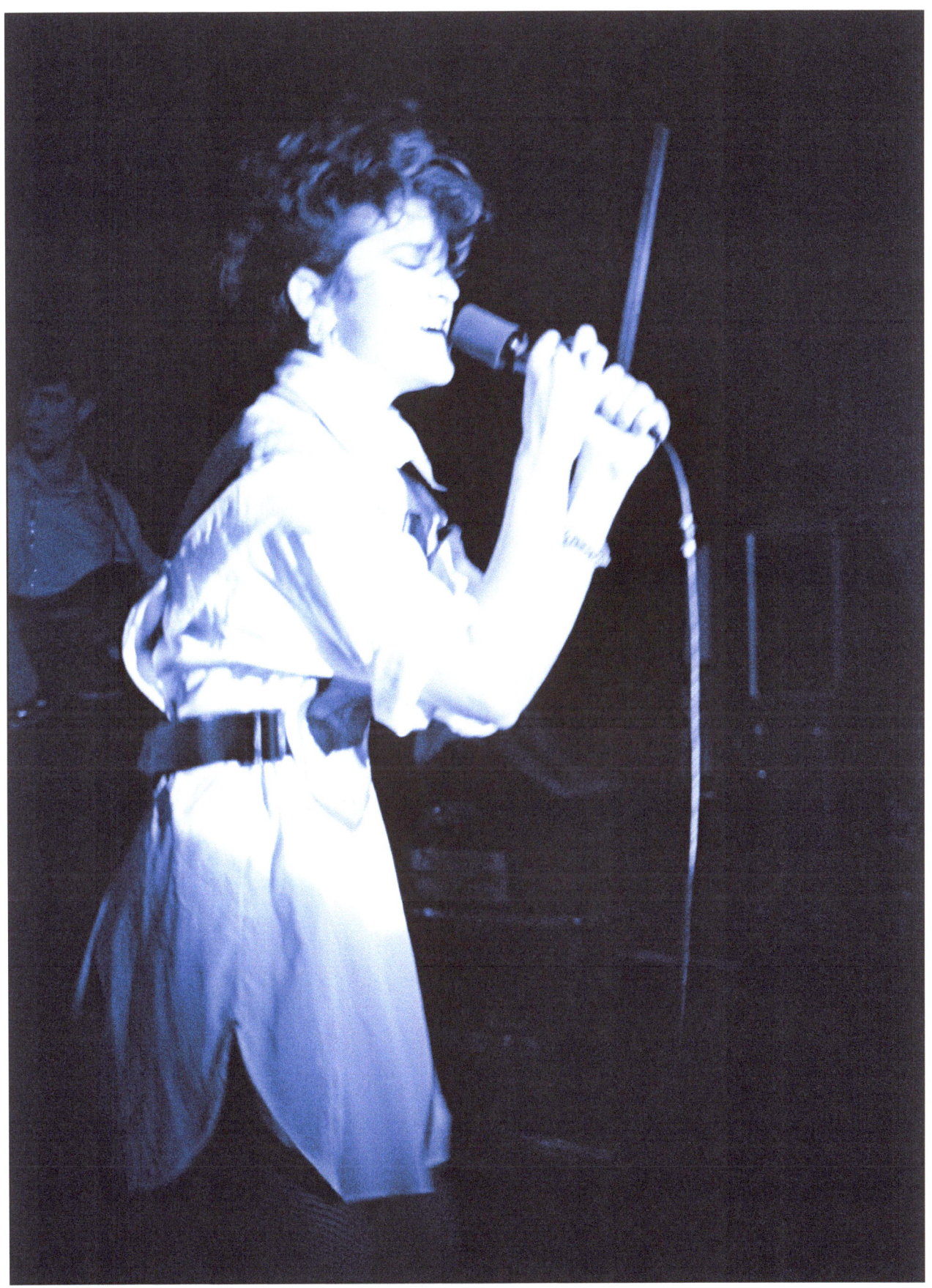

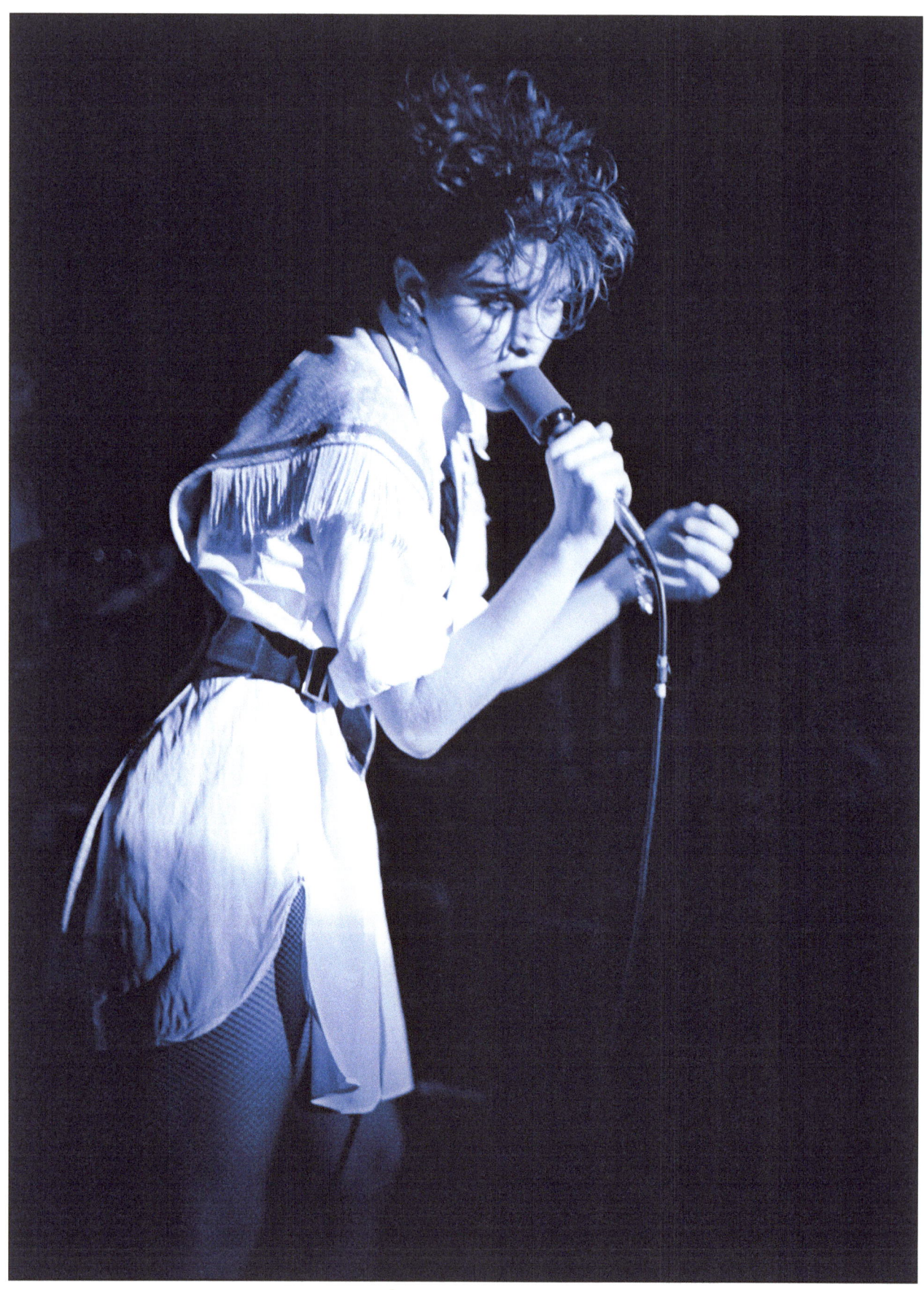

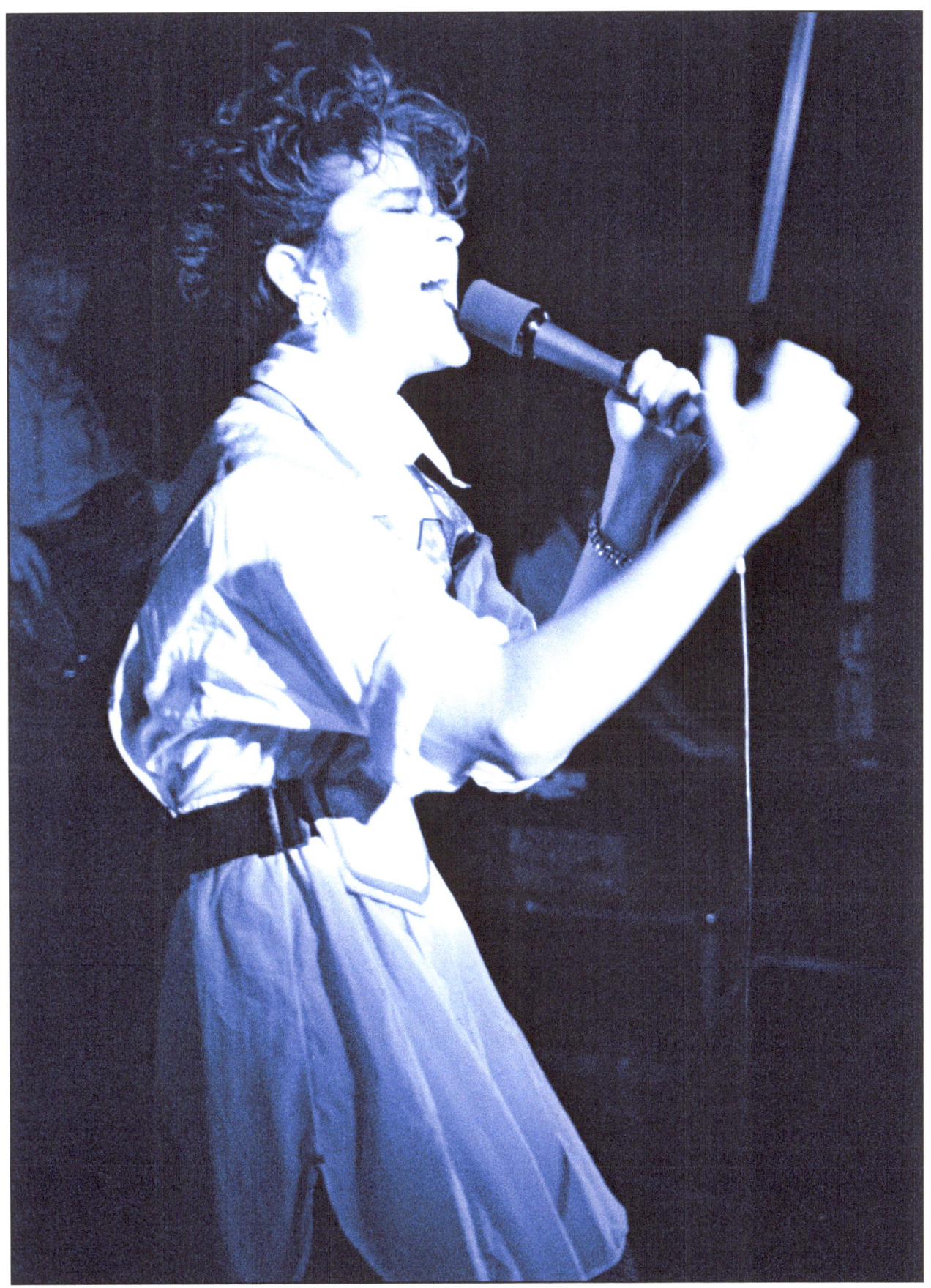

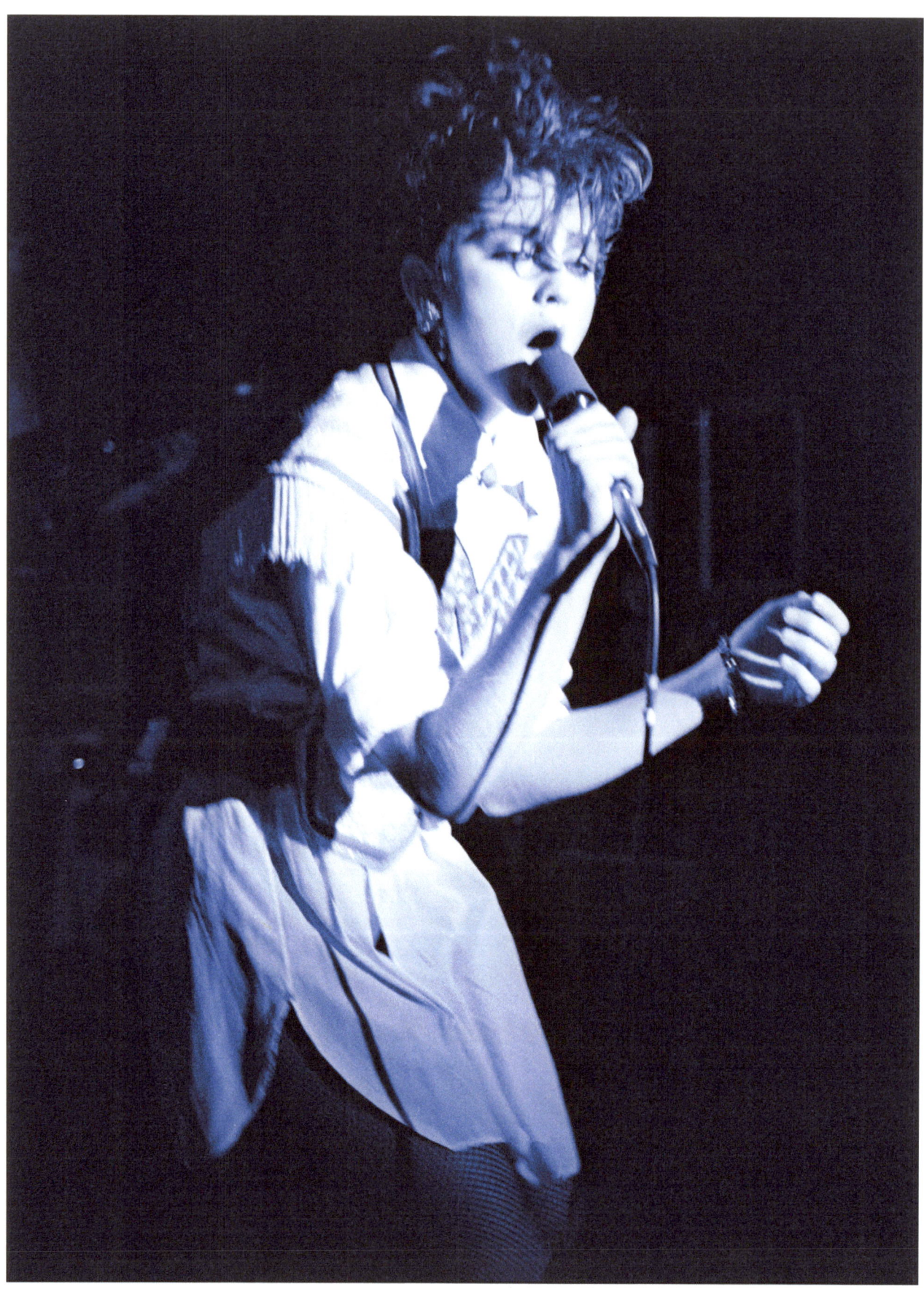

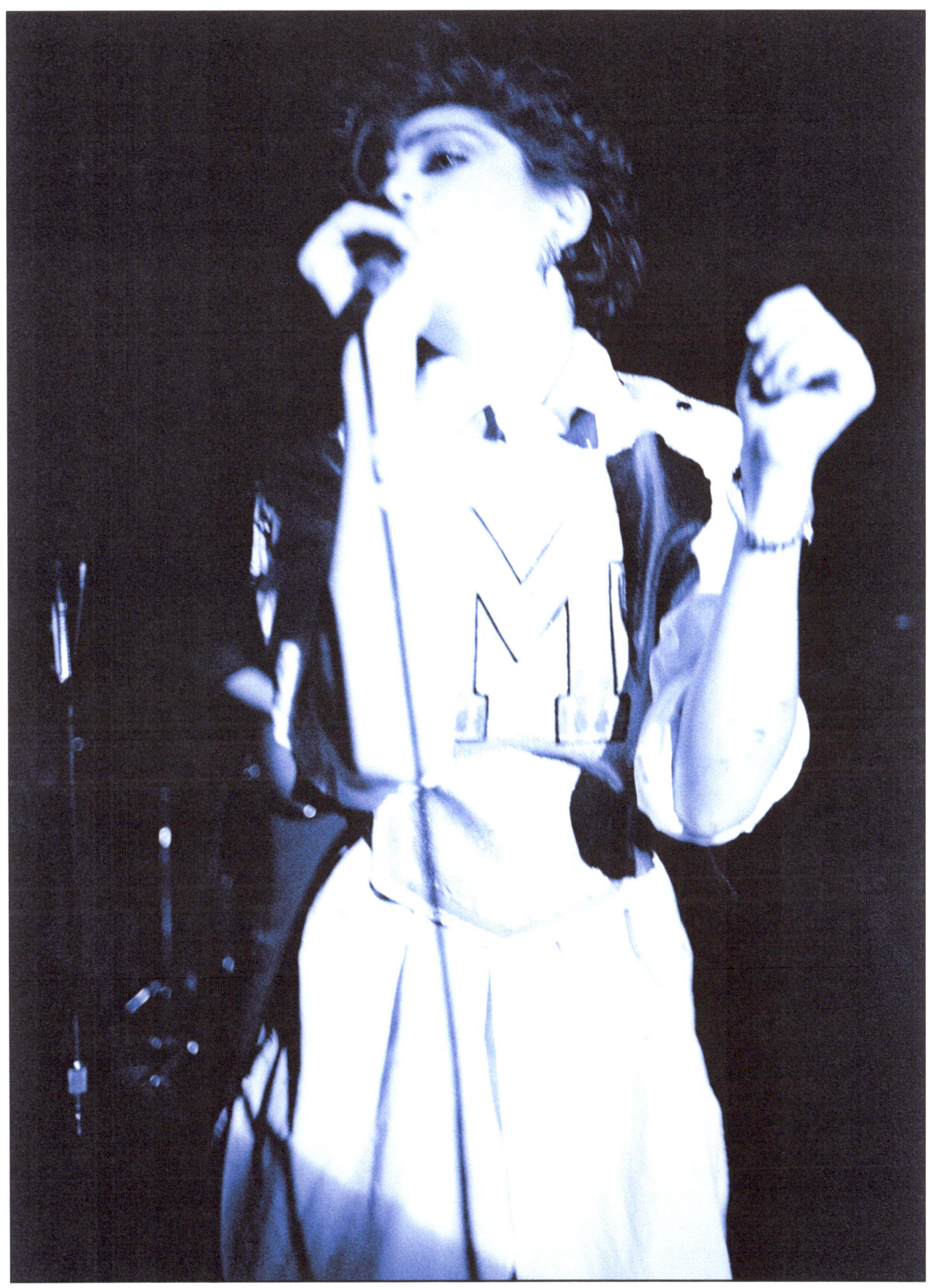

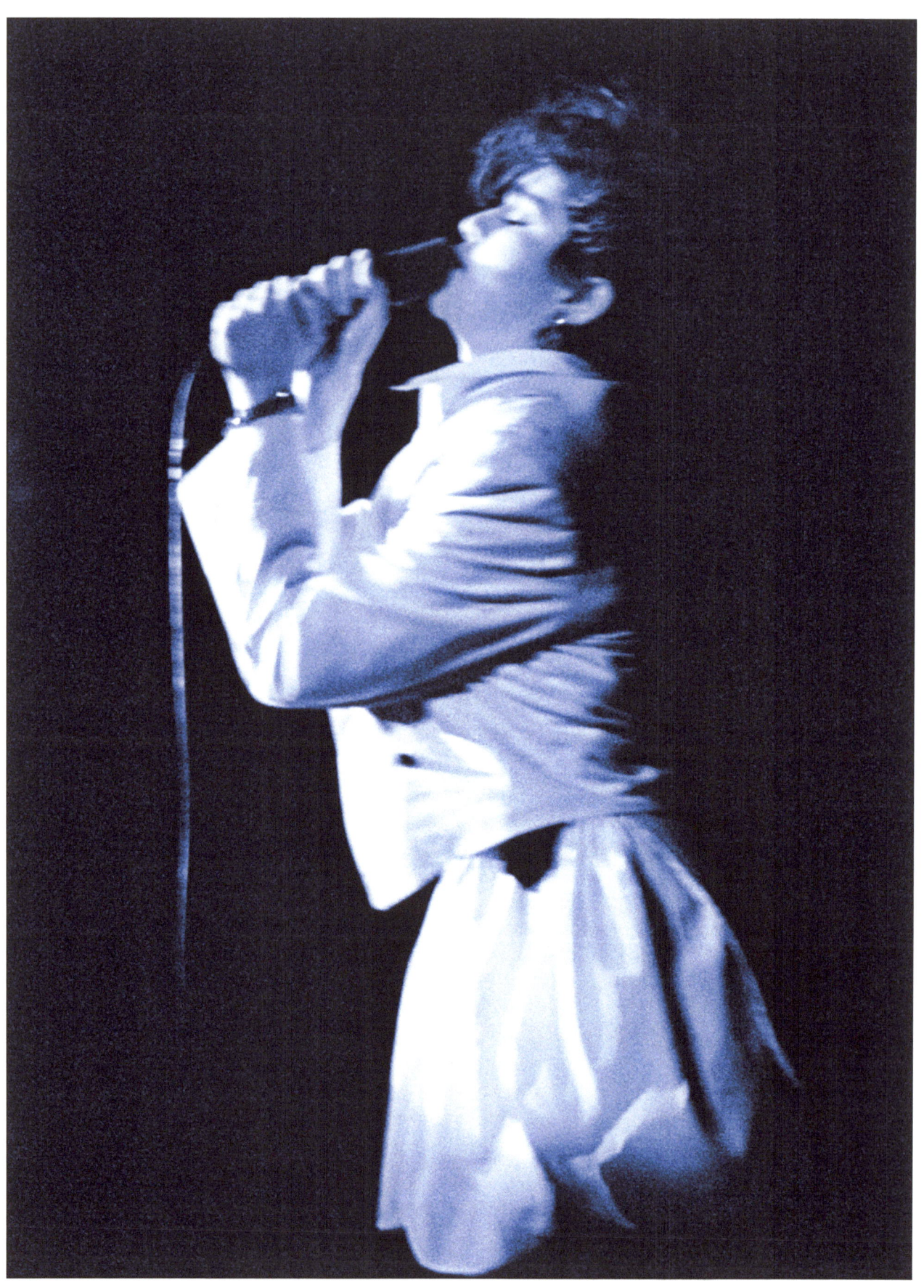

94

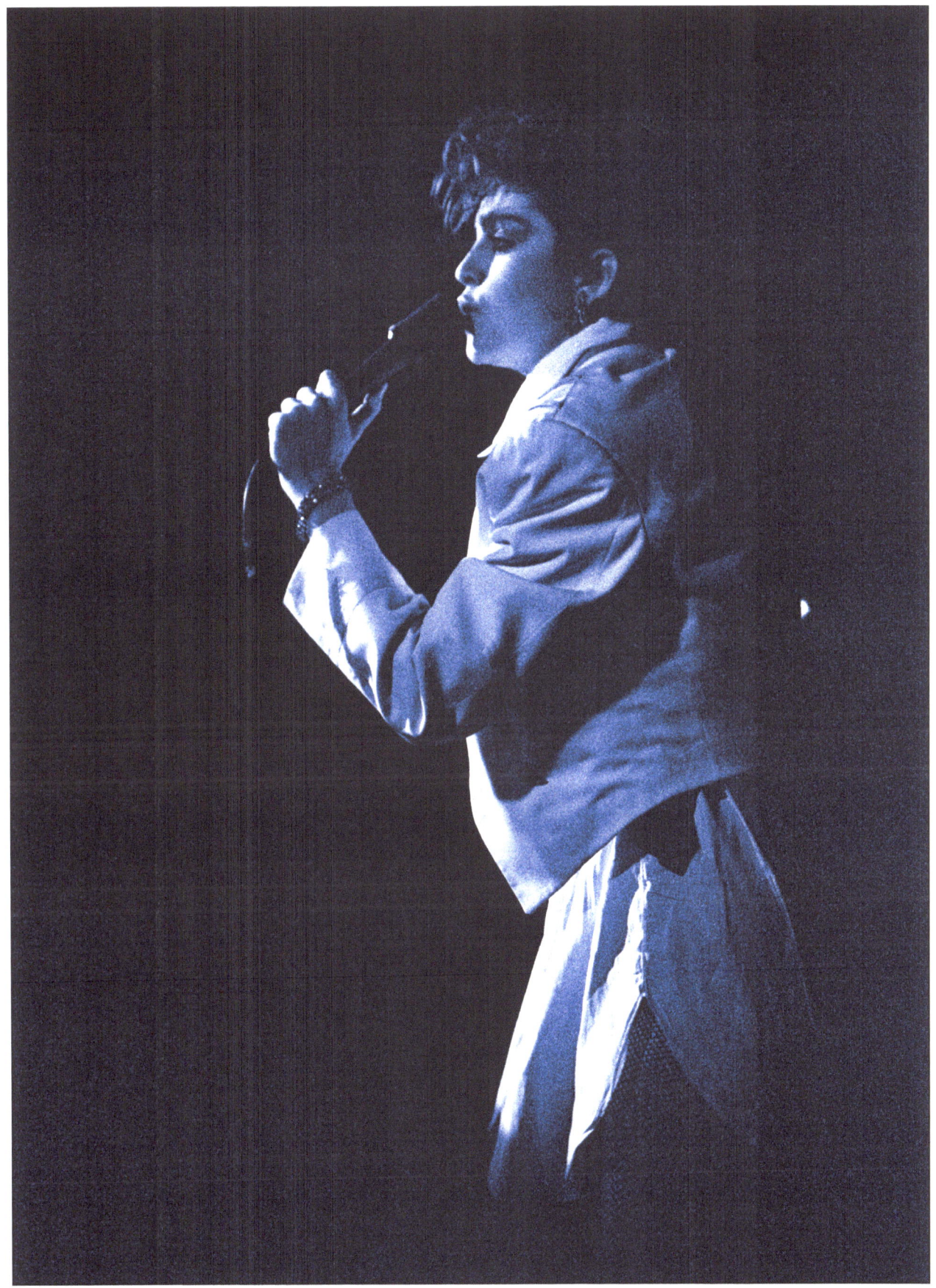

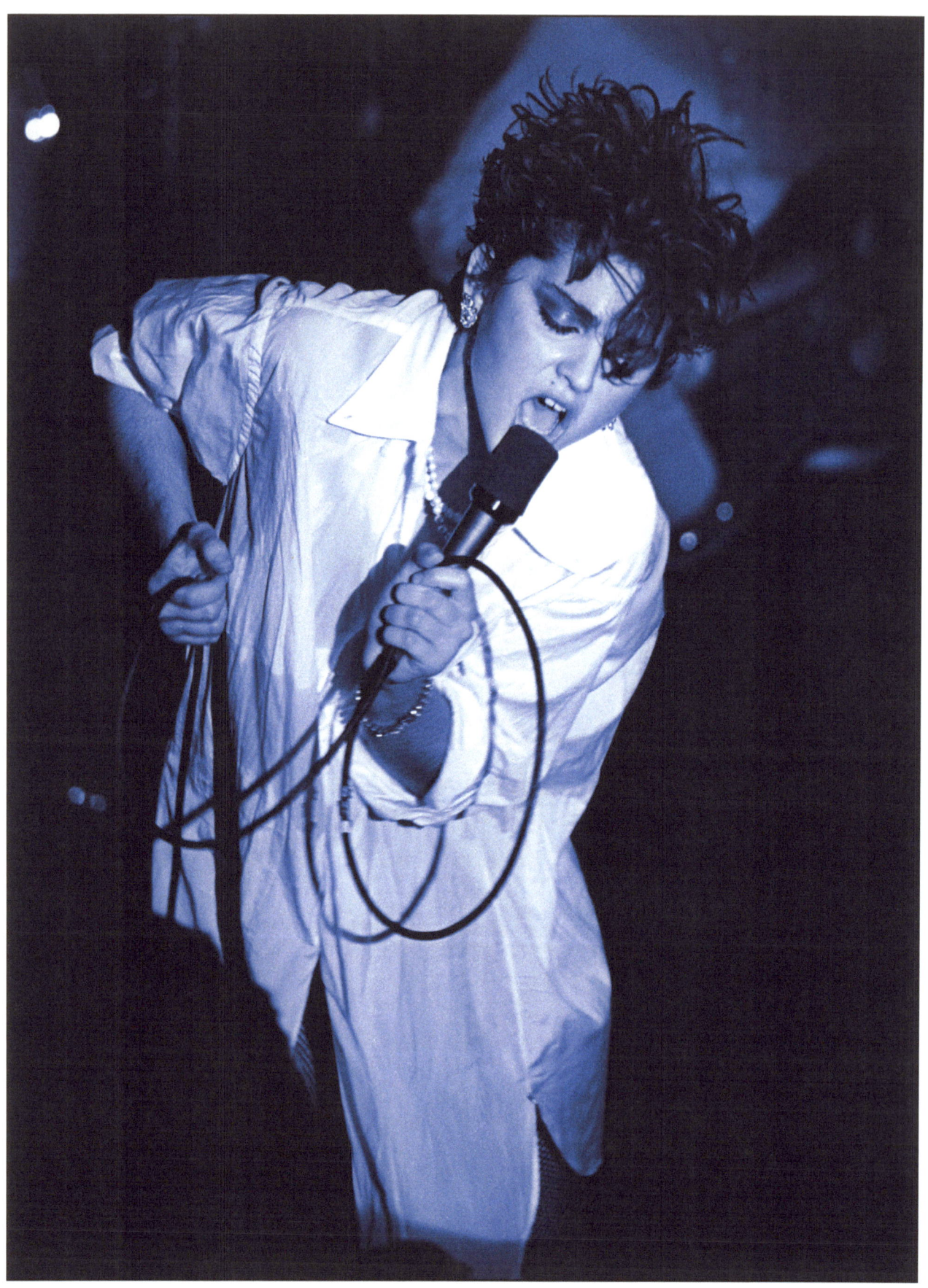

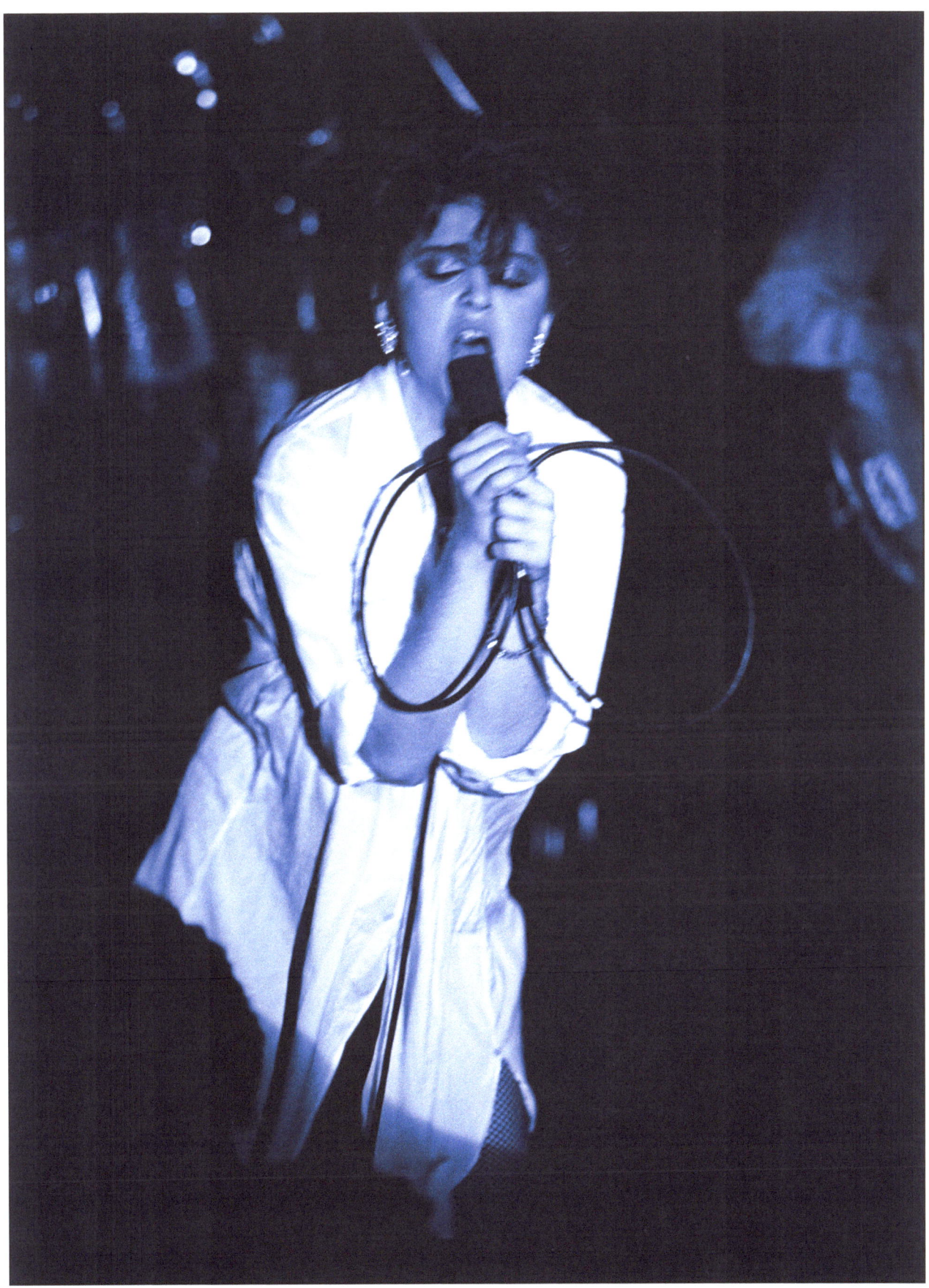

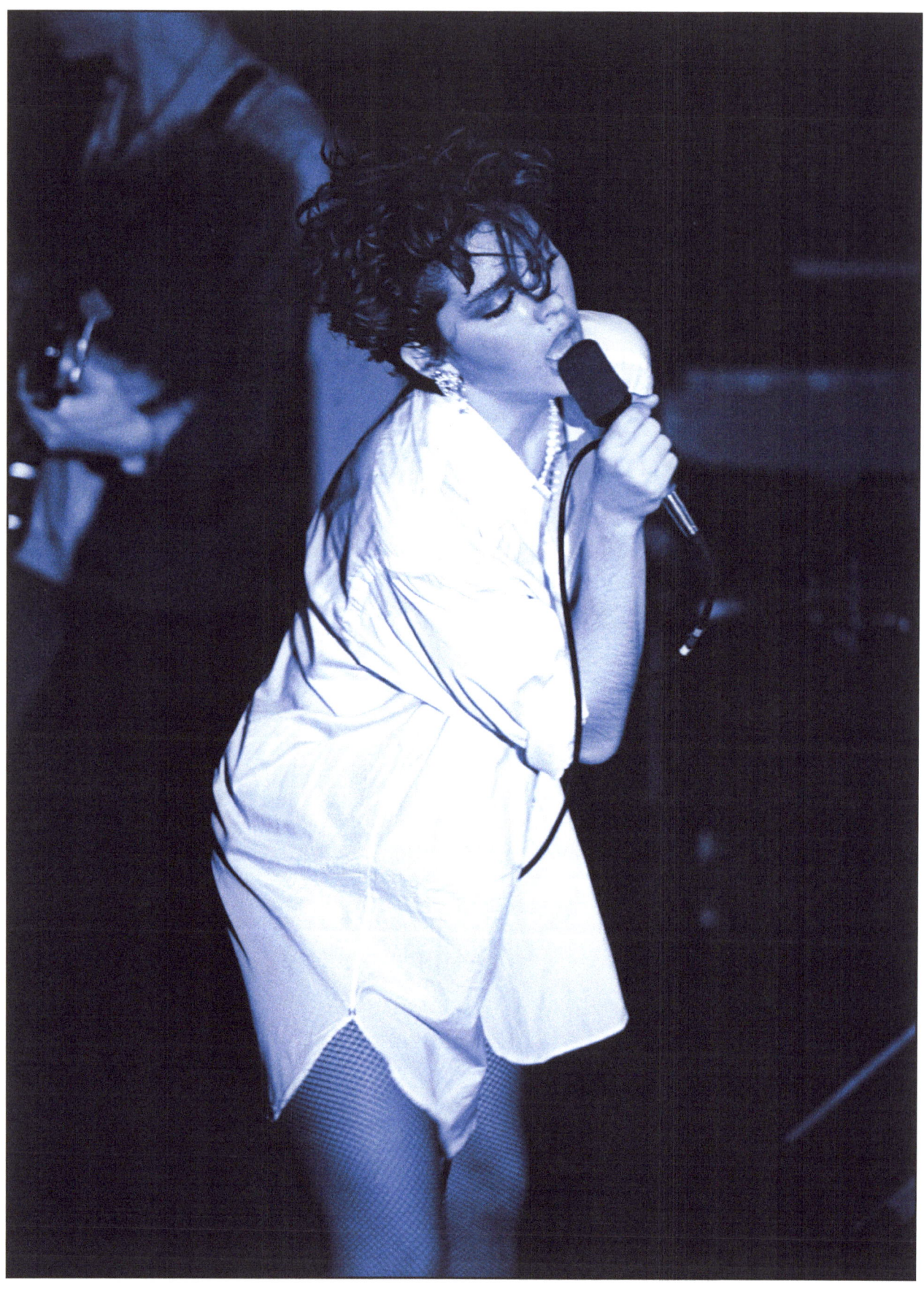

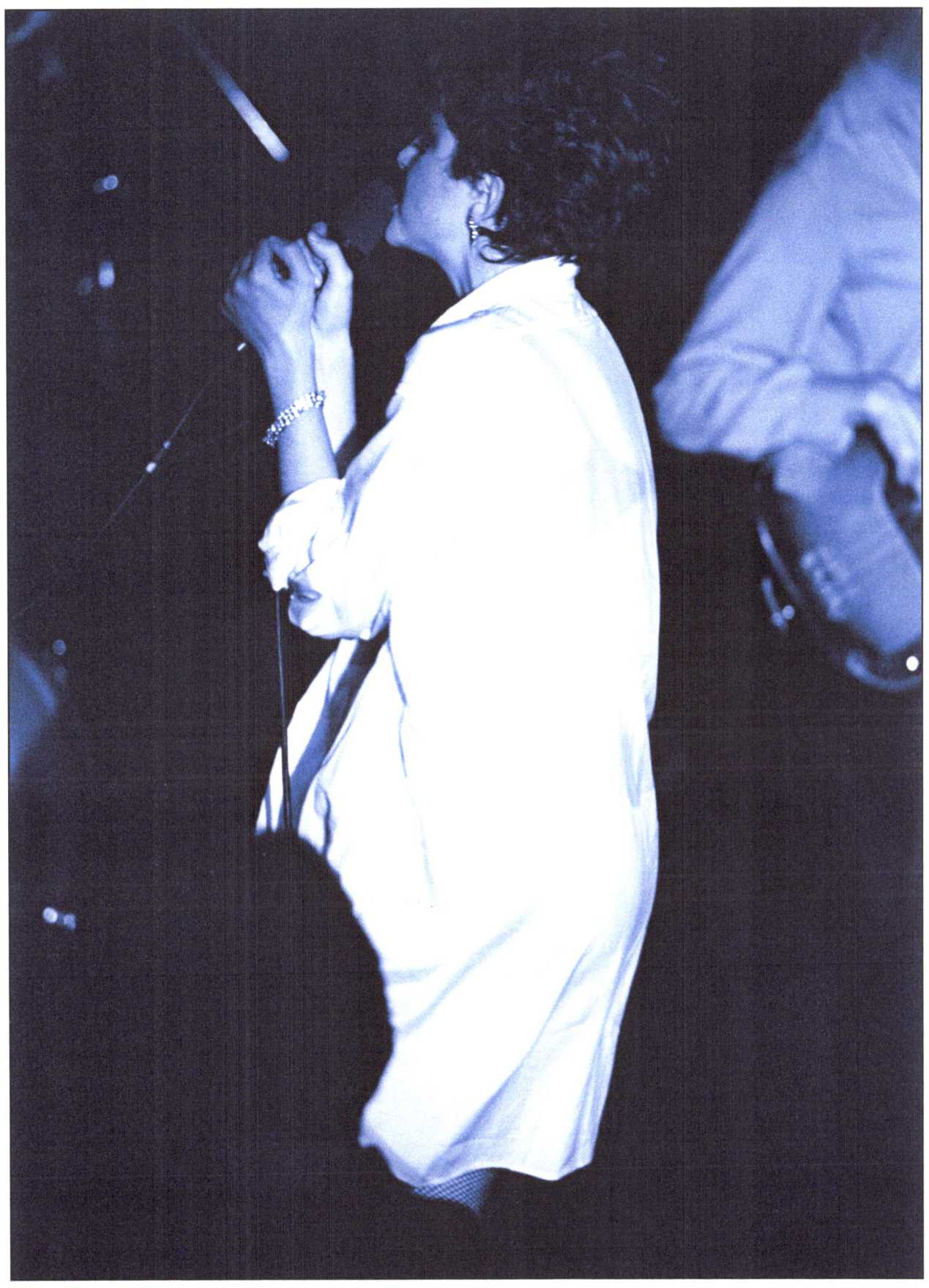

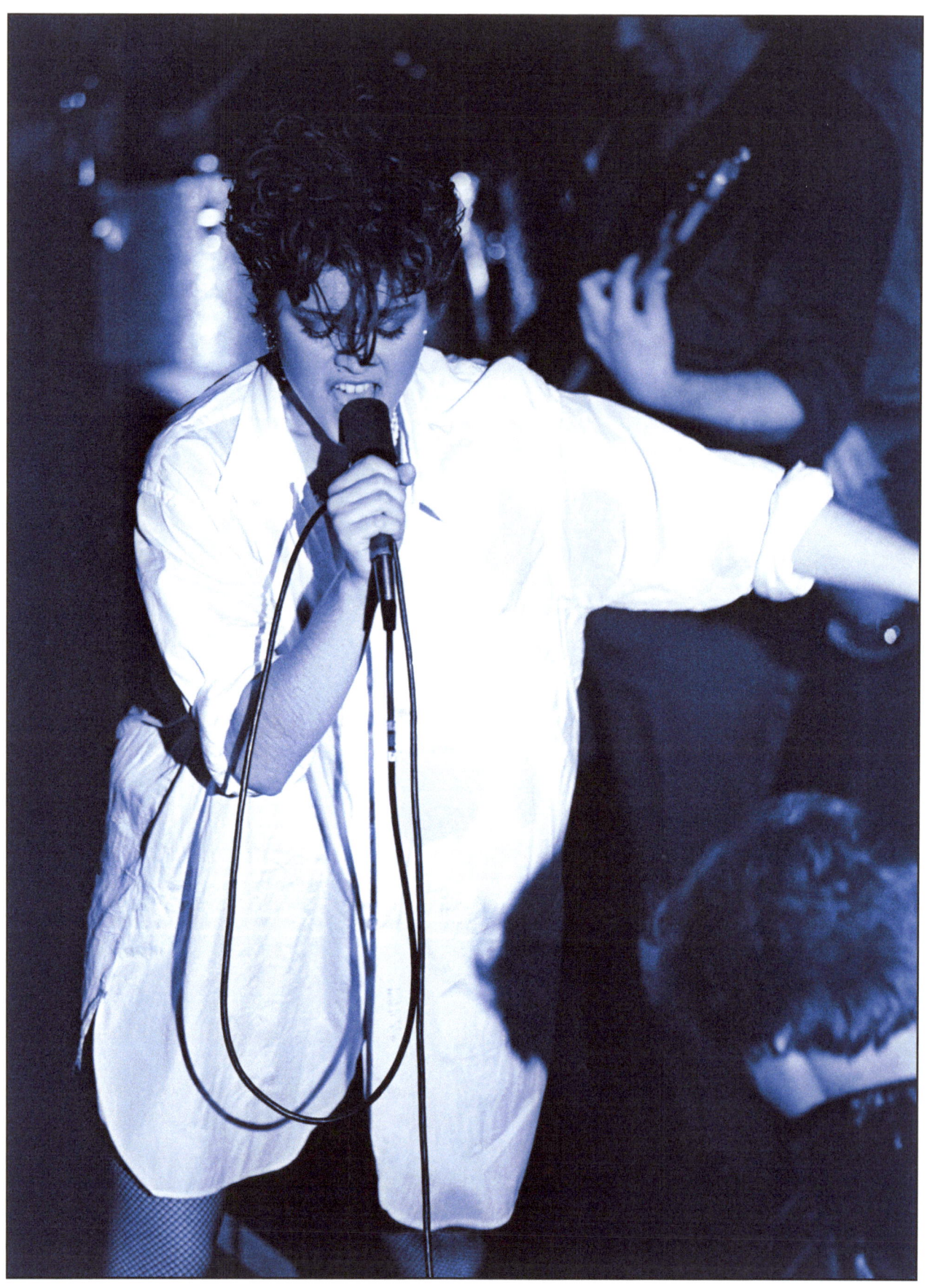

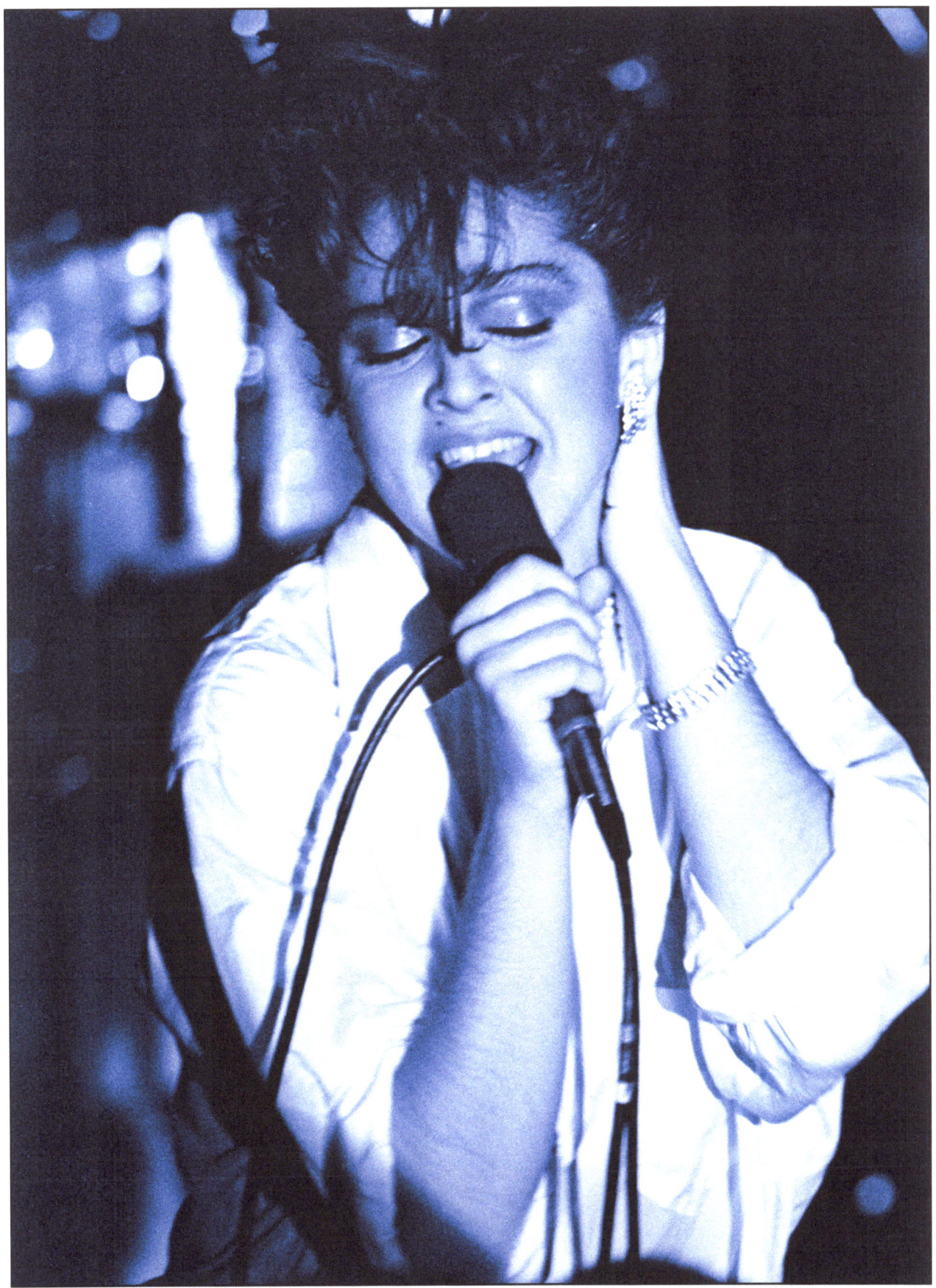

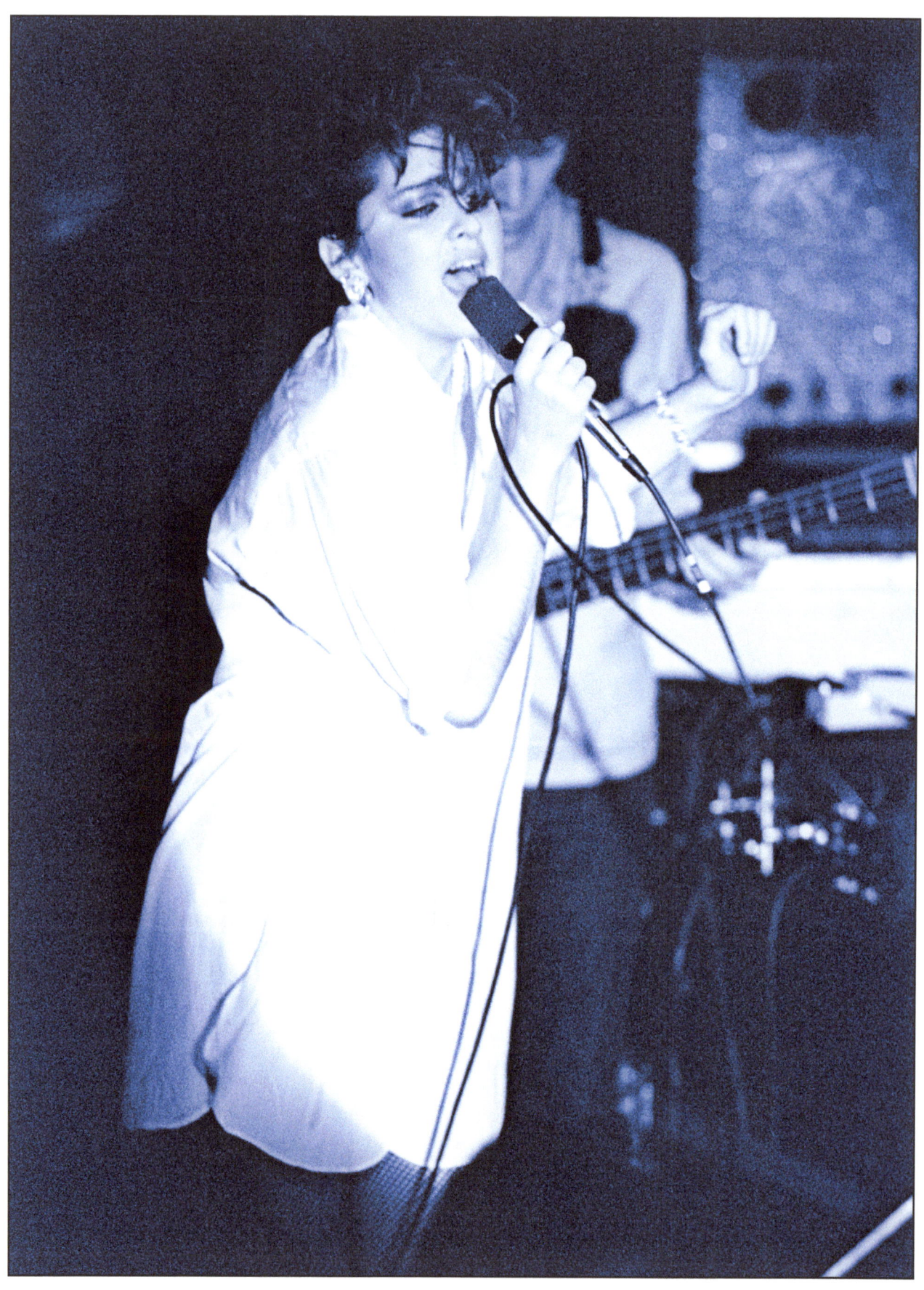

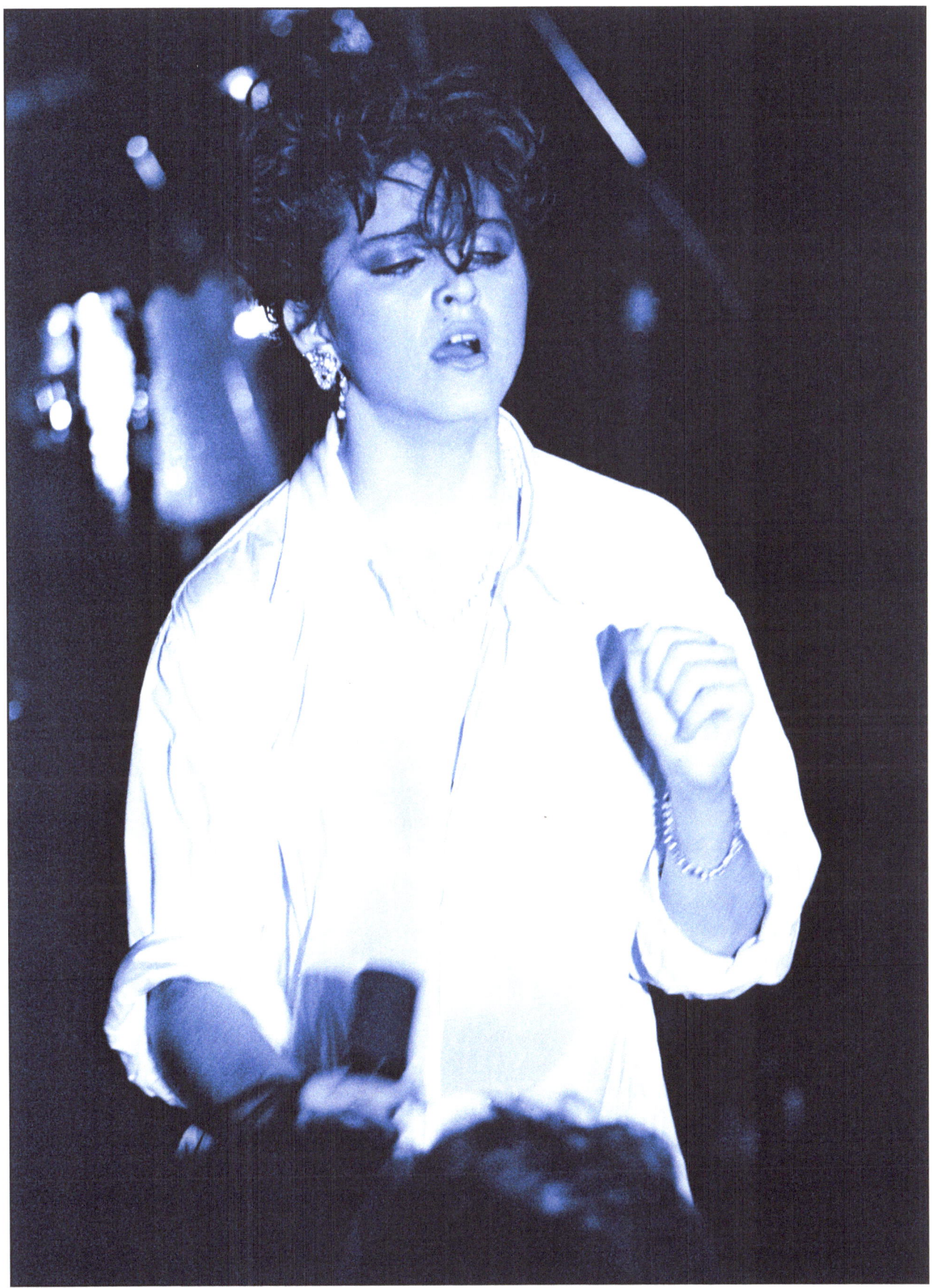

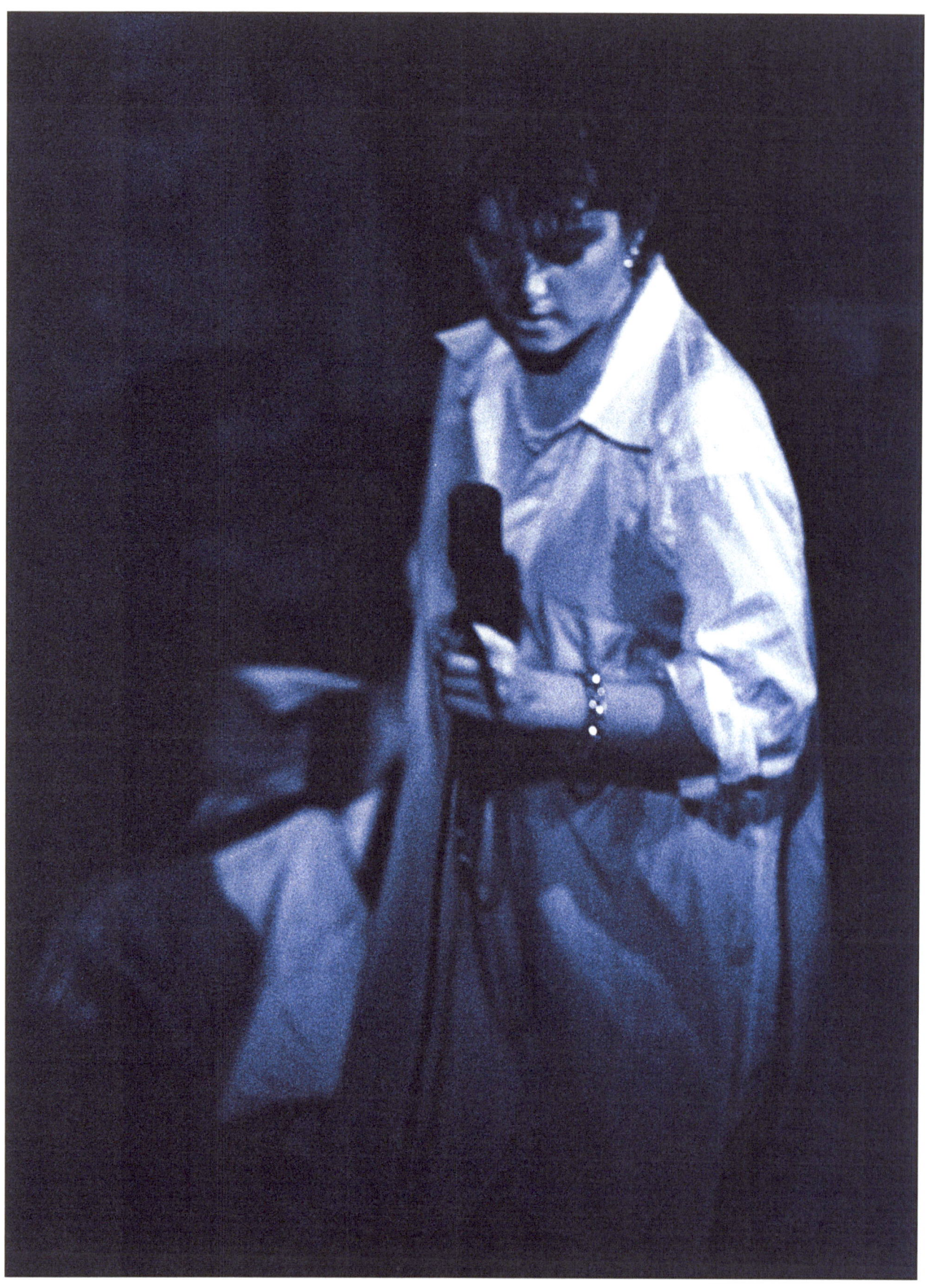

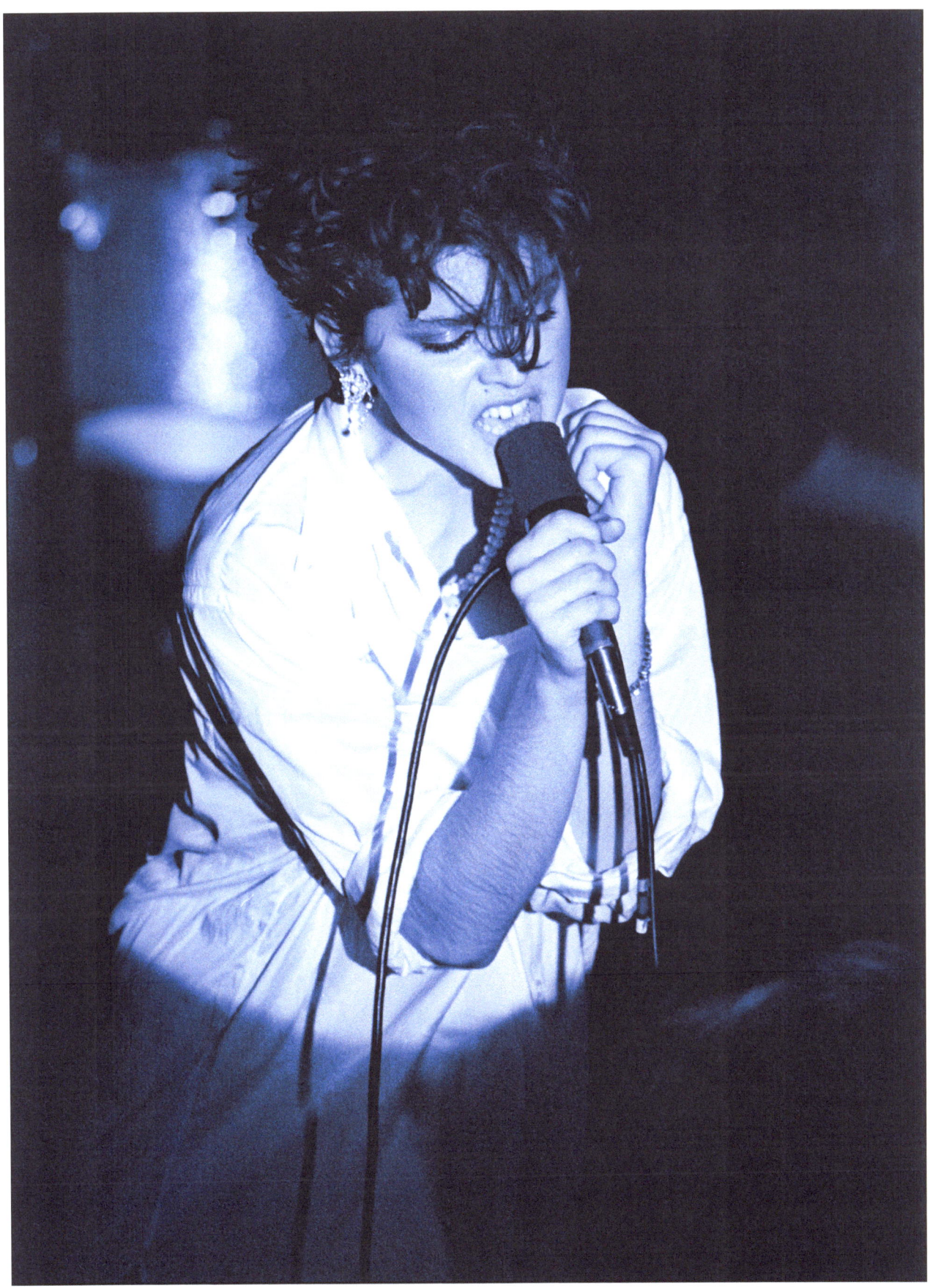

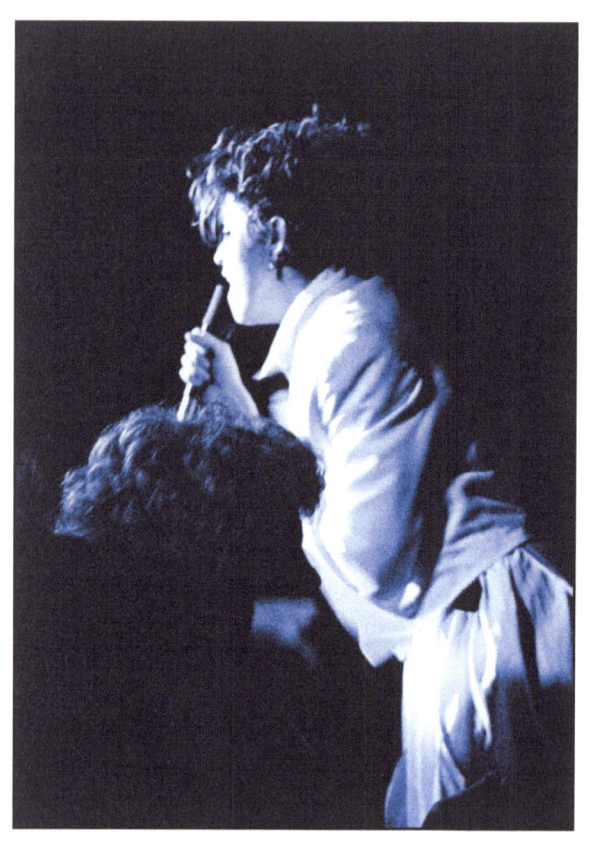 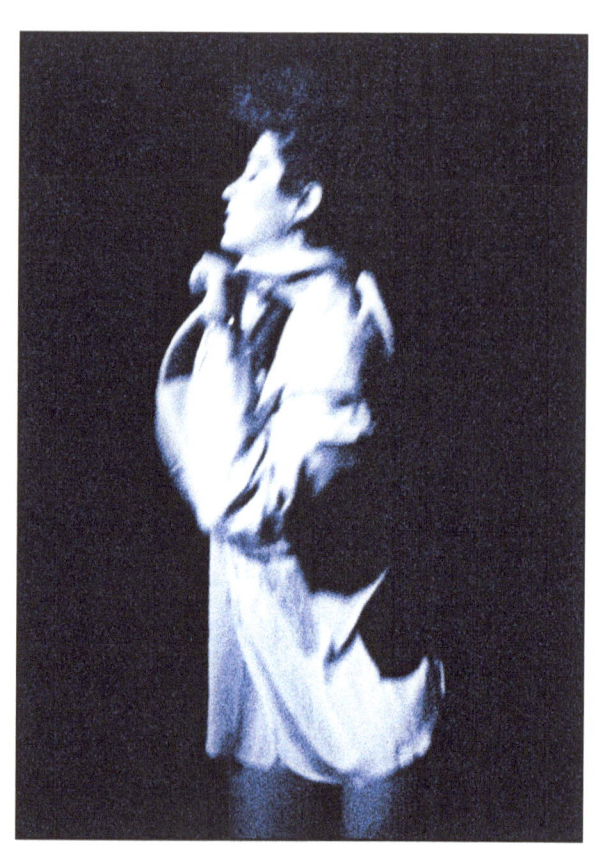

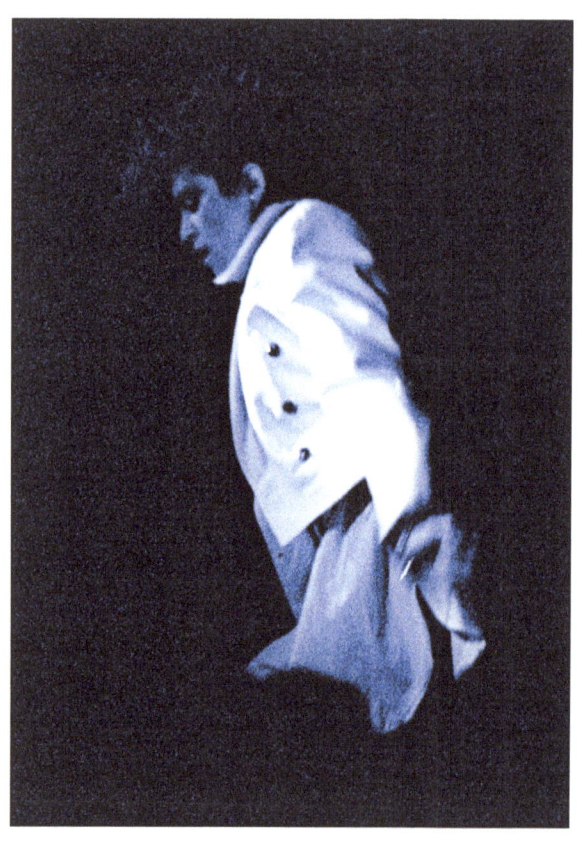 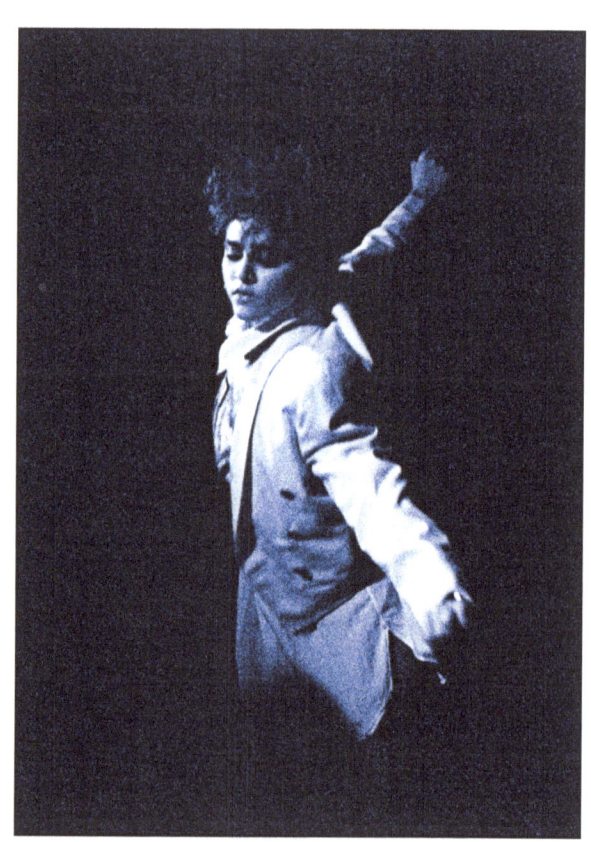

106

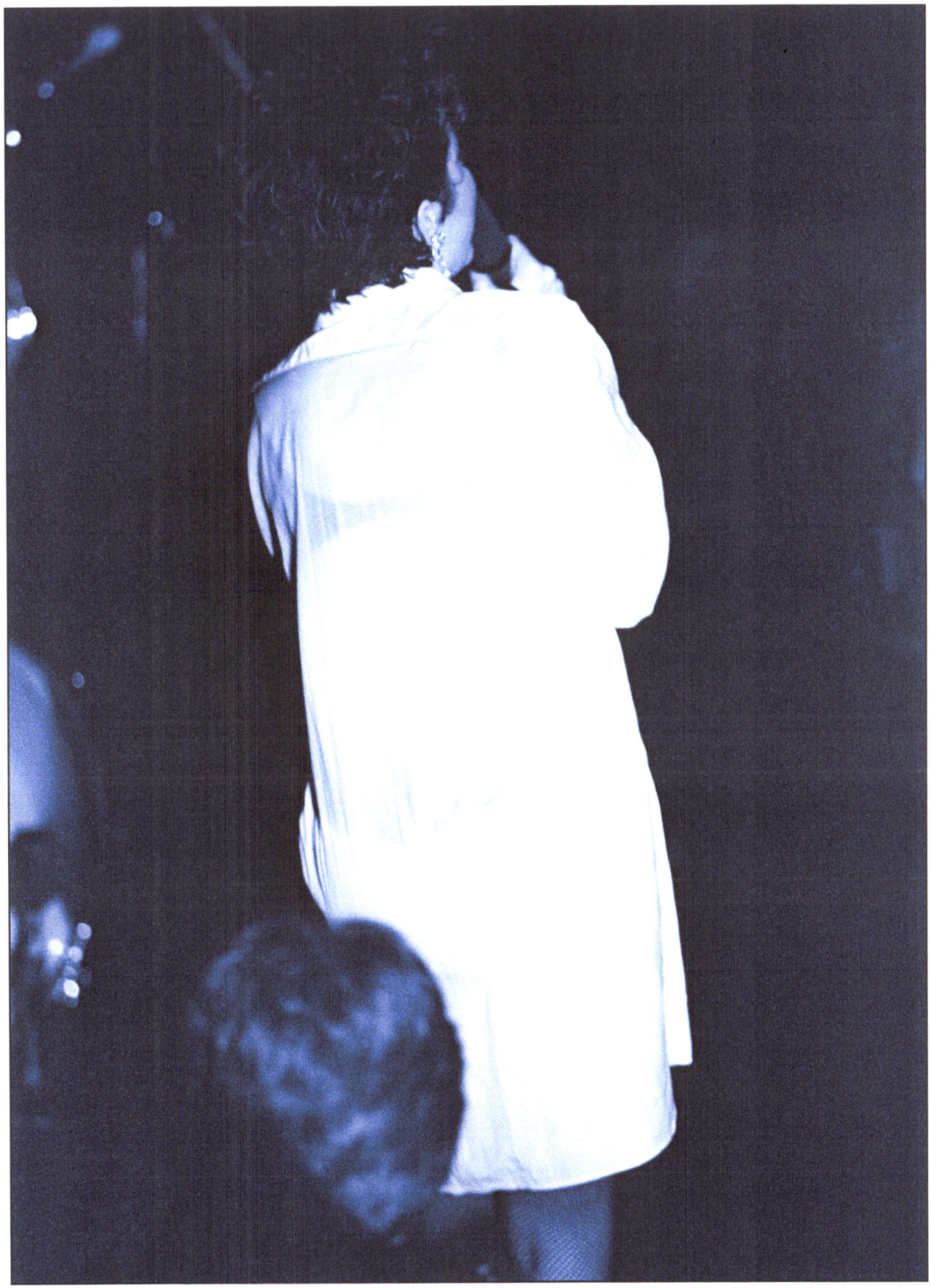

I am guessing that one evening on the roof of Danceteria in the summer of 1982, Madonna was now performing to music tracks of her songs.

There was no more band.

I was with Michael O'Brien and Yuki Watanabe. I had been hyping Madonna to anyone who would listen and Mike and Yuki were thinking of booking her to perform at their monthly event, "New York Nights" at various clubs in Boston.

It is clear in this photo from the roof of Danceteria that Madonna had been consulting with Maripol about her stage clothing and style.

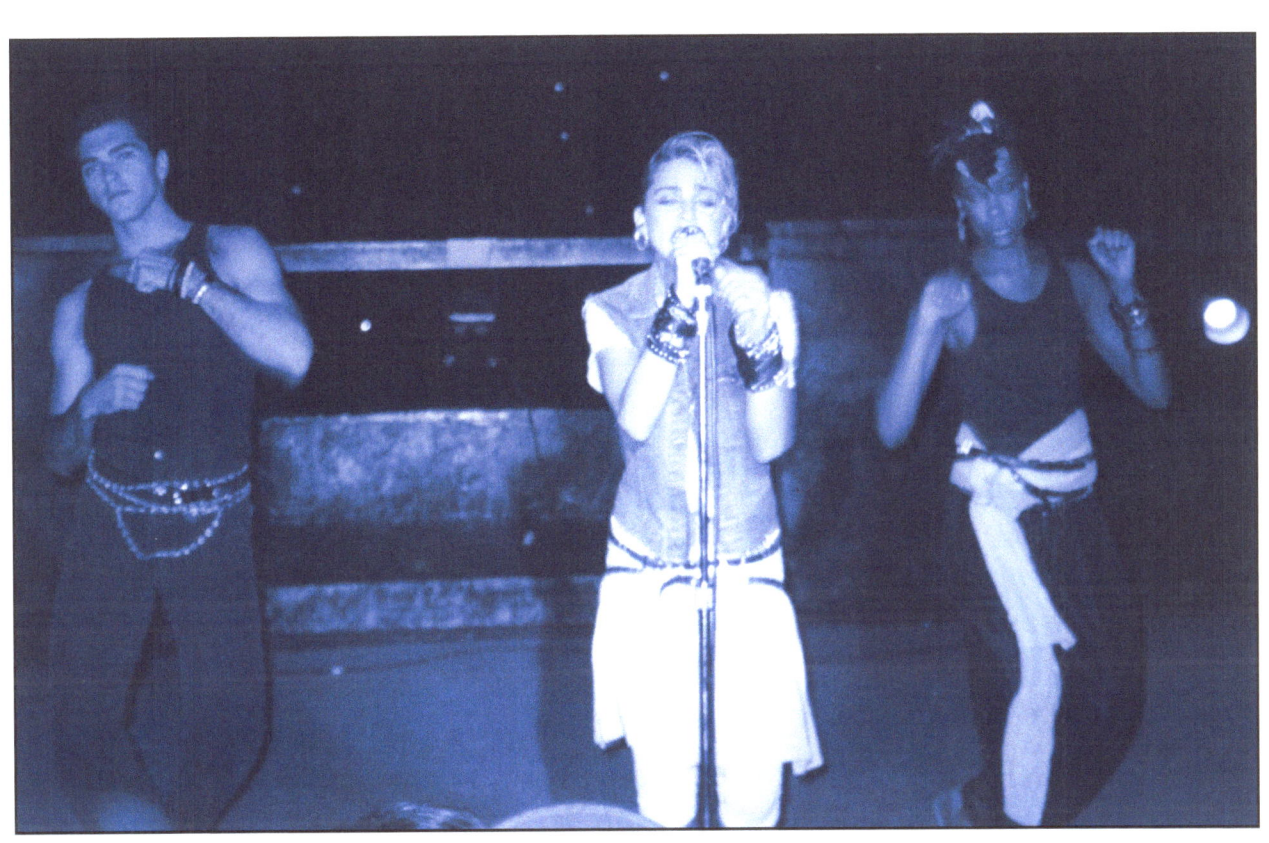

From the New York Nights show in Boston at the Metro, Madonna was running on all cylinders. She had her look together thanks to Maripol, she had her dancers organized.

Although, she still didn't have a record deal, it was pretty clear that this unique performer was going to be a success.

I had no idea how huge her success would become.

As you can see from the crowd at the Metro, the word was out.

Madonna was in town.

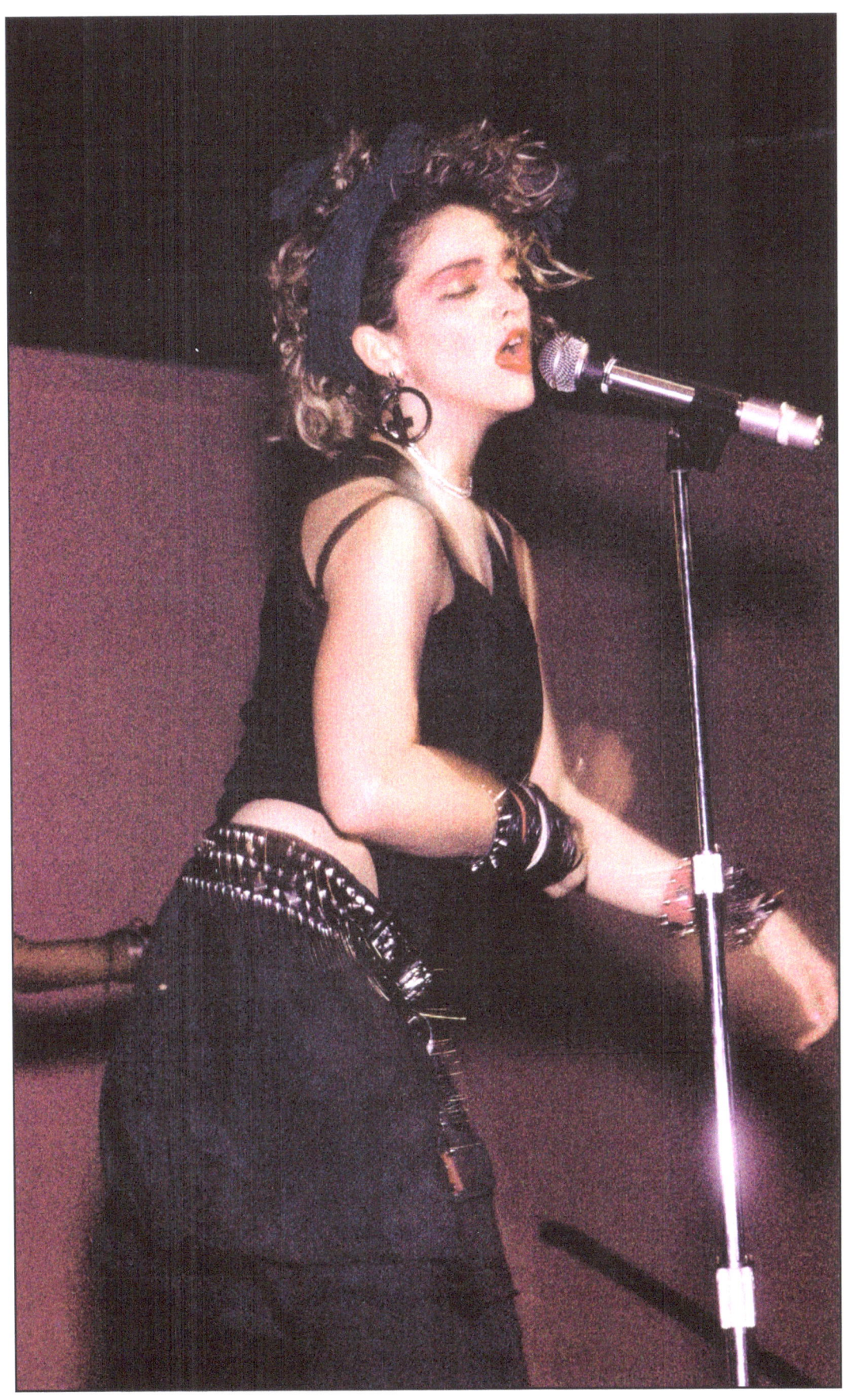

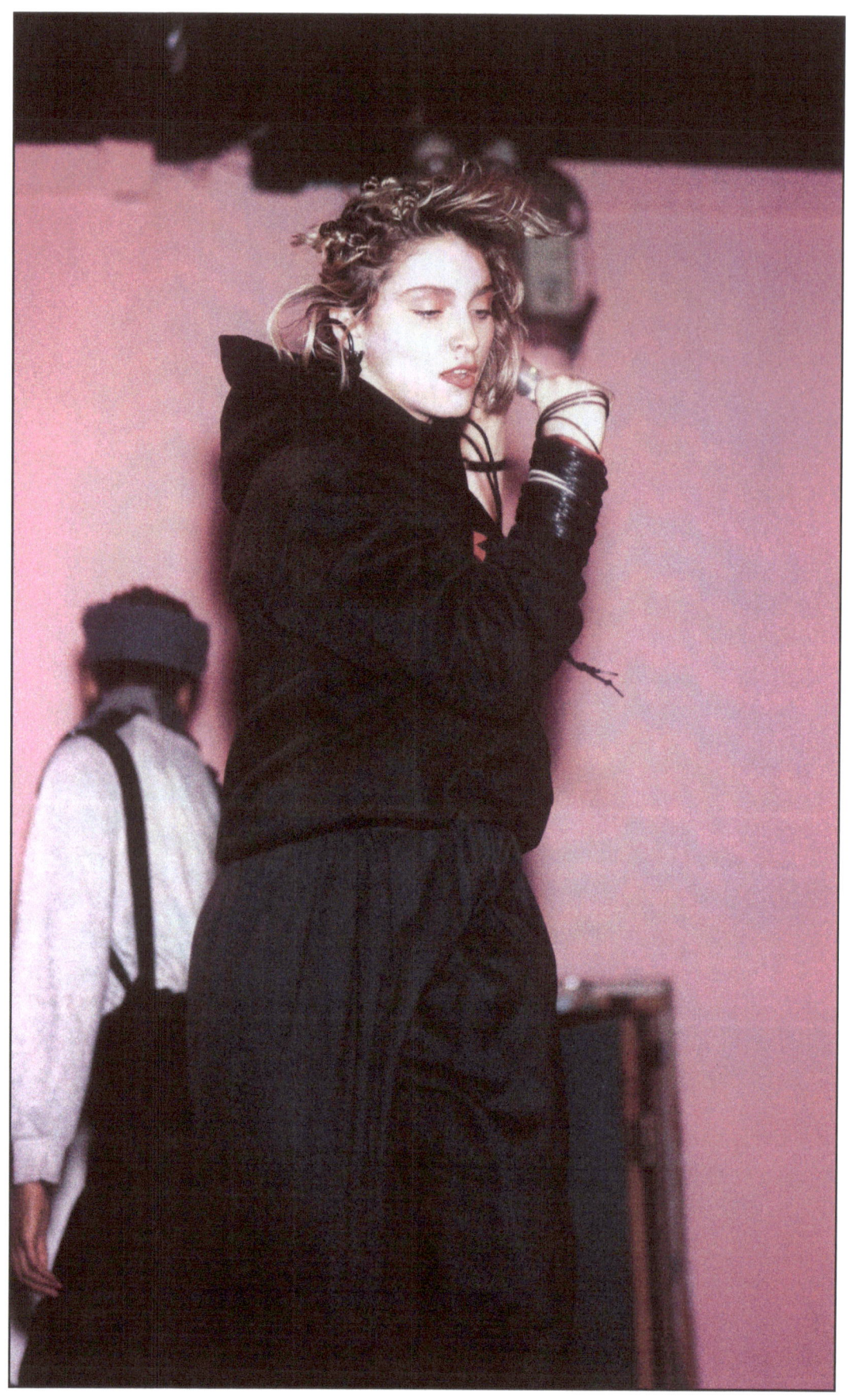

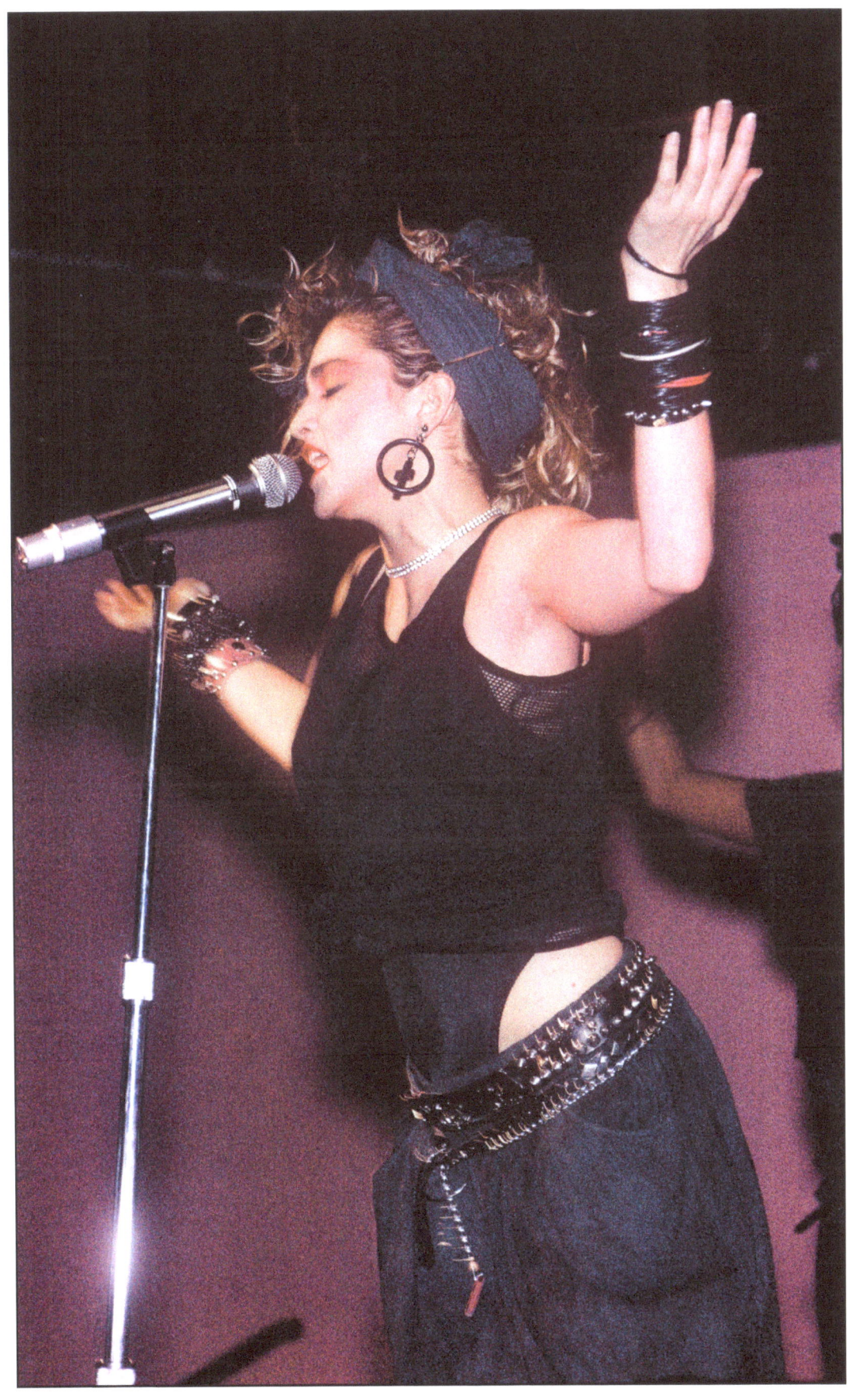

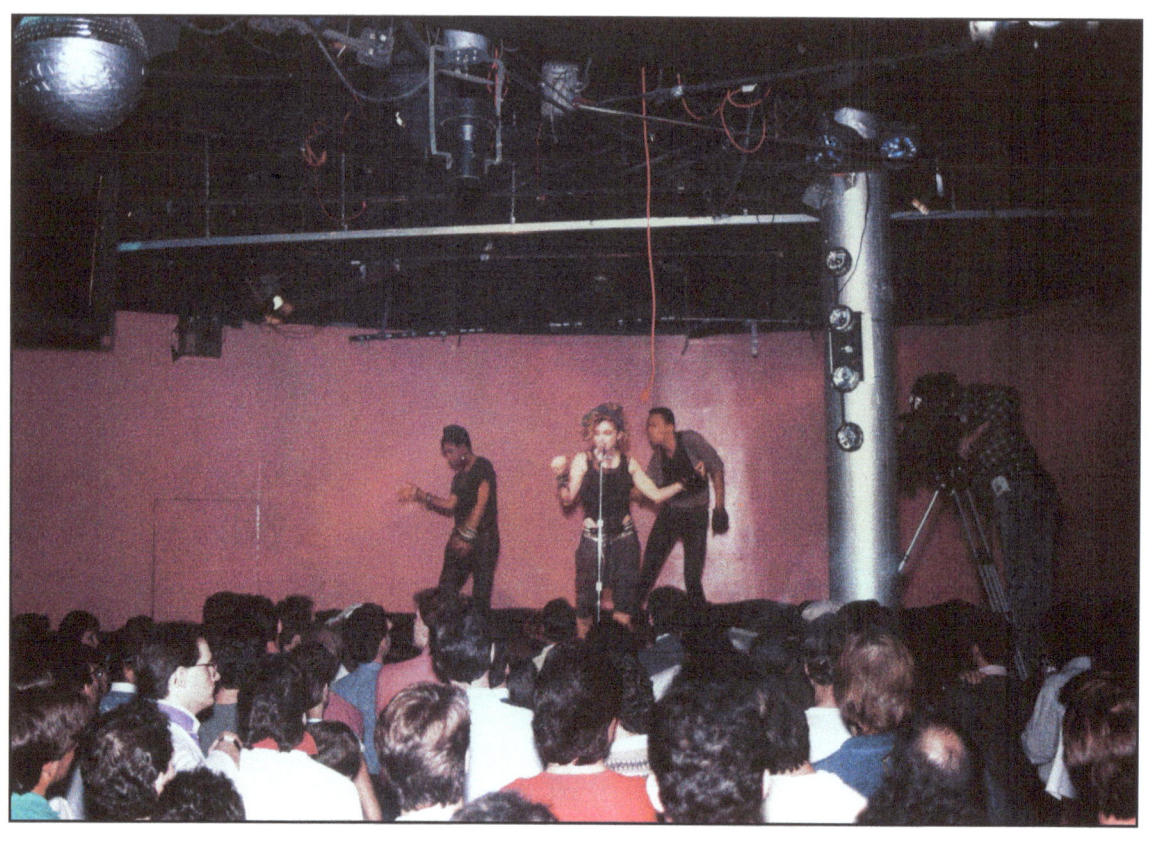

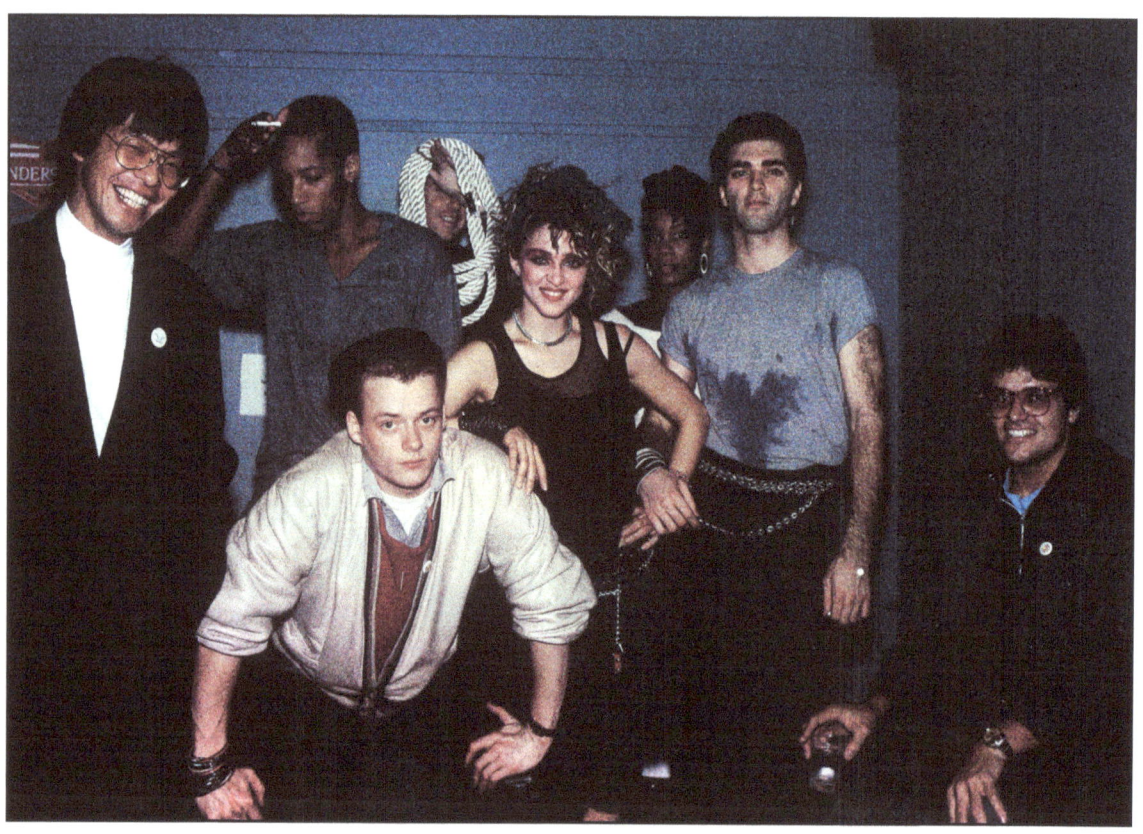

The author would like to thank:

Gerd Saller, for helping get this book together, retouching dozens of photographs and otherwise making this book look as good as possible. Gerd was instrumental in finding a way down the thorny path of self-publishing on demand.

Lane Pederson, my photography master, who took an interest in my career, shared a wealth of advice and knowledge with me and continues to be a friend and support all these years later.

Yuki Watanabe for taking my advice and Madonna to Boston.

Michael O'Brien R.I.P., for also supporting my career and for just being an unforgettable character in my life.

Deirdre DuBose, R.I.P., my mother. Even though she thought I should have been a lawyer, she always gave me the idea that I could do what I wanted with my life and she would still love me.

Glenn O'Brien, for being a friend. Glenn is and has been very supportive in many phases of my career and always encouraging. There is no writer that I admire more and enjoy reading as much. In my next life, I would like to be like him.

To all my fans and collectors of my work. You are helping me to survive.